CAR BUYER'S
AND LEASER'S
NEGOTIATING BIBLE

Third Edition

W. James Bragg

Random House Reference
New York

4/2004 GenFun $17

Car Buyer's and Leaser's Negotiating Bible, Third Edition

Copyright © 1999, 1996 by Cogito Ergo Sum, Inc.
Copyright © 2004, 1993 by Fighting Chance ®

This book is available for special discounts for bulk purchases for sales promotions or premiums. Special editions, including personalized covers, excerpts of existing books, and corporate imprints, can be created in large quantities for special needs. For more information, write to Special Markets/Premium Sales, 1745 Broadway, MD 6-2, New York, NY, 10019 or e-mail *specialmarkets@randomhouse.com*

Please address inquiries about electronic licensing of reference products, for use on a network or in software or on CD-ROM, to the Subsidiary Rights Department, Random House Information Group, fax 212-940-7370.

This is the third edition of *Car Buyer's and Leaser's Negotiating Bible,* originally published in 1996 by Random House, Inc.

Visit the Random House Information Group
web site at www.randomwords.com

Typeset and printed in the United States of America

Library of Congress Cataloging-in-Publication Data
Bragg, W. James (William James)
    Car buyer's and leaser's negotiating bible / W. James Bragg —
2nd ed.
      p.   cm.
    Includes bibliographical references and index.
    ISBN 0-375-72067-7
    1. Automobiles—Purchasing.   2. Automobile leasing and renting.
3. Negotiation. I. Title.
TL162.B7297   1998
629.222'029'6—dc21   98-49712
                                                     CIP

Third Edition
0 9 8 7 6 5 4 3 2 1

ISBN 0-375-72067-7

New York   Toronto   London   Sydney   Auckland

DEDICATION

- To every man who's ever bought a new car or truck and wondered whether the next guy got the same vehicle for a lot less.

- To every woman who's suffered through the purchase process and wondered whether she was a victim of gender-based price discrimination.

- To every member of a minority group who's wondered whether he or she has encountered race-based price discrimination when buying a new car or truck.

- To every young person who's about to buy that first new vehicle and wonders whether he or she will end up asking the same questions.

- To everyone who dreads walking into a new-car store to negotiate the price and wishes there were a better way.

This book is for all of you. After reading it, you'll wonder why no one ever told you this before.

Acknowledgments

- As difficult as this project was, it would have been impossible to accomplish without the support, encouragement, and love of my wife, who loses a husband for several weeks with each new edition. Thank you, Ricky, for understanding that perfection is the enemy of excellence and accepting me as I am.

- I must also acknowledge the patience and love of my surfer-girl teenage daughter, who loses a daddy, a ball game, and movie buddy for the same period. Thank you, Casey, for understanding that grownups can't come out to play every day and for giving me those rain checks.

- To my three grown children, Laurie, Karen, and John, who have watched their father write several editions of this book and start a very demanding national business at a time in life when other fathers are kicking back. Thank you for the encouragement and love I needed when I couldn't see the light at the end of the tunnel.

- Surf, our lovable female golden retriever, can't read this, but her constant companionship at my feet has helped keep my emotions on an even keel, even when I've had only four hours of sleep.

- Finally, I am grateful to my editors at Random House—partly for suffering through my missed deadlines, but mostly for believing this was still a book worth doing.

—W. James Bragg

Contents

identifying the right dealer contacts, preparing and sending the fax, fielding the responses, making the follow-up calls, and finalizing the deal by telephone to avoid unpleasant last-minute surprises.

20. Other Ways to Do It 158

Alternative ways to accomplish the same objective, either by doing it yourself or by hiring someone to do it for you. Why Internet car-buying services, auto brokers, and affiliation-group referrals may not be the best answer.

21. The Leasing Alternative: Breaking the Language Barrier 168

The basics of leasing demystified. Determining whether leasing makes sense for you. How to negotiate a favorable lease without letting dealers use the "boomfog" of leasing terminology to juggle you into a high-profit deal. How to do the arithmetic to check the monthly payment figure they are trying to sell you.

22. Are Extended Warranties Warranted? 195

How to determine whether you should buy an extended warranty contract and how to shop smart for the coverage you need. Why the safe bet is usually the automaker's contract, not the cheaper "no-name" alternatives you'll find on the Internet and elsewhere.

23. Resisting the Final Temptation 204

The preownership inspection. All the things to go over while they still own the car, before you give them the final check and sign the delivery receipt.

24. You've Got a Powerful Resource @www.fightingchance.com 208

How to get—directly from Fighting Chance, quickly and easily—the specific information package you need to negotiate from a position of strength for the vehicle you want: the most recent dealer invoice pricing and holdback data, details of manufacturer incentives in effect (customer rebates and traditional factory-to-dealer cash programs), and an updated overview of how your vehicle is doing in the marketplace, including a feel for the actual transaction prices paid by knowledgeable shoppers. Think of it as "the Swiss army knife for buying or leasing a new vehicle."

25. The Used-Car Alternative

The economic argument for buying or leasing a late-model used car instead of a new one. How to identify and find the most desirable previously owned vehicles. The growing importance of "factory-certified" used cars.

26. The Executive Summary

A brief reminder of the major points covered in the book, with referrals to the relevant chapters.

If a little knowledge is dangerous,
where are those who have so much
as to be out of danger?
                    —Thomas Huxley

Among new car buyers, it's those
who've read this book.

Introduction

This is the fourth version of this book—and the third edition under the title *Car Buyer's and Leaser's Negotiating Bible.* If another book provided all the insight you needed to buy or lease a new vehicle with confidence in today's auto market, we wouldn't have updated this one.

But we are in constant contact with new-car shoppers all over the country through Fighting Chance, an information service that has helped over 60,000 people buy or lease a new vehicle. We are reminded daily that no business is as dynamic as the automobile business, which continues to change dramatically. To help consumers negotiate the best deals, a book in this category needs to be up-to-speed on these changes. This one is.

Some of the key changes, which are covered in more detail later in the book, are noted briefly below:

• Spurred by the huge popularity of sport utility vehicles, the light-truck market segment (which also includes minivans and pickup trucks) exploded from 36 percent of new vehicle sales in 1992 to 51 percent in 2002. As a result, consumers have more makes and models of cars and trucks to choose from than ever before.

• Competition has become more brutal, as international automakers fight for a share of the huge, but slow-growing U.S. market. With the imports encroaching on the minivan, sport utility, and full-size truck segments that were once Detroit's exclusive high-profit domain, the competitive pressures intensify every year.

• Responding to these pressures, Detroit has escalated incentive values to levels that no one would have predicted several years ago.

Overall, these changes have benefited the new-vehicle shopper. A super-competitive marketplace tends to stimulate continuous product improvement and keep prices in line. But there have been other changes that are not so consumer friendly:

• Leasing has grown from relative infancy to become a major factor in new-vehicle sales. Leasing is a great idea for some people and a terrible idea for others. Unfortunately, many shoppers don't understand the language of leasing or how the monthly payment is determined, and they end up paying much more than they should. (There's nothing a car salesman likes more than customers who ask, "How much per month to lease that car?" It's as if they walk in with a sign reading, "I Just Fell Off the Turnip Truck.")

• The Internet has exploded as a source of automotive information, much of it free. You can even buy a new car on the World Wide Web. But those dealers you contact through Internet auto buying services have typically paid for the exclusive right to all the prospects from your zip code or telephone prefix. The price you get from them may or may not be a good one, but it's likely to be better when there's more than one dealer competing for your business.

• Detroit's Big Three have been eliminating smaller dealers and consolidating dealerships in several markets, making the business less competitive. In addition, some big publicly held companies have been buying many of the largest and most successful dealerships. Many of these stores have adopted a one-price, "no-dicker" sales policy, and there is a growing body of evidence indicating that no-dicker buyers pay significantly more than people who shop for the same vehicle at stores where prices are negotiable.

• The automakers' aggressive promotion of leasing over the past several years has created a steady stream of attractive vehicles for the used-car buyer. But dealers get used cars from several sources, and one used car can be a much smarter buy than its identically priced twin on the same lot, depending on who owned it first.

YOU'LL LEARN FROM OVER 60,000 AUTHORS

In this more complex market environment, the consumer must be better informed than ever to avoid getting taken. *The Car Buyer's and Leaser's Negotiating Bible* is loaded with inside information that will empower you in today's changing automotive market. Much of this information you won't find in any other book. Indeed, much of what we know about this business comes from the actual shopping experiences of the thousands of Fighting Chance customers—more than 60,000 at the time this book was published and increasing by about 10,000 each year. This gives us an unfair advantage over every other book in the category—and you an unfair advantage over those car salesmen.

STAY ON THE RIGHT SIDE OF THE RULE

There's an old maxim that applies here. We call it the 80/20 Rule of Life. Simply stated, it says that 20 percent of the people account for 80 percent of the activity, no matter what it is. For example, 20 percent of moviegoers buy 80 percent of the tickets and 20 percent of readers buy 80 percent of the books.

When the subject is the money dealers make from selling new cars, the rule says that 20 percent of the customers account for 80 percent of the profits. And every car salesman views every one of us as a prime candidate to join that unfortunate group. This book's reason for being is to keep you out of that group.

The one sure way for anyone to avoid getting taken is to become an informed and disciplined shopper. Period. This book can help you become that shopper. We will recommend strongly that you consider a vehicle's quality, dependability and crashworthiness as you narrow your choices, but we will *not* be steering you to any specific car or truck. *You* are the best judge of which vehicles fit your requirements. Do you like the way the vehicle looks? Is your body comfortable in the seat? Do you like its handling characteristics? Is it big enough for your needs? Is it too noisy or too quiet? Some of these are very personal questions, and many of these issues are quite subjective.

And we are not experts on fuel economy, maintenance and repair costs, or insurance ratings. These important issues are well covered in lots of other books and magazines.

Our focus here is primarily on the elements that influence the *financial* outcome of the purchase process—elements those other books and magazines often cover only superficially. Our job is to provide you with the knowledge that will give you real negotiating leverage in a transaction that traditionally has been stacked against the buyer.

We'll do that by bringing together all the relevant information, distilling and synthesizing it into one coherent presentation. We'll demystify the automotive purchase process thoroughly (in English, not Autospeak) and teach you how to use that information to negotiate from a position of strength, in the driver's seat. We'll even teach you how to do it without going anywhere near a car store, once you've chosen the vehicle you want.

SEVERAL SUBJECTS YOU'LL BE GLAD WE STUDIED

To illustrate, here are some important aspects of today's market reality— things you should know about to make good vehicle choices and negotiate from a position of strength.

1. The balance of power in the U.S. auto market today is substantially different from that of the early 1990s. Some manufacturers have gained ground, while others have slipped. Chapter 3 presents a comprehensive assessment of these important evolutionary changes and how they are impacting the vehicle choices of many consumers, as well as the prices they pay. Smart shoppers should be aware of these changes and the reasons for them as they come to grips with their purchase decisions.

2. Information on initial quality and longer-term durability has become more widely available in recent years. We cover this ground in chapter 4, including a section on customer satisfaction with dealer service.

3. The incentive landscape has shifted dramatically. Some vehicles seldom have incentives, while others have $1,000 (or much more) built into their pricing structure for customer rebates, cut-rate financing and subsidized leasing offers, and factory-to-dealer cash incentives. Many incentives are advertised and easy to learn about. But these days, manufacturers are putting money back in dealers' pockets in new ways—often ways that may have little or nothing to do with your specific purchase. It's usually impossible to know where any given dealer stands on these programs. Other books aren't telling you this, but we cover the subject in detail in chapter 16. We'll also teach you a negotiating method that will put most of that "secret" dealer incentive money in your pocket, even when there's no way to determine the exact amount any dealer gets.

3. Research shows that, compared to Caucasian males, women and minorities (who buy more than half of all new cars) face significant price discrimination in the purchase process—discrimination that may cost them over a billion dollars a year. This book presents these research results in chapter 2 and teaches readers how to turn the tables.

4. The fortunes of auto companies and their dealers ebb and flow from month to month, impacting price flexibility for each make and model. Disappointing sales typically lead to excess inventories and a greater willingness to deal. Chapter 15 explains this in detail, and chapter 24 provides a mechanism for obtaining the current sales status of the vehicle or vehicles on your shopping list—including information on what others have reported paying for those vehicles.

5. In this supercompetitive auto market, there's one thing no dealer wants you to know: Most dealers make several slim-profit deals every month with knowledgeable customers. In chapters 16 and 17, you'll learn why that's true and how you can turn this fact to your advantage.

6. Leasing now accounts for a major percentage of new vehicle purchases. While leasing isn't right for everyone, manufacturer-subsidized offers make it a very attractive alternative for many new-car shoppers. Chapter 21 is, hands down, today's bible on leasing.

7. The success of GM's Saturn division has encouraged many other dealers to adopt Saturn's one-price, no-dicker sales policy. But these Saturn wanna-bes don't have Saturn's crucial pricing umbrella working for them, and they don't offer the consumer the same pricing reassurance. Chapters 14 and 20 take you behind the curtain for a revealing look at how no-dicker pricing really works and why it's not as consumer-friendly as they'd like us to believe.

8. **Perhaps most important, it's time to dump the conventional wisdom about how to negotiate the price of a new car.** Those other books focus on telling you how to walk into a car store and do it face-to-face. Based on the collective experience of over 60,000 new-car shoppers, we've concluded that only a fool would do that. If you take our advice in chapter 19, once you've decided which car you want, you won't go anywhere near a car store till you're ready to sign the papers and drive that car home.

BUYING A CAR ISN'T ROCKET SCIENCE

In fact, buying a car ought to be fun! Our objective is to make this the most comprehensive, interesting and useful information package available for helping new-car and -truck shoppers save money. We won't talk down to you or tell you things you already know (such as, dress comfortably but conservatively when visiting showrooms). We'll just explain, as simply as we can, how the process works and how you can take advantage of it, instead of letting it take advantage of you.

We think you'll find this book fun to read, which may be a first for books in this category. It should help you relax about the entire car-shopping process, which is going to be much easier than you think because you'll know exactly how to complete the task successfully. And believe it or not, you'll find car dealers much easier to negotiate with when they know that you know what you're doing.

COMPLETING THE LOOP: FIGHTING CHANCE,® A UNIQUE INFORMATION SERVICE

To negotiate successfully, you'll need the most current, vehicle-specific information for the cars or trucks on your shopping list. When you're ready, our company, Fighting Chance, offers you an easy way to get that data by calling (800) 288-1134, by ordering through our web site on the Internet (www.fightingchance.com), or by writing to us. The Fighting Chance information package contains the up-to-date factory invoice pricing for the vehicles you're considering, a current report on manufacturers' incentive programs, and an updated sales and inventory picture for each make—including vehicle-specific pricing targets based on the feedback we've received on actual transaction prices from Fighting Chance customers. See chapter 24 for a complete description and ordering details.

In a time of turbulence and change, it is more true than ever that knowledge is power.
                    —John F. Kennedy

1

Everybody's Problem: An Uneven Playing Field

Quick! Can you name three things that are more fun than driving home in a brand-new car or truck? For most people, that's a tough call.

Now, can you name three things that are less fun than shopping for and negotiating the price of that new car or truck? For most people, that's even tougher.

We all suffer world-class anxiety in this process, with good reason.

Over the years, car prices have gone up faster than take-home pay. The average new vehicle's actual transaction price is now over $26,000. That's more than six months' wages for a typical household, enough to make anyone anxious. And there's little relief in sight. Despite evidence that "sticker shock" hurts new-car sales, you can expect automakers to continue hiking prices. (One key reason: the expanding number of costly built-in safety systems such as side- and head-level airbags and anti-lock brakes.) If the annual increases averaged only a "modest" 2 percent, they would add over $500 a year to the cost of the average car.

All automakers are focused on reducing production costs, but you can squeeze only so much juice from an orange. And the United Auto Workers union seems to fight every effort of Detroit's Big Three to improve productivity.

The vagaries of international monetary exchange rates can also have a major impact on auto pricing. In this arena, the Japanese manufacturers pull the strings. As the yen strengthens against the dollar, the Japanese receive fewer yen for each dollar they make here. For example, they took home over 250 yen for each dollar in the mid-1980s, but a decade later the yen was much stronger and the exchange rate went to 80 yen per dollar. In response, the Japanese were forced to raise U.S. prices continuously over that period to avoid big losses. The domestic makes should have seen this as an opportunity to gain a pricing advantage and recapture market share. But Detroit's response was to use the Japanese increases as an "umbrella" under which to raise prices and reduce incentive offers on domestic cars.

Conversely, as the dollar strengthens against the yen and the Japanese get more yen for each dollar they make here, there is no pressure to raise prices and the Japanese tend to hold the line. In that environment, Detroit must exercise price restraint or risk losing more market share to Tokyo.

What's the prognosis for the consumer? As automakers add new safety equipment and other bells and whistles, the cost of the average new car will continue to increase by $500 a year and maybe more. Is it any wonder that many of us would rather visit a dentist for root canal work than visit a showroom to shop for a new car or truck?

THE REAL PROBLEM: AN UNEVEN PLAYING FIELD

The gut-level issue, of course, is that the price of that expensive machine is negotiable, and therefore different for each buyer. By contrast, the price of just about everything else we buy is firmly established, and therefore the same for each buyer. That puts the pressure on us. We've got to do something we're not used to doing: negotiate the price of the second most expensive purchase most of us will ever make. And we're operating on unfamiliar turf, in a position of weakness, because we do it only once every few years.

But those salesmen we have to negotiate with are on very familiar turf, the car store, and in a position of strength, because they do it every day. (Yes, they call the dealership "the store." There are more than 40,000 new vehicle franchises nationally, and the average franchise for the top six selling nameplates sells over 700 cars and trucks each year. Many sell thousands!)

Those salesmen are trained to do one thing really well: maximize the car store's profit on each sale by separating us from as much of our money as possible. Their job is to determine how much is "as much as possible" for each prospect and, if the number is high enough, to close the sale at that price before the prospect gets away.

We make that job easier than it should be by giving them lots of important information they can use. We tell them exactly which car we want, and how much we can pay per month, and which vehicle we're trading in. In return, they give us no information we can use, such as how much that car really cost them, how low they'll really go to sell it, and what our trade-in is really worth. As a result, a playing field that was uneven from the start tips even further toward them. And when the transaction is over, most of us don't know whether we got a good deal or got taken.

EVERYONE DESERVES A FIGHTING CHANCE

As a *Motor Trend* writer said in an annual auto review issue, "Negotiating with terrorists is easier than bargaining with car dealers." That's why we wrote this book. We wanted to give the average new-vehicle shopper a fighting chance by making the playing field a little more level.

Our goal is to make the purchase process less painful and costly for you. To do that, we must change something important in that process. Since we can't change those salesmen and what they do, we've got to help change you and what you do.

THE OBJECTIVE: TO MAKE YOU MORE KNOWLEDGEABLE THAN THE CAR SALESMAN

That's not Mission Impossible. The average car salesman isn't that knowledgeable. He's trained to qualify, control, and close most of the people who walk in, prospects who just don't know much. But he's not well prepared to control and close people with solid knowledge of his business, a well-planned, disciplined approach, and insights that even he may not understand. Those shoppers can have real negotiating leverage.

(Incidentally, when we say "salesmen," assume we mean both sexes. There are successful auto saleswomen, but the male stereotype is still dominant. Also, when we say "cars," assume we're referring to both cars and trucks.)

How can we make you more knowledgeable than the car salesman? By giving you the attitude, facts, up-to-date insights, and advice you need to negotiate from a position of greater strength. We'll even show you how to handle the entire negotiation without walking into a car store and dealing face-to-face with a salesman.

We can't guarantee, of course, that you'll save hundreds or thousands more with this information than without it. That's up to you and what you do with it. The supply and demand conditions in your market for the vehicles you're interested in will also influence the outcome.

But remember, knowledge is power. The main advantage the salesman has over most buyers is that he thinks he's got all the knowledge. If you absorb the information we give you, you'll know more than most car salesmen. If you act on this information, you'll go into the process with real confidence in your ability to negotiate effectively. And if you believe you can, you will.

NO PAIN, NO GAIN

Most people work harder planning a $2,500 vacation than planning the purchase of the $25,000 car they'll be vacationing in for years. Why? For two reasons: (1) planning a vacation is more fun; and (2) they know how to plan a vacation, but they don't know how to shop for a car. If smart shopping were easy, everyone would do it.

The facts say everyone doesn't. Incredible as it seems, in a national survey conducted by the Dohring Company of Glendale, California, *one out of seven prospective new-car buyers was not aware that new-vehicle prices were negotiable!* And we'd bet that most of the other six frequently pay more than they realize, simply because they aren't focused on all the ways a car store can make money on a deal (more on this in chapter 7).

Smart shopping requires homework. Studying this book and acting on it intelligently will require more of your time than simply going out and buying a car next Saturday. The trade-off is between time and money, perhaps as much as several thousand dollars.

We'll assume that you wouldn't have bought this book if you weren't willing to trade time for money. Let's get on with your education.

*Everything is funny as long as it
is happening to someone else.*
—Will Rogers

2

The Other Problem: Price Discrimination

Our civil rights laws focus on the areas of employment, education, housing, and public accommodations. When it comes to the prices we pay for the things we buy, there's a comfortable assumption that good old American competition at the retail level tends to eliminate price discrimination.

Try telling that to women, who know they pay more for shoes than men do for theirs, even when the materials and workmanship are the same. Or to inner-city residents, who know that stores in their neighborhoods often charge higher prices for lower-quality goods than similar stores elsewhere.

Women and minorities will not be surprised to learn that they also face significant price discrimination in the automotive marketplace. *We believe a conservative estimate of the cost of this discrimination is over $1 billion a year, compared to the prices paid for the same vehicles by white males.*

WOMEN MAKE THE WHEELS GO ROUND

The female working population has grown dramatically over the last few decades, sparking a revolution in auto design and marketing strategies. With three out of four women between twenty and fifty-four years old in the labor force, women have become a key target for automakers.

Manufacturers now spend as much money researching women's automotive needs as men's, with good reason. Women purchase half of the new passenger cars sold and more than one-third of the light trucks, including some very profitable segments (minivans like the Dodge Caravan, Honda Odyssey and Toyota Siena and sport utility vehicles like the Ford Explorer and the Toyota Highlander).

Many vehicles are designed to appeal primarily to women. Female designers play important roles at automobile companies. They frequently supervise new-vehicle design teams, especially for sporty coupes—a market segment aimed directly at women that includes the Acura RSX, Hyundai Tiberon, Mazda Miata, Mitsubishi Eclipse, and Toyota Camry Solara.

The auto manufacturers have changed their ways to satisfy the needs of this powerful new economic force; they treat women differently from men. As a result, both win. Women get the products they want, and manufacturers sell more new cars and trucks.

The automakers' franchised *dealers,* however, are another story. Most women have always suspected that new-car salesmen treat them differently than men and that, as a result, they end up paying a different price from men—a higher price. That's why many of them drag along their husbands, boyfriends, or fathers when they shop.

Many members of minority groups have suspected they face similar price discrimination.

Now there's irrefutable evidence that substantiates these suspicions.

THE SEARCH FOR THE SMOKING GUN

Ian Ayres, a professor at Yale Law School and a research fellow of the American Bar Foundation, was interested in testing the ability of competitive market forces to eliminate gender- and race-based price discrimination in markets not covered by civil rights laws. Since a new-car purchase represents a large investment for most consumers, he saw the retail automobile market as "particularly ripe for scrutiny."

Between the summers of 1988 and 1990, when he was an associate professor at the Northwestern University School of Law, he conducted research to examine whether women and minorities were at a disadvantage in the process of negotiating the price of a new car.

He trained several college-educated testers of different genders and races to negotiate in the same way for specific models. They conducted 180 independent negotiations at 90 dealerships in the Chicago area, bargaining to each dealer's "final cash offer." To eliminate other financial considerations, no trade-in vehicles were involved.

THE FACTS OF PRICE DISCRIMINATION

The smoking gun wasn't hard to find. The results were published as the *Harvard Law Review*'s lead article in February 1991. They demonstrated that retail car dealerships systematically offered substantially better prices on identical cars to white men than they did to white women and African-Americans.

Specifically, final offers to white women contained about 40 percent more dealer profit than final offers to white men. Offers to African-American men contained more than twice the profit, and African-American women had to pay more than three times the markup of white male testers.

The tendency to charge African-Americans higher prices was echoed in this comment one dealer made to Professor Ayres: "My cousin owns a dealership in a black neighborhood. He doesn't sell nearly as many [cars], but he hits an awful lot of home runs. You know, sometimes it seems like the people that can least afford it have to pay the most."

The study also revealed that testers were systematically steered to salespeople of their own race and gender, who then gave them *worse* deals than others received from salespeople of a different race and gender. Consumers tend to feel more comfortable with someone of their own race and gender; salespeople take advantage of that implied trust and sell them higher-profit deals.

The major conclusions of this initial study were confirmed by a subsequent larger-scale test involving 400 additional negotiations in the Chicago area.

Years have passed since this research was completed, and you might wonder whether the result would be different if the study were conducted today. Based on our personal contacts with thousands of new-car shoppers each year, there is no evidence of significant changes. It would be easier to U-turn a supertanker in the Panama Canal than to change the way car salesmen operate.

GENDER DISCRIMINATION GETS A THEME SONG

On the assumption that our female readers have a sense of humor about this, we'd like to share the lyrics to a little song parody we've written. It's sung to the tune of that old standard "I Found a Million-Dollar Baby in a Five-and-Ten-Cent Store." We call it "I Made a Bundle on the Lady When I Put Her in a New Car." Imagine all those chauvinist car salesmen at their annual convention, hoisting their glasses to toast their male prowess and singing these lyrics:

> She was my lucky April shopper,
> It was my chance to be a star.
> I made a bundle on the lady
> When I put her in a new car.
>
> She thought she'd be here half an hour,
> We kept her here for three or four.
> We made a bundle on that lady
> With the deal she got at our store!
>
> She wanted basic transportation
> But much to her surprise,
> She drove home in a sports car
> With payments twice the size!
>
> So if you're looking for a bargain
> Our showroom isn't very far.
> I'll make a bundle on you, baby,
> When I put you in a new car!

THE ASSUMPTIONS BEHIND THE FACTS

Professor Ayres hypothesizes an explanation for this price discrimination. While there's no way to prove it, we think he's right on the money. Here's the essence of his reasoning.

- The dealer's objective is to maximize profits on each sale. (That's the American way, right?)

- The natural outcome of the bargaining process is that identical vehicles are sold to different buyers at different prices. Dealers make little or no profit on some sales, but a great deal of profit on others.

- The less the competition with other dealers for a given sale, the more profit the dealer is likely to make on the transaction.

- If a dealership can infer that some prospects are less likely to shop at other dealerships—because they aren't well informed about the dynamics of the retail automotive marketplace, or because they can't spend the time required, or because they simply hate the entire bargaining process and just want to get it behind them—that dealership is more likely to view these prospects as potential patsies for high-margin transactions. And that dealership is more likely to conclude that it can safely charge these prospects higher prices.

- Like it or not, our society is still rife with stereotypes about women and minority groups that provide at least a subconscious rationale for sales-people to view them as more likely candidates for high-margin, slam-dunk, sucker deals. Here are the most obvious assumptions they make:

  Women and minorities have less time to shop around for competitive bids. Compared to white men, they are less likely to be able to take time off from work to shop without losing wages. And women are more likely to have family responsibilities that further restrict their shopping time.

  Women and minorities are less sophisticated about the auto-shopping process. They are less likely to seek out information about the realities of the retail market and to understand that the sticker price is negotiable. They will be more passive in the sales situation and less likely to negotiate aggressively. That will make it easier for the salesperson to control the outcome.

  Women, in general, are more averse to the entire bargaining process. Haggling over the price of a new vehicle is a competitive ordeal. Some men relish the battle; for them it's one of the last macho things they can do without a gun. Most women simply hate it. They'll pay a higher cost just to get it behind them.

SUPPORT FROM MORE RECENT RESEARCH

In *Women Don't Ask: Negotiation and the Gender Divide,* a provocative book published in 2003 by Princeton University Press, authors Linda Babcock and Sara Laschever conclude from their research and the research of others that women are far less likely than men to initiate a negotiation about *anything.* Whether they want higher salaries or more help at home, they often find it hard to ask. They also cite evidence that women ask for less when they make the all-important opening offer, and then concede too quickly. (A survey by the Dohring Company showed that women are 40 percent more likely than men to accept the first car price a dealer offers.)

Babcock and Laschever note that in our society, women are expected to be selfless and nurturing, while men are selfish and competitive. This gives women "an impaired sense of entitlement." Their book offers sage advice on how best to bargain and overcome the fear of asking. This is an important book that will help anyone who fears negotiating, male or female.

THE LIGHT AT THE END OF THE TUNNEL

Women and minority readers shouldn't be discouraged by these revelations. Because if you take our advice and negotiate as we recommend in chapter 19, you are going to shake that car salesman's faith in his assumptions, putting him on the defensive. He'll be playing your game, instead of vice versa. You'll be that knowledgeable, disciplined shopper we promised you'd become, and his tricks won't work.

The road from here to there is straight and clearly marked. It begins on the next page, starting with an overview of the major changes that have been occurring in the U.S. auto market.

While the law of competition may sometimes be hard for the individual, it is best for the race, because it insures the survival of the fittest in every department.
—Andrew Carnegie

The Changing Face of the U.S. Automobile Market

The new-vehicle marketplace is the most competitive business you'll find anywhere. The main reason: worldwide production capacity exceeds demand by several million cars. When manufacturers can assemble many more cars than we can buy, there's a real dogfight for profits and long-term survival.

The U.S. is the world's largest new-car market. In 2002, 16,833,000 new vehicles were sold, the fourth highest total ever. Japan ranked a distant second, with 5,814,000 sales. U.S. sales even slightly exceeded the total sales of the seventeen countries in western Europe. That makes us the key target prospects for most of the world's automakers.

As a result, people living in the U.S. have many more nameplates, models, and dealers to choose from than any civilized society needs to get from point A to point B. In the 2003 model year, there were 1,366 models on sale in the U.S.—532 cars and 834 trucks. (Minivans, sport utility vehicles [SUVs], and pickups are all classified as trucks.) And on January 1, 2003, there were 42,864 retail new-vehicle franchises.

That's good news, because the competition between nameplates, models, and dealers for our business is especially fierce. In any business, that's the catalyst for better products that sell at better prices.

Although the U.S. new-car market is huge, it's also a mature market with limited growth potential. The year 2002 was the fourth consecutive year with sales exceeding 16,500,000 units, but sales were down 2 percent from 2001. Industry forecasts estimate annual U.S. sales in the range of 16,400,000 to 17,200,000 through 2007. (The industry's best year was 2000, with 17,400,000 sales.)

In a relatively stagnant market like this, there's a constant battle to maintain or increase market share, and the sands of fortune are constantly shifting between manufacturers. The sun doesn't shine on the same dog every day. There are winners and there are losers.

WHY DOES THIS MATTER?

When you're considering buying or leasing a new vehicle, start by checking the status of the overall market—understanding who's been gaining momentum and who's been losing it, and why.

Automakers that are gaining market share tend to have better brand images, mostly the result of building more appealing vehicles with better initial quality and long-term durability. They need fewer incentives to motivate purchase, so their vehicles typically sell for higher prices. But long term, they usually cost less to own, for three reasons: (1) they don't need frequent repair, (2) they last longer, providing more years of reliable service, and (3) they depreciate less rapidly and command higher prices as used cars when they are sold or traded.

By contrast, manufacturers that are losing share tend to have poorer brand images and reputations for building vehicles with subpar initial quality and long-term dependability. They typically need bigger incentives to motivate purchase, so their vehicles sell for lower prices. But for their customers, most of that advantage evaporates in more frequent repair bills, a shorter useful life, and higher depreciation when they sell or trade.

With new cars, as with most things you buy, you get what you pay for.

WINNERS AND LOSERS

Once upon a time, many decades ago Detroit had virtually all the new-car business in this country. Those days are long gone.

The Japanese and European automakers invaded the U.S. turf aggressively in the late 1950s and early 1960s and grew dramatically thereafter, with Toyota and Honda capturing leadership positions in passenger car sales. In more recent years, the import nameplates have successfully entered Detroit's most profitable market segments: luxury cars, SUVs, minivans, and full-size pickup trucks.

The table below shows how dramatically the sands shifted in the ten-year period between 1992 and 2002. Import nameplates accounted for 27.8

	Unit Sales (000)		Market Share (%)	
	1992	2002	1992	2002
Chrysler Corporation	1,713	2,205	13.3%	13.1%
Ford Motor Corporation	3,192	3,401	24.8	20.2
General Motors	4,398	4,782	34.1	28.4
Domestic Nameplates	**9,303**	**10,388**	**72.2%**	**61.7%**
BMW/Mini	66	257	0.5%	1.5%
Mercedes-Benz	63	213	0.5	1.3
Saab	26	38	0.2	0.1
Volvo	68	111	0.5	0.7
Volkswagen/Audi	91	424	0.7	2.5
Other European	22	123	0.2	0.8
European Nameplates	**336**	**1,166**	**2.6%**	**6.9%**
Honda/Acura	769	1,248	6.0%	7.4%
Mazda	339	258	2.6	1.5
Nissan/Infiniti	585	739	4.5	4.4
Subaru	105	180	0.8	1.1
Toyota/Lexus	1,024	1,756	7.9	10.4
Other Japanese	315	466	2.5	2.8
Japanese Nameplates	**3,137**	**4,647**	**24.3%**	**27.6%**
Korean Nameplates	**110**	**632**	**0.9%**	**3.8%**
Total Import Nameplates	**3,583**	**6,445**	**27.8%**	**38.3%**
TOTAL MARKET	**12,886**	**16,833**	**100.0%**	**100.0%**

percent of U.S. sales in 1992, but gained over ten share points to reach 38.3 percent in 2002. Domestic nameplates fell from 72.2 percent in 1992 to 61.7 percent in 2002, with General Motors surrendering 5.7 share points (54 percent of the domestic loss) and Ford giving up 4.6 points (44 percent of the loss).

It is reasonable to predict that this trend will continue through most of another decade. (In the first eight months of 2003, domestic nameplates slipped to 60 percent, while the imports edged up to 40 percent.)

The domestic brands could end up with 50 to 55 percent of the market.

AUTO MERGER MANIA

Detroit's Big Three have not been watching this happen while sitting still. Under the motto, "If you can't beat 'em, buy 'em," U.S. companies have been purchasing import nameplates and acquiring ownership stakes in import automakers.

• General Motors has purchased Saab and also owns 49 percent of Isuzu, 20 percent of Fuji Heavy Industries (Subaru's parent company), 20 percent of Fiat's auto division and 10 percent of Suzuki. GM also owns 42 percent of Korea's bankrupt Daewoo Motor Company and is importing Daewoo vehicles into the U.S. rebadged as Chevrolets and Suzukis.

• Ford has purchased Jaguar, Volvo and Land Rover and owns a 33 percent controlling interest in Mazda.

• In response, Daimler-Benz (Mercedes' parent) has merged with the Chrysler Corporation, taking control and changing the merged company's name to DaimlerChrysler. Daimler has also purchased a 37 percent interest in Japan's Mitsubishi Motors.

The consolidation argument is compelling. "Long-term, smaller companies can't survive in the automobile business. Brutal competition will soon leave fewer than a dozen car makers on the world stage," said the proponents. "Massive scale will yield massive economies of scale and massive profits. And the acquiring companies will benefit by offering a broader range of products and strengthening their own weaker product segments."

While this rationale makes sense, the results to date from most of these strategic alliances have been underwhelming.

• The Chrysler group was again registering big losses five years after its merger with Daimler.

- GM's entire $500 million investment in 49 percent of Isuzu has been erased by losses, and the Isuzu brand is flirting with extinction in the U.S. consumer auto market. Saab lost money in 2002 and in nine of the preceding eleven years. Fiat's auto division is in crisis in Europe, and GM has an option that may force it to buy the other 80 percent.

- Ford has not escaped problems with its acquisitions. The Jaguar brand lost about $500 million in 2002.

The major lesson from this industry consolidation may be that it's a real struggle to integrate two or more companies in different countries and with different corporate cultures. This daunting task diverts too much management energy and focus away from the primary job of designing and producing the diverse range of innovative new cars that today's buyers demand.

While the U.S. remains the key market for the most profitable high-end vehicles, the fastest-growing markets in the next few decades will be in developing countries like China and India, where the combination of a vast population and an emerging market economy is producing a burgeoning middle class of people hungry for their first new vehicles. Indeed, the Asia-Pacific region has the potential to become the world's largest automobile market. It's likely that in the long term, the most successful strategic alliances will be those forged by large automakers with companies whose expertise is in smaller vehicles best suited to capitalize on this opportunity.

The balance of this chapter provides an overview of the positions of the domestic and import nameplates. It should provide some interesting food for thought as you review the new-vehicle alternatives you are considering.

THE DOMESTIC BIG THREE

As shown in the table below, General Motors is still the king of the domestic-nameplate sales jungle, with Ford a distant second and Chrysler the runt of the Big Three litter.

	Share of Domestic Nameplate Sales - 2002
General Motors Corporation*	45.9%
Ford Motor Corporation**	32.9
Chrysler Group***	21.2
	100.0%

* Chevrolet, Buick, Pontiac, GMC, Cadillac, Saturn, and Hummer
** Ford, Lincoln, and Mercury
*** Chrysler, Dodge, and Jeep

Detroit's Biggest Problem

As a group, the domestic brands are not held in high esteem by large numbers of U.S. consumers. Many people under 50 years old matured driving import nameplates and associate GM, Ford, and Chrysler nameplates with the poor-quality cars their parents drove in the 1970s and 1980s. In more recent years, these negative impressions have been reinforced by Detroit's relatively poor quality and reliability ratings, compared to those of the leading import nameplates. Changing a brand's long-term image is extremely difficult, and Detroit has more negative baggage to overcome than most import brands.

Consider the situation General Motors faces. For at least a couple of decades, GM alienated many prospects by offering relatively dull, unreliable vehicles. It's the country's biggest auto manufacturer, yet GM's own research has indicated that about half of U.S. car buyers say they wouldn't consider buying a new GM vehicle. (GM noted that the other automakers in the U.S. market have even worse numbers, which may be true. In a market this big, with so many brand choices, no single company needs to—or can expect to—appeal to everyone.)

There is some evidence that GM nameplates can be a liability for prospective buyers. As an example, in consumer research conducted by GM in 2001, a new Pontiac design scored better than those of several import competitors. But when the respondents learned it would be a Pontiac, its ratings dropped substantially.

It's a safe bet that the Ford Motor Corporation and the Chrysler group carry similar negative-image baggage. As a consequence, Detroit's Big Three must rely much more heavily on incentives to move vehicles than the best of the Japanese and European automakers. With GM leading the charge, rebate values and cut-rate financing offers have reached new peaks in the past few years. It started just after the September 11, 2001 terrorist attacks, when GM launched its "Keep America Rolling" zero-percent financing campaign. Since then, the company has placed a heavy foot on the incentive accelerator periodically, and rebates on many vehicles have escalated occasionally to the $3,000 to $4,000 range—a level no one would have imagined just a few years ago.

Rival automakers have complained that GM's zero-percent loans and high rebates are trashing the industry's brands and profits. In response, GM's chairman bluntly told industry critics to "stop whining" in a January 2003 speech to the National Automobile Dealers Association.

GM has a strong rationale for its aggressive pricing action. Bigger incentives motivate people to buy pricier, higher-margin vehicles. They keep the factories running, getting production out of workers GM would have to pay if they didn't work. (Under its contract with the United Auto Workers, GM must pay laid-off hourly workers 95 percent of their normal pay.) Higher production volumes provide economies of scale that enable GM to reduce both the per-unit cost of parts and the per-vehicle cost of GM's heavy retiree pension and health care commitments. And keeping the sales momentum going boosts employee and dealer morale, as well as dealer profits. (Coincidentally, healthy new vehicle sales are the backbone of a healthy U.S. economy.)

Some industry observers believe there may be a more fundamental strategic consideration behind GM's actions. Their hypothesis goes like this: After a decade of cost cutting, GM has become the low-cost domestic producer, approaching the best of the import makes in efficiency. The company knows it's in a war of attrition with the imports, whose market share likely will continue to grow at the expense of the domestics as they invade more of the high-profit luxury vehicle, minivan, SUV, and full-size pickup segments. In this competitive environment, GM considers the Ford Motor Corporation and the Chrysler group as its major targets, not the Japanese and Europeans. They say GM would never admit this publicly, but it may feel its best chance at successful long-term survival lies in out-lasting its domestic rivals and stealing from them a bigger percentage of the shrinking domestic share. And as the low-cost domestic producer, GM will be hurt less by incentive wars than Ford or Chrysler.

GM's response to this speculation: "There's no calculated strategy to in-flict harm on some other manufacturer. We are playing the hand that we have." They've been playing it quite successfully so far. Despite its sky-high incentives, GM's net income from January 2001 through June 2003 was $4.7 billion, while Ford lost about $5.1 billion in that two-and-a-half-year period.

GM's critics are right when they claim there's a significant downside for GM and its domestic competitors, that these incentive wars are self-destructive in the long term. While big incentives help support today's sales and market share, there is strong evidence that heavy use of rebates has a negative effect on a nameplate's brand image. (In the J.D. Power & Associates 2001 Vehicle Quality Study, no nameplates for which customer cash was used for more than one-half of the vehicles had an image above the industry average.) A declining brand image depresses future sales and forces automakers to rely even more heavily on incentives, perpetuating a spiral that eventually can become the road to ruin.

Once consumers are conditioned to expect periodic $3,000 to $4,000 re-bates or zero-percent financing, it is very difficult to wean them from these drugs. Automakers paint themselves into a corner where they're no longer selling their vehicles, instead, they're selling their deals. This reinforces the consumer's impression that the real value is in the deal, not the product, and eventually no one will buy that brand unless there's a new incentive big enough to make the Guinness Book of World Records. But whenever the Big Three cut back on incentives, sales slip. It's a classic Catch-22.

Most car buyers don't realize that there's also a significant consumer downside to this price cutting. A rebate may save them $4,000 when they buy, but they'll give back about $3,000 of that saving when they sell or trade their vehicles. Big rebates and zero-percent financing make new vehicles relatively more attractive than used ones, severely depressing the prices of used vehicles. In addition, most buyers aren't aware that there will be constant price increases throughout the model year to help pay for these big incentive offers. (GM, Ford, and Chrysler each had six to seven price increases on 2003 models throughout the model year.)

It's safe to conclude that the competition will remain brutal and that the biggest incentives will continue to come from Detroit. If a big rebate or low-cost/no-cost financing rings your bell, shop for a GM, Ford, or Chrysler vehicle. If that incentive isn't there today, wait till tomorrow.

Here's an overview of the positions of the domestic and import nameplates:

GENERAL MOTORS
The domestic market leader and price setter.

- *Chevrolet*—The heartbeat of GM, if not of America, accounting for 55.3 percent of GM's 2002 domestic-nameplate sales. Business breakdown: 30 percent cars and 70 percent trucks, which deliver most of GM's profit. Held market share well in the 1998–2002 period (15.7 percent in 2002). Lacks a competitive minivan entry. Vulnerable to inroads from import-nameplate SUVs and pickup trucks.

- *Buick*—GM quality leader, along with Cadillac. 9.1 percent of GM's 2002 sales. Held share from 1998 to 2002 (2.6 percent in 2002). Car business slipping, with slack picked up by Rendezvous and Rainier SUV entries. Biggest problem: average 2003 Buick buyer was 63 years old.

- *Pontiac*—10.9 percent of 2002 GM sales, but losing ground. Market share fell from 3.5 percent in 1998 to 3.1 percent in 2002. Ugly-duckling Aztek SUV an embarrassing failure, and the Montana minivan doesn't measure up to competition. Needs truck-like vehicles, but retail-store pairing with GMC limits GM's options.

- *GMC*—11.4 percent of 2002 GM sales. Gained share in truck-favoring market (2.9 percent in 1998 and 3.2 percent in 2002). Like Chevy, vulnerable to inroads from import-nameplate SUVs and pickups.

- *Cadillac*—4.2 percent of GM's 2002 sales, but a much bigger percentage of profit. With the Escalade SUV addition, held market share (1.2 percent in 1998 and 1.2 percent in 2002). Critical issue: Prospects who grew up driving Hondas and Toyotas are not turning to domestic nameplates when they shop for luxury vehicles. Can GM attract enough of these younger buyers with SUV and CTS entries to offset the dwindling number of 60-plus-year-old DeVille customers? If it can't, does Cadillac have a future?

- *Saturn*—5.9 percent of 2002 GM sales. 1.5 percent market share in 1998 and 1.7 percent in 2002. A potentially good crop that GM has let lie fallow in the field. There's a bigger niche than 1.7 percent for a one-price, no-dicker brand, but a better sales experience alone won't get GM there. Saturn needs a more compelling vehicle lineup.

FORD MOTOR CORPORATION
A strong #2, but usually must play follow-the-leader to GM.

- *Ford*—87.7 percent of Ford's 2002 domestic-nameplate sales. Business breakdown: 29 percent cars, 71 percent trucks, which account for 90 plus percent of Ford brand profits. Lost market share from 21.1 percent in 1998 to 17.8 percent in 2002, mostly the result of dropping money-losing passenger cars (Escort and Contour). F-Series pickups and Explorer SUV are #1 sellers in their segments. New family sedans (Accord and Camry fighters) planned as 2005 models. Vulnerable to inroads from import-nameplate minivans, SUVs, and pickups.

- *Lincoln*—4.4 percent of 2002 Ford sales, but a higher percentage of profits. Market share 1.2 percent in 1998 and 0.9 percent in 2002. LS sedan and Navigator SUV additions not enough to offset loss of bread-and-butter 60-plus-year-old Town Car buyers. Aviator SUV selling poorly and probably will be dropped. Critical issue is the same as Cadillac's: Lincoln isn't on the shopping lists of enough younger prospects. Can Ford reinvent the brand relatively quickly to appeal to a younger audience? (That's no slam dunk.) If it can't, does Lincoln have a future?

- *Mercury*—7.7 percent of 2002 Ford sales, but fading. Market share dropped from 2.6 percent in 1998 to 1.6 percent in 2002. Problem: no unique vehicles, just clones of Ford nameplates. Minivan and small SUV additions will help, but will still be Ford dittos. Ford needs to shore up the entire Lincoln-Mercury franchise.

CHRYSLER GROUP

The domestic company least able to weather incentive escalation, but must go along to get along. Plagued by a long-term record of below-average dependability. Profits have been hard to come by since the DaimlerChrysler merger in 1998.

- *Chrysler*—21.8 percent of Chrysler group sales in 2002. Business breakdown: 66 percent cars, 34 percent trucks. Market share up from 2.0 percent in 1998 to 2.9 percent in 2002. Major concern: Two vehicles account for over 60 percent of sales: PT Cruiser, potentially a fad-type vehicle vulnerable to new competitive "retro" designs, and Town & Country minivan, under attack from strong Japanese entries. If GM ever figures out how to build an appealing minivan, Chrysler will be in big trouble.

- *Dodge*—Chrysler group leader with 57.3 percent of 2002 sales. 28 percent cars, 72 percent trucks. Market share down from 9.3 percent in 1998 to 7.5 percent in 2002. Like Ford, vulnerable to inroads from import-nameplate minivans, SUVs, and pickups.

- *Jeep*—20.9 percent of Chrysler group sales. Market share 3.0 percent in 1998 and 2.7 percent in 2002. Legendary brand name, but the lowest overall image scores among domestic nameplates and third lowest of all brands in the J.D. Power 2001 Vehicle Quality Study—below Hyundai and above only Isuzu, Suzuki, and Kia. Off-road product focus out of sync with increasing consumer demand for more refined SUVs with car-like ride and handling. (Fording water, climbing rocks, and slogging through sand are not high on the wish lists of most prospects.) Major challenge: improving product quality.

THE JAPANESE CHALLENGERS

With Toyota/Lexus leading the way, the relentless Japanese companies are forging ahead in all market segments and account for the lion's share of sales of import nameplates.

There are four tiers of Japanese competitors, based on sales volumes and market strength.

- The Tier 1 leaders, Toyota/Lexus and Honda/Acura, accounted for 64.6 percent of Japanese-nameplate U.S. sales in 2002.

- Nissan/Infiniti is alone in Tier 2 (15.9 percent of Japanese sales), well behind the two leaders but leagues ahead of the rest.

- Mitsubishi (7.4 percent), Mazda (5.6 percent), and Subaru (3.9 percent) populate Tier 3.

- Suzuki (1.5 percent) and Isuzu (1.1 percent) lie at the bottom in Tier 4.

Japanese Tier 1

TOYOTA MOTOR SALES, U.S.A. (TOYOTA & LEXUS)

Toyota, the world's third largest auto manufacturer, is closing in on Ford's #2 global position (6,168,000 sales in 2002 vs. 6,820,000 for Ford) (GM is #1). With its healthy sales growth in Europe and Asia as well as in North America, Toyota is probably the strongest global automaker. Toyota accounted for 37.8 percent of Japanese-nameplate sales in the U.S. in 2002, but U.S. sales represented just 28.5 percent of its worldwide total. Fortunately for Toyota, the increasing demand for its products is based mainly on their legendary quality and reliability, not on the size of Toyota's rebates.

Toyota and the other Japanese manufacturers are not immune to the U.S. incentive frenzy. But in the wild discounting battle in the April–June quarter of 2003, Toyota spent only one-fourth as much per car as Detroit did on incentives (rebates, dealer cash, and cut-rate financing). And Toyota's net income for that quarter was greater than the *combined* incomes of GM, Ford, and DaimlerChrysler.

Think of Toyota as a boxer—pound for pound, the best in the ring. It is an international heavyweight that is giving the domestic heavyweight division all the fight it can handle and winning more often than not.

- The Toyota brand had a 9 percent share of the U.S. market in 2002. Business breakdown: 55 percent cars, 45 percent trucks. The Camry is in a perennial battle with Honda's Accord for supremacy in the midsize sedan segment. The Corolla is one of the best-selling compact cars. And Toyota covers the SUV spectrum like a blanket, from compact (RAV4) to midsize (4Runner and Highlander) to full size (Sequoia) to luxury (Land Cruiser).

- Toyota's Lexus luxury-nameplate landed on our shores in late 1989 and had surpassed both Cadillac and Lincoln in sales by 1999. 2002 U.S. market share: 1.4 percent.

- Toyota is also a world leader in developing and marketing fuel-efficient, low-emission hybrid powertrains for vehicles like the Prius sedan. Look for a hybrid to be an option on most Toyota vehicles over the next few years.

There are no charity cases among dealers who sell Toyota's products. Measured by the average number of vehicles sold per dealership in 2002, Toyota was the #1 nameplate (1,265 per dealer) and Lexus was #2 (1,171 per dealer). The late Janis Joplin sang, "Lord, won't you buy me a Mercedes-Benz?" If she were alive today, she'd ask instead for a Toyota or Lexus dealership.

AMERICAN HONDA MOTOR COMPANY, INC. (HONDA & ACURA)
Toyota is Japan's U.S. leader, but Honda is a strong runner-up, accounting for 26.8 percent of Japanese-nameplate U.S. sales in 2002. Honda is much more dependent on the U.S., which represented 44.3 percent of the company's worldwide sales in 2002. Like Toyota, Honda's growth is based mainly on its reputation for quality and reliability. Honda vehicles sell quite well without incentives.

- Honda's midsize Accord and compact Civic are among the ten best-selling vehicles year after year. As the light truck segment grew dramatically in the early 1990s, Honda realized that it would lose market share in the U.S. if it didn't develop attractive entries. The key additions so far: the popular CR-V and Pilot SUVs and the Odyssey minivan. Honda's U.S. market share in 2002: 6.4 percent. Business breakdown: 67 percent cars, 32 percent trucks.

- Honda was the first Japanese company to launch a luxury division (Acura), recognizing that it couldn't successfully sell a $30,000 or more vehicle under the same nameplate as a $12,000 compact car. Today, Acura enjoys top ratings on quality and reliability, and its TL sedan and MDX SUV are strong sellers. Acura's 2002 U.S. market share: 1 percent.

Japanese Tier 2

NISSAN NORTH AMERICA, INC. (NISSAN & INFINITI)
With 15.9 percent of Japanese-nameplate U.S. sales in 2002, Nissan has Tier 2 to itself. (The U.S. accounted for 27 percent of the company's global total in 2002.)

Nissan has always made reliable vehicles, but its quality scores, while good, have not been among the leaders. Since most consumers don't rate Nissan as highly as Toyota and Honda, Nissan and its dealers have been more likely to fall back on price as a major reason to buy.

The company's major problem over the years has been its product strategy: the vehicles it offered didn't hit the nail on the head in the segments they were aimed at. For years, the Sentra was a very spartan car, compared to the Corolla and the Civic. The Altima was sized and priced between Civics and Accords, and Corollas and Camrys. And the Maxima was at the high end of the midsize segment. In short, these cars didn't compete effectively against the key Japanese alternatives most of their prospects were considering.

Nissan has effectively addressed this issue in recent years.

• The Sentra is now a worthy competitor to the Corolla and Civic. The Altima is Camry-and-Accord sized and priced. With these changes, the Maxima is now properly positioned at the high end of the midsize segment. And all Nissans are designed to appeal to people who actually want something that's fun to drive. (Think of the Maxima as "the poor man's BMW.") Nissan's 2002 U.S. market share: 3.9 percent. Business breakdown: 64 percent cars, 36 percent trucks.

• Nissan has entered the full-size pickup segment with the Titan and the full-size SUV segment with the Pathfinder Armada, which is larger than a Ford Expedition. These will hit Detroit where it hurts most: in the wallet.

• Infiniti was introduced in 1989, the same year as Lexus, but Nissan's luxury-vehicle division has been much less successful. In 2002, Lexus sales were 2.6 times those of Infiniti. The problem: again, product strategy. The quality and reliability scores were sky-high, but most Infiniti offerings were gussied-up versions of Nissan vehicles, and the consumer wasn't that impressed. Nissan has been busy cleaning up that act, and Infiniti now has several unique, compelling vehicles in the lineup. 2002 U.S. market share: 0.5 percent.

Japanese Tier 3

The combined U.S. sales of the three Japanese companies in this group are about equal to those of Nissan/Infiniti.

MITSUBISHI MOTORS NORTH AMERICA, INC.
Mitsubishi had 7.4 percent of Japanese-nameplate U.S. sales in 2002, but hasn't had a strong enough model lineup to generate sustained consumer enthusiasm. (The U.S. represented 18.7 percent of Mitsubishi's 2002 sales

worldwide.) 2002 U.S. market share: 2.1 percent. Business breakdown: 75 percent cars, 25 percent trucks.

• The Galant midsize sedan has never been the bread-and-butter traffic draw Mitsubishi needs to expose the entire product line to a wider range of prospects. (The Accord does that for Honda, the Camry for Toyota.)

• This brand's biggest problem: a long-term record of poor-quality and -reliability scores. As a consequence, Mitsubishi typically needs substantial incentives to sell cars, and it becomes the fall-back choice for those who don't want to pay the price for a Toyota, Honda, or Nissan. Mitsubishi occasionally reports huge losses due to its deep discounting in the U.S.

Mazda Motor Corporation
Ford owns a 33 percent controlling interest in Mazda, but this brand has been losing ground or treading water in the U.S. market for years. Mazda sold 342,000 vehicles in the U.S in 1989, the year the Miata roadster arrived to start a widely hyped new-product blitz. By 2002, U.S. sales were down to 258,000, just 5.6 percent of Japanese-nameplate units (but 26.8 percent of Mazda's worldwide sales). Through most of the intervening years, Mazda's product line was heavy on sporty two-door cars and out of sync with a market that wanted more SUVs and trucks. In short, Mazda almost "niched" itself to death. (Evidence: the Miata product name has better unaided recall among most consumers than the Mazda brand name.)

• Like Mitsubishi, Mazda has needed a midsize family sedan that competes effectively with the Camry and the Accord. The 626 wasn't the answer, and the jury is out on the Mazda6. The MPV is a nice minivan that sells relatively poorly. And Ford has been unwilling to give Mazda a midsize SUV that would compete with the Explorer.

• With only so-so quality ratings, a somewhat uninspiring model lineup, and a limited advertising budget, Mazda and its dealers must use price as a major sales motivator. 2002 U.S. market share: 1.5 percent. Business breakdown: 61 percent cars, 39 percent trucks.

Subaru of America, Inc.
Subaru accounted for just 3.9 percent of Japanese-nameplate U.S. sales in 2002, but it's probably the strongest brand in Tier 3. That's because it has the clearest brand identity: it sells only all-wheel drive (AWD) vehicles. (U.S. sales accounted for 32.4 percent of Subaru's global total in 2002.)

- In 1996, only two of twenty Legacy models came with AWD. Today, all Subarus do. With AWD its reason for being, Subaru has created appealing products for its core sales area: the snowbelts in the Northeast, the Midwest, and the Northwest. With their above-average dependability ratings, Subaru vehicles typically sell well without big incentives. 2002 U.S. market share: 1.1 percent.

Japanese Tier 4

The two companies at the bottom of this ladder accounted for just 2.6 percent of Japanese-nameplate sales in 2002.

AMERICAN SUZUKI MOTOR CORPORATION

Suzuki represented 1.5 percent of Japanese-nameplate U.S. sales in 2002. The company's internal slogan: "Committed to Superior Value." You can interpret this as, "Our cars are cheaper to buy than their cars." One reason: Suzuki's incentives are typically high in relation to the price of its vehicles. 2002 U.S. market share: 0.4 percent.

Unfortunately, Suzuki's quality and reliability scores have always been well below average. As a result, Suzuki's vehicles depreciate very rapidly, and most of those front-end "superior value" savings evaporate when you sell or trade them. Worth noting: the U.S. is a relatively unimportant market for Suzuki, accounting for just 4 percent of worldwide units in 2002.

AMERICAN ISUZU MOTORS, INC.

As noted earlier, the value of GM's 49 percent investment in Isuzu has been wiped out by losses. Isuzu's U.S. sales plummeted from 117,000 in 1994 to just 53,000 in 2002 (1.1 percent of Japanese-nameplate units and a U.S. market share of 0.3 percent), with no bottom in sight. Plagued by poor-quality and -dependability scores and hamstrung by a lack of marketing dollars, Isuzu may not survive much longer in the U.S. market, which represented just 11.6 percent of its global sales in 2002. Isuzu has a reasonably successful commercial truck business. GM may decide that's where Isuzu's focus should be and take the company out of the passenger vehicle business.

THE EUROPEAN ROYALTY

If you asked Americans to name the auto brands they'd most aspire to own someday, European nameplates would rate high on that list. Despite the recent high-end gains by the Japanese, the luxury-car heritage associated with nameplates like BMW and Mercedes-Benz gives those brands a permanent "cachet halo" among U.S. consumers.

This was illustrated dramatically in the 2001 Vehicle Quality Study conducted by J.D. Power. Respondents were asked to rate their feelings about the "overall image" of 34 brands on a scale from 1 ("Unacceptable") to 10 ("Outstanding"). J.D. Power then ranked each nameplate based on the percentage of respondents rating a brand 9 or 10. The European brands captured eight of the top twelve "image" positions:

1. Mercedes-Benz

2. BMW

3. Lexus

4. Porsche

5. Jaguar

6. Volvo

7. Acura

8. Audi

9. Cadillac

10. Lincoln

11. Saab

12. Volkswagen (Land Rover was number eighteen)

Most of us would probably be surprised to hear that all nine European nameplates combined accounted for only 6.9 percent of U.S. car sales in 2002. But of course, exclusivity breeds cachet. If everyone drove them, they wouldn't be considered so special.

Likewise, if we were asked to name the auto brands with the highest dependability ratings, many of those European nameplates would be among the first few mentioned. And most of us would be surprised to learn that few Europeans are among the quality leaders today. (See the next chapter for more on this subject.) But perception hasn't caught up with reality on these brands. They still retain their strong positive images, built over many decades. As a result, compared to the domestic nameplates, the

Europeans typically sell for higher prices, need fewer incentives, and retain their value better as used vehicles.

As with the Japanese, there are a few tiers of European competitors, based on sales volumes and market strength.

• The Tier 1 sales leaders, Volkswagen/Audi, BMW, and Mercedes-Benz, accounted for 76.7 percent of European-nameplate U.S. sales in 2002.

• Volvo is alone in Tier 2 (9.5 percent of European-brand U.S. sales in 2002), well behind the leaders but ahead of the rest.

• Jaguar, Land Rover, Saab, and Porsche are at the bottom in Tier 3 and combined they represented 13.8 percent of 2002 European-nameplate sales in the U.S.

European Tier 1

VOLKSWAGEN OF AMERICA (VW & AUDI)

Volkswagen AG is the world's fourth largest auto manufacturer. VW accounted for 36.4 percent of European-nameplate sales in the U.S. in 2002, but its U.S. sales represented just a small fraction (8.5 percent) of VW AG's worldwide total.

• Volkswagen is the only European brand making cars aimed at the big, fat middle of the market, with a lineup stretching from the Golf at the bottom through the Jetta and the Beetle to the Passat. It's also a nameplate that has come back from the almost-dead. In 1986, VW sold 217,000 cars in the U.S., but had plunged to just 50,000 by 1993. By the end of the 1990s, however, the Jetta, Passat, and reincarnated Beetle were all solid sellers. Aided by advertising deemed "cool" by VW's young target audience, this lineup sold 338,000 cars in 2002, giving the VW brand a 2 percent U.S. market share. VW's biggest problem: an ongoing history of poor-quality ratings—a heavy load to carry when your key competitors are named Toyota and Honda.

• In 1985, Audi sold 74,000 cars in the U.S. Then *60 Minutes* dealt the brand a near-fatal blow with a charge of "unintended acceleration," and sales dropped like a stone, bottoming out at 12,000 in 1991. It's been a long road back, but with the popular A4 sedan and its Quattro AWD transmission leading the way, Audi sold 86,000 cars in 2002—a 0.5 percent share of the U.S. market. A nice recovery, but like VW, Audi's reliability ratings trail those of most of its major competitors. That's not good news for a name-plate aspiring to luxury-brand status.

BMW OF NORTH AMERICA (BMW & MINI)

The BMW group is the world's fourteenth largest automaker. It accounted for 22 percent of European-nameplate U.S. sales in 2002, when the U.S. represented 24 percent of BMW's global sales.

• After peaking at 97,000 U.S. sales in 1986, the BMW brand slipped to just 53,000 in 1991, shocked by the Japanese luxury introductions of Lexus and Infiniti cars, which offered better quality at lower prices. But BMW responded smartly with a line of cars consistent with its heritage and designed and priced attractively for its natural constituency: folks who want cars they can actively enjoy *driving*. In 2002, BMW sold 232,000 cars in the U.S., for a market share of 1.4 percent—the same as Lexus and well ahead of both Cadillac and Lincoln.

• The MINI Cooper compact car joined the BMW lineup in 2002, registering a 0.1 percent share of the U.S. market.

MERCEDES-BENZ

Reeling from the impact of the Japanese luxury-car invasion, Mercedes sold just 62,000 cars in the U.S. in 1993 and was no longer considered the import luxury car leader in either resale value or value for the dollar. It started to revamp its product lineup in 1994, and it's been on a roll ever since, selling 213,000 vehicles in the U.S. in 2002 and accounting for 18.3 percent of European-nameplate sales. 2002 U.S. market share: 1.3 percent.

• Mercedes' biggest challenge: improving the surprisingly poor-quality and -reliability ratings it has registered in recent years.

• Worth noting: In 2002, Mercedes asked dealers to sell their cars at the full sticker price, as Saturn does. Benz apparently believed it had the only luxury cars anyone wanted. They said they did this "to increase customer loyalty." Yeah, sure. The real purpose: To eliminate retail price competition between dealers by fixing prices at a level that maximized the automaker's and the dealers' profits, all at the expense of you, the customer. (Would paying thousands more increase *your* loyalty?) This policy has been a failure; consumers wouldn't buy it in the supercompetitive U.S. luxury car market. It's safe to assume that Mercedes dealers are dealing, but you'll seldom find incentives on the brand.

European Tier 2

VOLVO

This Ford-owned nameplate stands alone in Tier 2, selling 111,000 cars in the U.S. in 2002—9.7 percent of European-nameplate sales. Volvo's U.S. market share: 0.7 percent. Volvo's image strength is still based on its safety heritage, though the addition of air bags and antilock brakes in most new cars has eroded Volvo's once-exclusive ownership of the safety position. The brand's dependability ratings have slipped to below average in recent years. Volvo tends to employ significant dealer cash incentives on slower-selling models, especially late in the model year.

European Tier 3

JAGUAR

In 2002, Jaguar sold 61,000 cars in the U.S., accounting for 5.3 percent of European-brand sales and a 0.4 percent U.S. market share.

• Jaguar has always been a niche player in the luxury segment, separated from the pack by its distinctive styling. Ford purchased the brand to provide a luxury-car option with more youthful appeal in case the Lincoln nameplate continues to sink slowly in the West. Some industry observers described Ford's view as, "Let's make Jaguar our global luxury brand and keep Lincoln as long as it will go."

• The best reason for buying a Jag: not many folks do. (Where's the exclusivity in driving a Lexus, when over 230,000 of your neighbors buy one every year?)

• Ford wants to increase Jag sales significantly, but moving down market too quickly in the quest for more volume risks eroding Jaguar's high-end image. That could become an issue with the entry-level X-Type, which boosted Jaguar to a 37 percent sales gain in 2002, but may be viewed longer term as a gussied-up Ford, not a true Jaguar. (Porsche almost ruined its reputation by selling high volumes of cheaper cars with the Porsche name over two decades ago. And Acura is still rebuilding its image as a luxury nameplate, which slipped badly when the $15,000 to $20,000 Integra grew to over 60 percent of Acura sales.)

• To Ford's credit, it has improved Jaguar's quality significantly—no small feat for a nameplate that used to log more time in the dealer's service department than in useful service to its owners. But as noted earlier, Jaguar profits have been elusive.

LAND ROVER

Land Rover is a tiny dot on the U.S. new-vehicle landscape. Its 41,000 sales in 2002 represented 3.6 percent of European-brand sales and a 0.3 percent U.S. market share. Ford purchased the brand in early 2002 from BMW, for whom it was a substantial money loser. (For perspective, Ford sold 41,000 Explorers every seven weeks in 2002.)

• Ford wants to ramp up Land Rover sales, but as with Jaguar, it must do that carefully. The entry-level Freelander increased brand sales dramatically in 2002, but may not enhance Land Rover's position long term—especially given the nameplate's dismal long-term record on quality and dependability.

SAAB

In 2002, Saab, which is owned by GM, sold 38,000 cars in the U.S., 3.3 percent of European-brand sales and a 0.2 percent U.S. market share. That's not enough. A U.S. sales total under 40,000 is the sign of a car company flirting with extinction in the competitive luxury-car segment. To become a more significant factor, Saab needs greater penetration outside its traditional Northeast stronghold. To become profitable, it also needs a wider product line.

• The main reason for buying a Saab remains what it has always been: "It's different, which says I'm different." But over the years the number of people making that statement has dropped as the price of Saabs has escalated. The challenge for GM as it expands the Saab line is to deliver vehicles that have the drive and feel of a Saab, which is known for its sporty handling and performance.

• Barely on the radar of most new-car shoppers, Saab needs the highest incentives of any European nameplate to sell its cars. Most are probably sold to current Saab owners.

PORSCHE AG

Like Audi, Porsche has come back from the near-dead in the U.S. After plummeting from 30,000 sales in 1986 to 4,000 in 1993, Porsche has turned its business around and was back up to 21,000 U.S. sales in 2002 (1.8 percent of European-brand sales). That was 39 percent of Porsche's global units.

- Porsche is a tiny factor in the car business, but the brand has more cachet—and testosterone—than any other. It's everyone's fantasy nameplate, one that few can afford and even fewer can rationalize buying. (Imagine how differently your friends would view you if you showed up tomorrow in your new Porsche.) A Porsche is an emotional, right-brain purchase decision, but many prospects want it so much it becomes a real need. The dealers' assumption is that the purchasers' right brains are in control, while their left brains are unplugged.

- With fewer than 200 Porsche dealers nationally, there's little real competition for your business in many markets. Transaction prices tend to get more flexible in economic downturns. But if you want one and can't postpone gratification until the next recession, go for it. Life was made to be gulped, not sipped.

THE KOREAN PRETENDERS

Korean manufacturers Hyundai and Kia accounted for 3.7 percent of U.S. auto sales in 2002. They are the low-price leaders in an expanding number of small and midsize market segments. Both use incentives frequently. (Daewoo sold 20,000 cars in the U.S. in 2002, a 0.1 percent market share, but has since gone into bankruptcy.)

HYUNDAI MOTOR AMERICA

Hyundai came to the U.S. market with the entry-level Excel subcompact, 264,000 of which were sold in 1987. But the Excel was a poor-quality product, and Hyundai sales slipped below 110,000 in 1992. Since then, the company has added several higher-priced vehicles, improved its quality somewhat, and strengthened its warranty substantially to build consumer confidence. Sales have responded well (375,000 in 2002, a 2.3 percent U.S. market share). Hyundai's major appeal is its relatively low price. While the brand's quality and reliability scores have been improving, they remain well below average, and that is reflected in higher depreciation and relatively low resale values.

KIA MOTORS AMERICA

Kia arrived in 1994 and was selling 83,000 vehicles in the U.S. by 1998, but struggling financially. In a closed bidding in October 1998, Hyundai purchased a controlling 51 percent of parent Kia Motors Corporation. Kia's U.S. sales grew to 237,000 in 2002, a 1.4 percent share of the market. (Hyundai and Kia's combined U.S. sales in 2002 represented 20.8 percent of their worldwide units.) Kia's Achilles heel: quality. From its introduction through the 2003 model year, Kia has been rated dead last on every quality and reliability study we have seen.

WHEN IS AN IMPORT NAMEPLATE NOT AN IMPORT VEHICLE?

This question is worth considering.

My brother wouldn't consider buying a car with a Japanese nameplate. He was born after December 7, 1941, but he still can't forgive the attack on Pearl Harbor. (His home has Japanese-brand televisions, stereos, and DVD players, so go figure.)

He's not alone. There are lots of folks who have personal reasons for avoiding imported brands in many product categories—many of them simply patriotic Americans who are tired of seeing that so many things they want or need are made in China, Taiwan, or Tierra del Fuego, instead of in the good old U.S.A.

But today we live in a global-economy world, where many brands are sold almost everywhere and the economic and political realities argue for producing products in the countries where they'll be sold. Most of the major Japanese and European players have established manufacturing beachheads in the U.S. to insulate themselves from the pricing dilemmas caused by unpredictable fluctuations in international monetary exchange rates and, in some cases, to escape higher labor costs in their countries.

As a result, a high percentage of the "import-nameplate" vehicles sold in the U.S. are assembled in factories in the U.S. and other parts of North America. Of the 4,647,000 Japanese-nameplate vehicles sold in the U.S. in 2002, only 1,765,000 (38 percent) were assembled in Japan. The other 2,882,000 (62 percent) were built in North America.

Granted, the profits from selling these vehicles to dealers are repatriated to those other countries. But it's also true that tens of thousands of Americans have steady jobs because of those production facilities.

Toyota, for example, has assembly plants in Cambridge, Ontario (Corolla, Matrix, and Lexus RX), Georgetown, Kentucky (Camry, Camry Solara, and Avalon), Princeton, Indiana (Tundra, Sequoia and Sienna), and

Fremont, California (a joint venture with GM where Corollas, Tacomas, and Pontiac Vibes are built). Toyota builds V6 and V8 engines for its vehicles in Jackson, Tennessee. A Tacoma assembly plant will start up in Tijuana, Mexico, at the end of 2004. And Toyota will begin assembling Tundras in a new San Antonio, Texas, facility in 2006, bringing the company's total North American production capacity to about 1,650,000 units per year.

Toyota employs some 34,000 people throughout North America, and the San Antonio plant will create another 2,000 jobs. These production facilities represent a direct investment of nearly $14 billion, and Toyota's annual purchase of parts, materials, goods, and services from North American suppliers totals nearly $20 billion.

Similarly, Honda has assembly plants in Alliston, Ontario, Marysville and East Liberty, Ohio, El Salto Jalisco, Mexico, and Lincoln, Alabama. Subarus and Isuzus are built in Lafayette, Indiana, and Mitsubishis in Normal, Illinois. Nissans are assembled in Smyrna and Decherd, Tennessee, Aguascalientes and Cuernavaca, Mexico, and Canton, Mississippi. Mazdas are built in Flat Rock, Michigan, Edison, New Jersey, and Kansas City, Kansas, and Suzukis in Ingersoll, Ontario. And Hyundai is building an assembly plant in Montgomery, Alabama, that will produce 300,000 vehicles a year starting in 2005.

Among the Europeans, BMW assembles its Z-Series and X5 in Spartanburg, South Carolina, and Mercedes-Benz builds its M-Class in Vance, Alabama, and most Volkswagens sold here are put together in Pueblo, Mexico.

This is a two-way street. The domestic manufacturers produce many of the vehicles they sell here outside of the U.S. Chrysler builds PT Cruisers in Toluca, Mexico, Ram pickups in Lago, Alberto, and Saltillo, Mexico, passenger cars in Brampton, Ontario, and minivans in Windsor, Ontario. Ford assembles minivans and pickups in Oakville, Ontario, and passenger cars in Hermosillo, Mexico, and St. Thomas, Ontario. And GM builds SUVs in Ramos Arizpe and Silao, Mexico, and Ingersoll, Ontario.

So when is an import nameplate not an "import vehicle"? And when is a domestic nameplate not a "domestic vehicle"?

Not easy questions to answer, are they?

The next two chapters will address important issues you should consider as you narrow your new-vehicle choices: product quality and crashworthiness.

4

Whatever is worth doing at all, is worth doing well.
—Philip Dormer Stanhope
Earl of Chesterfield

What They Don't Want You to Know About Product Quality

n the early 1980s, when GM was making cars to quality standards that would have embarrassed even the Russians, GM's market research chief tried to inform Chairman Roger Smith of the problems. As those who were there tell the story, Smith actually put his hands over his ears so he wouldn't hear the bad news!

More than twenty years later, GM was still dealing with that legacy of poor quality. In mid-2003, the company aired *a mea culpa* "Road To Redemption" advertising campaign, conceding that it had produced a lot of lousy vehicles over the years. (That wasn't new news to most Americans.)

Today, GM and all automakers pay closer attention to quality for two key reasons. First, the Japanese have captured a major market share based mainly on their fanatical attention to quality, "raising the bar" for all manufacturers. Second, J.D. Power & Associates' new-vehicle research has put the spotlight on quality, and companies scoring well trumpet their success in advertising. As a result, everyone is building better cars today.

Does that mean that relative quality has become a nonissue in the consumer's choice of a new vehicle? Nope. If it were a nonissue, why would companies scoring well spend all those advertising dollars celebrating their scores? The fact is, perception is reality for consumers, and they vote their perceptions with their wallets. So all manufacturers want to magnify positive impressions.

WHY ADDRESS QUALITY?

My job is to help you spend your money more intelligently. And product excellence—or the perceived lack thereof—can impact you financially in this, typically the second largest purchase you'll make in your lifetime (the first is your house). That's because the biggest cost item involved in owning a car isn't gasoline, repairs, or insurance. It's *depreciation*—the difference between what you pay for it when you buy it and what you get for it when you sell or trade it. (This is true even if you're leasing, since the biggest chunk of your monthly payment is for depreciation.)

As noted in the previous chapter, vehicles from automakers with higher quality and reliability ratings may cost more initially, but eventually return much of that price premium to their owners because people are willing to pay more for them as used vehicles. They also tend to need fewer expensive repairs and deliver longer useful lives. Add all these potential savings, and it is not unusual for folks comparing cars in different price segments to discover that the total cost of ownership over several years is less for a vehicle they initially thought was out of their price range.

Quality is difficult for us to judge subjectively. New cars appeal first to the eye, then (as we sit in them and drive them) to our other senses. When you step out of that five- or ten-year-old beater with the engine rattle that you've been driving, slip into one of those sexy cockpits with the lumbar support, inhale that new car smell, hear the silky-soft purr of that brand-new engine, and insert a CD into that 250-watt sound system, it's easy to believe that all new cars are built with exceptional quality. (That smell comes mainly from the new upholstery and the glues automakers use to attach the inside headliner fabric to the roof.)

But all new vehicles are not created equal. The gulf between the best and the worst is narrower than it was years ago, but it's still a gulf. My role is to make you aware of facts that many manufacturers and dealers might not want you to know. And the relative quality of the vehicles they build is often at the top of the list.

The best way to judge a vehicle's quality is to survey a large sample of its owners about their experiences. You and I can't do that, but the research firm of J.D. Power & Associates does it each year. J.D. Power's three key studies cover initial quality, longer-term dependability, and customer satisfaction with dealer service. The nameplate-by-nameplate results from these surveys have been difficult to uncover in the past. But in recent years they've been reported in detail in several national publications—among them *USA Today,* the *Wall Street Journal,* and *Automotive News,* the industry's weekly newspaper, as well as in *The Power Report,* published monthly by J.D. Power. We've used all of these sources to gather the information in this chapter.

INITIAL QUALITY

Initial quality is one important criterion prospects use in their purchase decision. About one-third of them cite "defect-free when new" as a reason to prefer one nameplate over another.

To measure initial quality, every year J.D. Power asks 50,000 new-vehicle buyers about problems experienced in the first 90 days, then ranks nameplates by the average number of problems per vehicle. The best models average one-half of a defect per vehicle, the worst average two to three. Those differences may seem small, but going from near-bottom to near-top would require a monumental change in the way an automaker operates and several years to accomplish.

These early problems tend to be relatively minor—electrical glitches, wind noise, a rattle in the glove compartment, etc. (Does anyone actually put gloves in there?) No new cars fall apart in the first 90 days. But industry experts believe attention to detail on little things likely to go wrong in the first 90 days usually correlates well with attention to detail on bigger things likely to go wrong thereafter.

Here are the nameplate rankings from J.D. Power's 2003 Initial Quality Study for 2003 models. (The 2002, 2001, and 2000 model rankings are shown in parenthesis.)

1. Lexus (1, 1, 2)	19. Dodge (23, 29, 28)
2. Cadillac (7, 9, 16)	20. Nissan (28, 19, 19)
3. Infiniti (2, 7, 3)	20. Lincoln (10, 20, 13)
4. Acura (2, 3, 1)	22. Pontiac (18, 27, 25)
5. Buick (9, 7, 8)	23. Hyundai (28, 32, 34)
6. Mercury (21, 16, 15)	23. Volkswagen (27, 26, 33)
7. Porsche (12, 14, 6)	25. GMC (25, 21, 27)
8. BMW (7, 4, 4)	25. Suzuki (35, 36, 36)
9. Toyota (4, 5, 5)	27. Jeep (26, 23, 29)
10. Jaguar (19, 2, 10)	27. Subaru (30, 31, 32)
11. Honda (6, 11, 7)	29. Mazda (31, 35, 20)
11. Volvo (5, 22, 17)	29. Mitsubishi (24, 28, 23)
13. Chevrolet (13, 18, 26)	31. Saturn (10, 13, 23)
14. Audi (16, 14, 13)	32. Saab (21, 5, 11)
14. Mercedes-Benz (13, 10, 9)	33. Mini (new make in '03)
16. Oldsmobile (17, 24, 21)	34. Kia (36, 37, 37)
17. Chrysler (15, 12, 18)	35. Land Rover (32, 34, 30)
17. Ford (20, 25, 22/tie)	36. Hummer (new make in '03)

Note: Isuzu, which was not rated in 2003 because the sample size was too small, was #33 in 2002, #32 in 2001, and #31 in 2000.

LONG-TERM RELIABILITY

While initial quality is one key quality measurement, most car buyers put more stock in how a vehicle performs over a longer time period, when the problems encountered are likely to be more expensive and aggravating. According to J.D. Power research, 52 percent of consumers place long-term reliability high on their criteria list, well ahead of both initial quality and technology.

In the cutthroat U.S. auto market, nameplates that score poorly in reliability surveys can develop a stigma that's hard to erase, lowering the perceived value of their vehicles, both new and used.

J.D. Power's Vehicle Dependability Studies address this issue by measuring the average number of problems per vehicle over several years. In the 2003 study, 55,000 respondents were asked about the reliability of 2000 models after three years of ownership. The nameplate rankings, from top to bottom, were:

1. Lexus	13. BMW	25. Dodge
2. Infiniti	14. Subaru	26. Audi (tie)
3. Buick	15. Nissan	26. Mercedes-Benz (tie)
4. Porsche	16. GMC	28. Jeep
5. Acura	17. Chevrolet	29. Volvo
6. Toyota	18. Saturn	30. Mitsubishi
7. Cadillac	19. Oldsmobile	31. Hyundai
8. Lincoln	20. Mazda	32. Isuzu
9. Honda	21. Pontiac	33. Volkswagen
10. Mercury	22. Chrysler (tie)	34. Suzuki
11. Jaguar	22. Ford (tie)	35. Daewoo
12. Saab	24. Plymouth	36. Land Rover
		37. Kia

Reviewing the rankings of the "European Royalty" nameplates, many are probably surprised to see: (1) Jaguar so near the top, (2) Audi, Mercedes-Benz, and Volvo so far down the list, and (3) Volkswagen so close to the bottom. Here's a bigger surprise from this study: on average, models produced by the Big Three domestic manufacturers had fewer problems than the Europeans at three years of ownership.

PERCEPTION VS. REALITY

Over the years, some nameplates have developed reputations for producing "bulletproof" vehicles, while others are known for building cars that cause continual problems for their owners. These perceptions impact consumers' behavior in the selection process as they consider, then reject certain vehicles, narrowing their choices.

In J.D. Power's 2001 Escaped Shopper and Owner Loyalty Study, an average of 14.5 percent of respondents cited reliability concerns as a reason for rejecting vehicles they had considered initially. For most nameplates, consumers' perceptions of reliability closely matched the reality revealed in the dependability study results shown above. For example, fewer than 5 percent of Honda, Toyota, Lexus, and Acura shoppers rejected those brands for reliability reasons. But 30 to 40 percent cited reliability as a reason for removing Land Rover, Suzuki, and Kia from their shopping lists.

This study also illustrates how far consumers' quality perceptions can lag behind reality for some nameplates. Specifically:

- 30 percent of Jaguar shoppers rejected the brand because of reliability concerns. Throughout most of the 1980s and 1990s, Jaguar's reliability was dismal. You needed to own two because one was always being repaired. Under Ford's stewardship, Jaguar's quality and dependability have improved dramatically, but the stigma from the past continues to haunt the brand.

- By contrast, Mercedes-Benz is rarely rejected for reliability concerns, but no longer warrants its bulletproof reputation. In the J.D. Power Initial Quality Study, Mercedes' 2000 models ranked #9 of 37 nameplates. Three years later, those same cars had plummeted to #26 in the Dependability Study, behind midpriced brands Subaru, Chevy, Mazda, Ford, Dodge, and twenty others. (Back in 1990, Mercedes ranked #1 in J.D. Power's first Vehicle Dependability Study.)

- Volkswagen has always ranked well below average in both Initial Quality and Vehicle Dependability studies, but is seldom rejected for reliability reasons. It has the youngest owner profile of any nameplate and a "cool" image, and its customers either aren't aware of VW's reliability issues or are willing to overlook them.

CUSTOMER SATISFACTION WITH DEALER SERVICE

In recent years, a few companies with lower quality rankings have improved their initial bumper-to-bumper warranties, hoping that this would reassure their prospects about quality and increase sales. As examples, Hyundai and Volkswagen have done this, but with very different results.

- Effective with 1999 models, Hyundai improved its basic bumper-to-bumper warranty to 5 years/60,000 miles, with a powertrain warranty of 10 years/100,000 miles. When Hyundai bought Kia in 2000, it placed the same coverage on Kia vehicles. (Not a single luxury nameplate offers warranty coverage this comprehensive.) This change led to an immediate and dramatic increase in Hyundai and Kia sales, even though Hyundai's quality position was still well below the industry average and Kia's was dead last.

- Taking a page from Hyundai's book, Volkswagen increased its basic warranty from a stingy 2 years/24,000 miles to a generous 4 years/50,000 miles, starting with 2002 models. But this upgrade did not have the same effect. VW sales fell 4.9 percent in 2002 and were down 13.9 percent in the first eight months of 2003. Unlike Hyundai, VW had no poor-quality image to overcome among its prospects. The consumer's perception of VW's quality has always been much higher than the reality exposed in J.D. Power research. In that situation, a better warranty seemed to have little or no leverage on sales. It was a solution in search of a problem.

Many car shoppers may find these improved warranties reassuring enough to tip the scales in favor of a vehicle with poor-quality scores. ("If it breaks, no problem. They'll fix it, for free, right?") But how satisfied will they be with the service they get when they need it?

J.D. Power addresses this issue in its annual Customer Service Index (CSI) study, which focuses on consumers' experience with dealer service departments during the first three years, when the majority of vehicle warranty work is performed.

The 2003 CSI Study was based on the responses of almost 106,000 new-vehicle owners and lessees, who reported their experiences with both warranty repairs and routine maintenance. In recent years, industrywide quality improvements have changed the nature of the service business. On average, warranty repairs accounted for 53 percent of dealer service work in 1999, but just 43 percent in 2003. Note, however, that the service mix between repairs and maintenance can differ substantially from one nameplate to another.

• Brands that perform well in J.D. Power's Initial Quality and longer-term Vehicle Dependability studies have fewer quality problems and therefore need fewer warranty repairs. The bulk of their dealer service visits will be for regular scheduled maintenance. For routine maintenance, nameplates that score well in the 2003 CSI study are those that schedule appointments within a short time frame and get customers in and out of the service department quickly on their visits. If a brand with few quality problems ranks poorly in the CSI study, that's probably because its dealers don't perform well on these two criteria.

• Brands that perform poorly in the quality and dependability studies have more problems, and most of their service visits will be for repairs, not routine maintenance. For warranty repairs, the highest ratings go to brands that diagnose the problem correctly and fix it right the first time. If a poorer quality nameplate has a low ranking in the CSI study, that's probably because it needs repair frequently.

The brand rankings from the J.D. Power 2003 CSI study are shown below. Scores are based on a 1,000-point scale. The industry average score: 851.

1. Infiniti (900)	11. Volvo (868/tie)	24. Ford (845/tie)
2. Saturn (896)	14. Mercury (867)	26. Subaru (841/tie)
3. Acura (895/tie)	15. Oldsmobile (863)	26. Mazda (841/tie)
3. Lexus (895/tie)	16. Chevrolet (858/tie)	28. Toyota (838)
3. Lincoln (895/tie)	16. GMC (858/tie)	29. Mitsubishi (833)
6. Cadillac (893)	18. Chrysler (857)	30. Hyundai (832)
7. Saab (892)	19. Honda (854)	31. Nissan (831)
8. Buick (889)	20. Audi (852)	32. Land Rover (812)
9. Porsche (874)	21. Jeep (851)	33. Volkswagen (795)
10. BMW (873)	22. Pontiac (849)	34. Kia (786)
11. Jaguar (868/tie)	23. Plymouth (846)	35. Suzuki (781)
11. Mercedes (868/tie)	24. Dodge (845/tie)	36. Isuzu (780)
		37. Daewoo (737)

This study suggests that putting a longer warranty on a poorer quality brand does not result in high consumer satisfaction with dealer service.

Note also that Toyota dealers' service ranked relatively poorly in this study. This certainly suggests that dealers selling relatively bulletproof, problem-free vehicles don't necessarily deliver great routine maintenance service. One possible reason for Toyota's poor showing: Toyota, with 1,203 dealers, sold more new vehicles per dealer (1,265) than any other nameplate in 2002, which means the average Toyota dealer has to deal with many more service customers than other dealers. (For perspective, Chevrolet sold 2,633,000 vehicles in 2002 vs. 1,522,000 for Toyota. But Chevy had 4,180 dealers selling an average of just 630 per store, half the total of the average Toyota dealer.)

ONE MORE WORTHWHILE SOURCE OF RELIABILITY DATA

In its April annual auto issue, *Consumer Reports* predicts the reliability of current-year models, based on frequency-of-repair data from subscriber responses to an annual questionnaire. Vehicles are ranked in one of five quintiles: much better than average, better than average, average, worse than average, or much worse than average.

We would be sure to check the reliability data in this issue, which you probably can find at your local library, and I'd avoid any vehicles rated below average. Alternatively, you can visit the *Consumer Reports* web site, www.consumerreports.org, where you can purchase access to all the data for a modest fee. While there, you should also check to see if recent models of your vehicle are on their list of "Used Cars To Avoid."

5

Once harm has been done, even a fool understands it.

—Homer, *The Iliad*

Right Brain,
Left Brain

After talking with thousands of car shoppers, we are convinced that the purchase of a new car is primarily a right-brain decision.

If your left brain could talk, it would say that no one needs a new car to get from point A to point B, that there are plenty of good used cars that will do the job just as well and save you a bundle, too. In response, your right brain would say that life is to be gulped, not sipped— that our time on earth is too short to drink wine from a box, eat any ice cream but Häagen-Dazs, or drive someone else's problem.

People buy new cars because they feel they deserve them. New cars are about self-esteem and reward for hard work. They are toys that provide gratification for the kid who lives inside every grownup. They are also accessories that we wear like suits, dresses, or cellular phones—visible statements of who we are, or at least who we'd like others to think we are.

Given the strong emotional tug of the product, our selection criteria tend to be more subjective than we admit. Do I like the way that car looks? Do I look great in it? Has it got an awesome stereo system? Do I like the way it handles? Will the trunk hold four bags of golf clubs? Does it have enough cupholders?

Of course, we all claim to have practical criteria. But, truth be told, often the only controlling one is whether we can afford the monthly payment. If we can, and it's a great-looking car that fits our image of the perfect personal chariot, we'll buy it. We justify that right-brain decision with some left-brain rationale ("It's got four-wheel drive, so it'll go better in the snow"). But mainly we're buying what we want, not what we need.

On one level, there's nothing wrong with that. All the fun stuff happens on the pleasure side of the brain, and what's life without pleasure? It's only natural for someone who spends the equivalent of three or four weeks in a car each year to want a comfortable "home away from home." *But in that decision process, most of us don't give enough consideration to the critical issue of the safety differences between one car and another.*

BE SAFE, NOT SORRY

The time to research the safety question is *before* you form an emotional attachment to a specific vehicle. New cars are very seductive, and once you've committed to one in your mind, it's difficult to view it objectively. The kid in you wants it in your garage *now.* And if safety negatives turn up late in the selection process, it's easy to rationalize that the safety equipment mandated in the last couple of decades has made all cars safe.

True, every new passenger vehicle must meet the federal standards that specify minimum safety levels. Those standards now include the installation of air bags, the highest-profile auto safety devices in history— and a high-tech panacea. We've got front-impact air bags and side-impact air bags and head-impact air bags, and someday we'll probably have roof-impact air bags. Encouraged by the government's PR campaign and the automakers' marketing hype, lots of Americans think they're riding around in a bubble-wrapped cocoon, insulated from harm.

Wrong.

Air bags work, but not nearly as well as originally projected. When the National Highway Traffic Safety Administration (NHTSA), part of the U.S. Department of Transportation, mandated air bags back in 1977, the agency calculated that air bags alone would reduce the fatality risk in all crash modes by 40 percent. As reported in the *Wall Street Journal,* NHTSA's subsequent study of accident experience found that an air bag reduces this risk by 13 percent for unbelted drivers and by just 9 percent for the other two-thirds of drivers who use their seat belts. These reductions are certainly worthwhile, but they're a far cry from the original promise. Some auto safety experts have concluded that the same increase in protection could be obtained simply by driving a car that's 200 pounds heavier. And they worry that air bags encourage a false sense of security among drivers of smaller cars.

Safety Lesson 1 is a no-brainer: *Just as rock beats scissors and match beats paper in that old kids' game, big beats small in a car crash.*

We can't repeal the laws of physics. When a big car and a small car smack into each other at highway speeds, the folks in the big car will probably walk away, but all the king's horses and all the king's air bags might not be able to save those in the small car. In relation to their numbers on the road, small cars experience more than twice as many occupant deaths each year as large cars. So everything else being equal, you should buy the biggest, heaviest car you can afford. If you're considering buying a cute little subcompact for a teenage daughter or son, you'll sleep much better if you spend the same amount on a used Ford Crown Victoria. (Your child won't like it as well, but heck, it's still free wheels.)

GIVE SERIOUS WEIGHT TO RELATIVE CRASHWORTHINESS

Unfortunately, most of us can't afford leviathans-of-the-road like Cadillac Devilles, Lexus LS Sedans, and Chevy Suburbans. So we need to pay close attention to Safety Lesson 2: *All autos are* not *equally safe, even if they're essentially the same type, size, and weight.* Some vehicles are inherently safer than others in a serious crash because they are structurally sounder, and the choice you make could turn out to be a life-or-death decision for you or someone you love.

Fortunately, reliable crash test data are available from two main sources.

One is the National Highway Traffic Safety Administration (NHTSA), which has been conducting head-on tests since 1978. In these simulated tests, the entire front of each vehicle hits a rigid barrier at 35 miles per hour. That's equivalent to a head-on collision between two similar vehicles each moving at 35 mph. Instruments measure the force of impact to each dummy's head, chest, and legs. The resulting information indicates a belted person's chances of incurring a serious injury in the event of a crash. (A serious injury is one requiring immediate hospitalization and may be life threatening.) Tested vehicles receive scores from five stars (10 percent or less chance of serious injury) to one star (46 percent or greater chance of serious injury).

The NHTSA started conducting side-impact crash tests on passenger cars in 1997 and on pickups, SUVs, and vans in 1998. This test represents an intersection-type collision with a 3,015-pound barrier moving at 38.5 mph into a standing vehicle. The barrier is covered with material that has "give" to replicate the impact-absorbing area in the front of a vehicle. Side-collision ratings indicate the chance of a life-threatening chest injury for the driver, front-seat passenger, and driver's-side rear-seat passenger. Tested vehicles receive scores from five stars (5 percent or less chance of serious injury) to one star (26 percent or greater chance of serious injury).

We are not safety experts, but we wish the NHTSA's side-impact test also measured head injuries. The main reason it doesn't is probably because few automakers provide head-level side air bags. Surely one's head is particularly vulnerable in a side-impact crash. Most broken-bone injuries are survivable, whereas brain injuries frequently are not. The worst crashes often seem to be those where one car runs through a red light or stop sign at a high rate of speed and hits another vehicle broadside. If you always look to your left before proceeding from a stop sign or traffic light, you will minimize your risk of being in that situation.

The NHTSA also provides a "Rollover Resistance Rating," an estimate of your risk of rolling over if you have a single-vehicle crash. Most of these crashes occur when the vehicle runs off the road and is "tripped" by a ditch, curb, soft soil, or other object, causing it to roll over. Rollovers have a higher fatality rate than other kinds of crashes, usually because people not wearing seat belts get thrown from the vehicle. (You'll reduce your chance of being killed in a rollover by about 75 percent just by wearing your seat belt.) The Rollover Resistance Rating essentially measures a vehicle's center of gravity and tire track width to determine how "top–heavy" it is. Vehicles receive ratings from five stars (rollover risk of less than 10 percent) to one star (risk greater than 40 percent). SUVs are the most top-heavy vehicles and have the highest rollover rates, followed by pickups, vans, and passenger cars, which have the lowest centers of gravity.

The other major source of crash test data is the Insurance Institute for Highway Safety (IIHS), an independent, nonprofit research and communications organization wholly supported by automobile insurers and dedicated to reducing crash deaths, injuries, and property damage losses. Since 1995, the IIHS has been conducting 40 mph "offset" crash tests in which only part of a vehicle's front end hits a formidable barrier, simulating a two-vehicle collision at an angle, driver's side to driver's side. This frontal offset test provides a good indication of a vehicle's structural performance in serious crashes. Results are scored good, acceptable, marginal, or poor. Many of these tests have been shown on prime-time network news magazine shows.

The NHTSA full-front and the IIHS frontal-offset crashes complement each other, but they measure much different crash scenarios. The NHTSA's test crashes the full width of the front of a vehicle into a rigid barrier. This maximizes the energy absorbed by the crumple zone in the front of the vehicle so that the occupant compartment is more likely to remain intact. The full-frontal tests produce high-level occupant compartment decelerations, making them very demanding on the restraint systems, thus providing better information on the safety features and their performance. In the IIHS offset crash tests, only one side of a vehicle's front end is hit, thus a smaller area of the structure absorbs the energy from the crash. Offset crashes are more demanding on the structure of a vehicle, and intrusion into the occupant compartment is more likely in these crashes.

Again, we're not safety experts, but we give somewhat more weight to the IIHS offset test. We ask ourselves, "If we saw a vehicle coming at us head-on, wouldn't we naturally take some evasive action? If we still got hit, wouldn't that more likely be at an angle?" Ideally, a vehicle should perform well in both tests. You can find the results in magazines like the *Consumer Reports* annual auto issue, published each April. But these tests are conducted year-round. For the most recent information, we strongly suggest that you visit the web sites of these organizations. You will find the NHTSA data at www.nhtsa.dot.gov/cars/testing. The IIHS is at www.hwysafety.org.

With limited budgets, neither the NHTSA nor the IIHS can afford to test all vehicles. In deciding which new vehicles to test, both organizations choose those that are predicted to have high sales volumes or vehicles that have been redesigned with structural changes or improved safety equipment. These vehicles are purchased from dealerships, just as a consumer would, not supplied by the manufacturers.

How much stock should you put in these crash test results?

A great deal, we believe. You will probably be surprised at some of the vehicles that score poorly. Based on the results, there are always several relatively popular automobiles that we would not drive around the block if the automakers gave them away free. Of course, those automakers will claim that the tests are flawed, while the ones whose vehicles score well will use the results in their advertising. But the tests are what they are. One vehicle scores better than another because it's structurally sounder in that crisis situation, period. And if the manufacturer of the low-scoring vehicle has better results from its own crash tests, it can show us the film. (Strangely, manufacturers never do.)

This isn't a money issue; it's about your life and the lives of your loved ones. The purchase of a new car may be mostly a right-brain decision, but this is the one area where you should give your left brain total control early in the selection process. You may not decide to buy the highest-scoring vehicle, but you definitely should avoid any vehicle that gets the worst score on either test (one star on the NHTSA tests or poor on the IIHS test), even if you love everything else about it and have a $2,000 rebate coming on that automaker's affinity VISA or MasterCard.

Your chance of being in a similar crash is relatively small. But you can't control what another driver does on the open road, and if one ever crosses that double yellow line and plows into your family car, you'll be glad it didn't get one star or a poor rating in these tests.

6

*Necessity never made a good
bargain.*

—Benjamin Franklin

Attitude

Adjustment

Here are six basic principles of automotive negotiating that you
must burn into your brain. Think of them as the key facts that
will transform you attitudinally from a potential pushover into a
tower of strength. Make them your mantra.

ECONOMICS 101

First, understand that you are shopping for a commodity. Car dealers don't
want you to think that way, but in fact, every new car is a commodity.
Whether it's a compact pickup or a luxury sedan, it's essentially the same

product with the same basic pricing structure at every dealership selling that nameplate.

You will always get a better price on a commodity if you make it a competition between suppliers. Would a food company talk to just one sugar manufacturer? Would Random House contact only one paper company? Would an automaker get bids from just one tire supplier? Of course not. Yet, every day thousands of people walk into a car store to negotiate the price of a car, flunking Economics 101. They don't know any better. That's what they've always done, just like their parents did. Pity them, but don't follow them.

> ONLY A SOLID, GOLD-PLATED FOOL WOULD WALK INTO A CAR STORE TO NEGOTIATE THE PRICE OF A CAR.

If you take our advice, once you decide which car you want, you'll negotiate the price by making it a competitive bidding situation among several dealers. But you won't go anywhere near a car store. We'll tell you how to do this in chapter 19.

If the idea seems strange to you, ask yourself this question: If there were fifteen dealers selling the car you wanted on one street in your hometown, would you walk into each one to negotiate the price? Wouldn't you have to be a certified lunatic to subject yourself to that much pain?

GEOGRAPHY 101

If your first inclination would be to buy your new car from the nearest dealer, put that idea on hold for awhile. The reason: Often the best deal will come from dealers who are further away—maybe much further away. They'll look at you as "found business," a prospect who would never walk in their door. They might give you a deal they'd never give to someone in their town. (Since you don't live there, you won't be telling everyone that they're almost giving cars away.)

Contact your local dealer only after canvassing the others. If they can meet your best out-of-town offer or come reasonably close, why not buy from them? If they can't, why not take the better offer?

> HOME IS WHERE THE HEART IS, BUT THE BEST DEAL MAY BE ELSEWHERE. CASTING A WIDER NET OFTEN LANDS A BIGGER FISH.

TIMING 101

Car dealerships are sales-driven enterprises with monthly sales goals. Early in the month, optimism rules. But in the last week, dealers who aren't approaching their sales targets get more anxious to sell, and transaction prices get more attractive.

> ONLY A FOOL WOULD SHOP FOR A NEW CAR BEFORE THE LAST WEEK OF THE MONTH.

PSYCHOLOGY 101

Of course, you have to visit car stores to test drive the vehicles you're considering and finalize your choice. As we recommend in chapter 13, you will announce up front that you're there only to test drive, not to buy—that you've got an appointment to test another car in 90 minutes and that you're going to keep the appointment.

On those visits, avoid showing even the smallest display of enthusiasm for any vehicle. Car salesmen are trained to make the purchase process as emotional as possible. They believe that if they can get you excited about that car, they can sell it to you before you leave for that next appointment.

How do you avoid giving salespeople that signal? *By projecting total emotional detachment.*

In the showroom, on the lot, and during the test drive, your behavior should say: A car is a car, something that gets me from point A to point B. Lots of cars will do that, including many that this store doesn't sell. I'm going to check them all out and make the best deal.

(Ask your friends who shop for antiques about the "Don't-let-'em-know-what-you-really-want-as-soon-as-you-walk-in" rule. They'll tell you it also works well at estate sales, swap meets, and garage sales.)

> HEAVY BREATHING SHOULD BE RESERVED FOR MORE APPROPRIATE OCCASIONS. IN CAR STORES, IT LEADS ONLY TO HEAVY PAYMENTS.

That doesn't mean you can't fall in love. Just don't let the salesman know.

ANATOMY 101

Look down at the floor right now. That's where you'll find the most powerful negotiating tools you'll ever own: your feet.

> ONE REASON GOD GAVE YOU FEET WAS TO WALK AWAY FROM CAR SALESMEN.

Every car salesman dreads watching you walk out of his store, into the arms of another salesman at another store. He's got bags of tricks to keep you there for hours. (Dealers sometimes *require* that their salesmen *not let you leave* without seeing a sales manager!)

After your test drive, many salesmen will say, "Let's just take a minute to look at some numbers. You won't believe the deal we can give you on this car."

That may sound like a reasonable next step, but don't even think about traveling down that slippery slope. Just say, calmly but firmly, "No thanks. I don't want to waste your time or mine today. I've got some other cars to test. If I decide I want to buy this car, I'd be happy to give you a shot at selling me one."

Then remember that reason God gave you feet, and leave.

REALITY 101

Pick up any buyer's guide to this year's models, and you will find a mind-boggling offering of new cars and trucks. As noted earlier, there are many more choices than any civilized society needs to get around town. That's because the people who run car companies are terminal optimists who believe that if they build them, we will buy them—all of them. They eventually learn, painfully, that building them is easy, but selling them is hard. Then they are fired and replaced by a new crop of terminal optimists.

The reality is that there will be more car production capacity than car buying capacity for as long as anyone can see into the future. We'd have to take the minimum driving age down to three years old for all the manufacturers to realize the sales projections they made when they built their production facilities.

> THE REALITY IS THAT IT'S MUCH EASIER FOR YOU TO FIND SOMEONE
> WHO WANTS TO SELL A NEW CAR THAN FOR A CAR SALESMAN TO FIND
> SOMEONE WHO WANTS TO BUY ONE.

The reality is that you can walk away from any deal, or any car, and be absolutely certain there is one just like it, and probably better, around the next corner.

Trust this reality.

*The time is long overdue for this
industry—the largest and most
important industry in the
world—to erase the popular idea
that its No. 1 priority is to pull
the wool over everyone's eyes.*
　　—Automotive News editorial

7

The

Juggler

When you're buying a new car, the salesman has three balls in
the air, three important areas of opportunity where he can
make money on the transaction.

1. He can make money on the front end, on the difference between your
purchase price and the dealer's cost on that new vehicle.

2. He can make money on the back end, selling you things like financing (with related life and disability insurance), extended warranty coverage, and dealer add-on options like rustproofing and fabric protection.

3. If the deal includes your trade-in vehicle, he can make money on the difference between what the car store really pays for your car and what they get for it, either by retailing it through their own used-car department or by wholesaling it to a used-car dealer.

If it surprises you to learn that there can be more profit potential in the second and third areas than in the first, you are in the group that needs this book the most.

Think of the salesman as a juggler, trained to keep all these balls moving so fast that you can't tell which is which.

He wants to make a good profit on all three if he can. But the total gross is what counts, and there isn't a dealer alive who wouldn't give up profit on one of these balls to swing a deal if he knew he could make a killing on the other two.

The world is full of naive but happy car buyers who think they got a great deal because they bought "below dealer invoice." Or because they got a "fabulous trade-in allowance." Or a "big discount" on an extended warranty policy.

They watched only the ball that they were interested in. But the salesman watched them all.

We'll cover how to watch . . . and even control . . . what happens with each of these balls. But first you need an overall shopping plan.

Ninety-nine percent of the people in the world are fools, and the rest of us are in great danger of contagion.

—Thornton Wilder

If You Haven't Got a Plan, You Haven't Got a Prayer

The subject here isn't cars, it's your money, and how a big chunk of it will be divided between you and a car store and a bank or financing company (unless you're among the roughly one in five buyers who pays cash).

THE 80/20 RULE OF LIFE

The 80/20 Rule of Life is one of those maxims that applies to just about any subject you can name. It says that whatever the activity, 80 percent of it is accounted for by 20 percent of the people. Here are some examples:

- 80 percent of the beer is drunk by 20 percent of the drinkers.

- 80 percent of the auto accidents are caused by 20 percent of the drivers.

- 80 percent of the wealth is owned by 20 percent of the people.

- *And 80 percent of a dealer's profits on new-car sales comes from 20 percent of his customers.*

Remember, the salesman's goal is to maximize profit on every deal. He gets paid to determine the highest amount a prospect might be willing to pay and to get that customer's commitment to pay it.

To that salesman, every prospect represents a "slam-dunk"—a potential high-margin sucker deal.

To avoid waking up on the wrong side of Life's 80/20 Rule in this competition, you need a plan. Most people don't have one.

Here's the way most people approach the purchase process:

- They start by visiting car stores and getting excited about specific cars in the presence of car salesmen. *(That's a really bad idea.)*

- Then, still in "new-car heat," they wonder out loud how they'll pay for that pretty thing, and (you guessed it) the salesman tells them how easy it'll be. *(Another bad idea.)*

- Finally, too confused to turn suddenly rational, they wonder out loud what their current car is worth in trade, and they accept the number the salesman gives them without checking it out themselves. *(More bad ideas.)*

They'll repeat this behavior at several car stores and think they're out there dealing. The lucky salesman who gets them at 3:00 P.M. on Sunday will make his weekend quota, and the happy buyers will drive their new cars into the sunset without a clue that they are exactly the kind of prospects that every salesman dreams about.

YES, VIRGINIA, THERE IS A BETTER WAY

Smart buyers don't rely on car salesmen for any important information. They don't give them any either. Smart buyers have a shopping plan that reverses the sequence that most people follow:

- They start by focusing on the car they've got. They know that they're either going to sell it themselves or trade it in, and that the proceeds represent an important part of the new car's down payment. So they begin by finding out how much their vehicle is really worth in their market today, both at retail and at wholesale.

- Then they decide whether they'll sell it themselves at retail or trade it in at wholesale. (They know the difference affects the money available for their down payment.)

- Then they turn to the essential financial questions. They decide on the monthly payment they can handle comfortably, including auto insurance, which costs a lot more for new cars than for old ones. They also determine the down payment they can afford. They know that bigger is better, so they find some loose cash to add to what they'll get for their current car.

- They take all this information and shop for money before they shop seriously for a car or truck. This gives them a good fix on the maximum amount they can pay for a new vehicle, including all the miscellaneous sales taxes and license fees that many salesmen don't mention until you're committed to a price for the car. It also provides a basis for measuring the attractiveness of the financing offered by the dealer or manufacturer.

- They study the advantages and disadvantages of leasing versus buying and decide whether they are candidates to lease. If they are, they do additional homework to understand the key elements of leasing, including exactly how to do the arithmetic to determine the monthly payment.

- Concurrently, they're reading articles on the vehicles they're interested in for information to help narrow their choices, and they're visiting car stores to obtain brochures and take test drives. But they make it clear from the start that they are not going to buy on those visits, and they avoid getting into any salesman's "closing room" because they know they're not ready.

- They decide on at least two or three finalists, including the trim levels and optional equipment they'd like on each. They pick their first-choice vehicle and at least one attractive fallback alternative, based on both emotional appeal and rational analysis.

• Next, they find the dealer invoice cost for those vehicles and gather any available information on current factory-to-dealer incentives, as a basis from which to negotiate a purchase price confidently and aggressively. They also bone up on any direct consumer incentives being offered by the manufacturers.

• With solid knowledge of the wholesale and retail values of their current cars and the best financing they can arrange independently, they plan an aggressive approach that will get several car stores to bid competitively for their business.

• They understand the potential value of proper timing, in relation to both incentive programs and dealer sales targets, and they plan their approach accordingly.

• They understand the ways car stores try to boost their profits, including all the high-cost/low-value add-on options they'll try to sell, and they are ready to handle them.

• Finally, they go into the negotiating process determined to let the guys at the car store do the stewing. They know that those guys need us more than we need them.

For typical buyers, the serious shopping phase takes an average of about five weeks, from the time they start visiting car stores for test drives until the day they drive a new car home.

Following the smart buyers' lead, let's focus now on the car you drive today. We'll start with an illustration of what can happen when you don't keep a close eye on that ball.

Training is everything. The peach was once a bitter almond; cauliflower is nothing but cabbage with a college education.
— Mark Twain

Divide
and
Conquer

Read the next paragraph twice.

Even if you're the world's worst price negotiator when buying a new vehicle, the car store probably will make as much profit or more selling your late-model, well-maintained trade-in to someone else as it will make selling you a new car or truck. *And that profit will come directly out of your pocket.*

It's a fact. Today, the average dealer sells almost as many used cars as new. And although dollar sales of new cars are twice those of used, used-car departments deliver about as much total gross profit as new-car departments.

This is illustrated clearly in the tables below, which outline the key elements of the average dealership financial profile for 2002. The source of this data is the Industry Analysis Division of the National Automobile Dealers Association, the dealers' trade organization.

As shown in this first table, new-car sales accounted for almost 60 percent of a dealership's gross sales in 2002, used cars just under 29 percent, and service and parts almost 12 percent.

	Sales	% of Total
New-Vehicle Department	$18,651,091	59.6
Used-Vehicle Department	8,942,973	28.6
Service and Parts Departments	3,681,518	11.8
Totals	$31,275,582	100.0

Over the last several years, automakers have been raising dealer invoice prices by more dollars than they've been raising retail sticker prices, squeezing dealers' profit margins while also acknowledging tacitly that the manufacturers' suggested retail price (MSRP; sticker price) is pure fiction. Since only the retail prices get reported broadly in the media, they apparently think this will fool consumers into believing they are raising prices very little, or not at all. Which is nonsense, since what we pay for new vehicles is highly dependent on what dealers pay for them, not what it says on the fictional sticker. (If the MSRP were unchanged, but the dealer invoice price was raised by $500, transaction prices would go up by at least $500.)

As a result of these pricing decisions, today there's typically less than 12 percent gross profit built into the MSRPs for new cars. (For Mercedes-Benz, it's just 7 percent.)

As outlined below, the average negotiated new-car transaction price in 2002 delivered just under a 6 percent gross profit. But a few years later, dealer asking prices on those same cars as *used* vehicles will include a gross profit of 20 percent or more, and the average-transaction gross profit will be about 11 percent, as it was in 2002. So they'll earn as much gross profit selling them the second time as they did the first.

	Number Sold Per Dealer	Avg. Retail Selling Price	Gross Profit Per Vehicle	Profit % of Selling Price
New Cars	713	$26,163	$1,531	5.85
Used Cars	646	13,840	1,530	11.06

This third table shows the result: almost equal gross profits per year from used-vehicle and new-vehicle departments. But note one other key item: parts and service account for only about 12 percent of sales, but deliver half of the average dealer's gross profit. Keep this in mind as you go through the car-buying process. Remember that, for most dealers, it is better to sell one more car at a slim profit than not to sell it. More cars on the road mean more cars in the service department, where the most profit dollars are generated.

	Gross Profit	% of Total
New-Vehicle Department	$1,091,450	26.1
Used-Vehicle Department	988,638	23.7
Service and Parts Departments	2,095,368	50.2
Total	4,175,456	100.0

Okay, so the average dealership earned a *gross* profit of $4,175,456 in 2002. But that was before deducting overhead expenses—rent or mortgage payments on the land and building(s), utilities, management salaries and benefits, business insurance, interest on short-term loans, etc. Deducting those expenses, the average dealership's *net* profit in 2002 came to $599,210, 1.9 percent of total sales.

Total Dealership Sales	$31,275,581
Total Gross Profit	4,175,456 (13.4 percent of sales)
Less Dealer Overhead	3,576,246 (11.4 percent of sales)
Net Profit Before Taxes	599,210 (1.9 percent of sales)

While new-car and used-car departments provide almost equal *gross* profits, used-car departments typically deliver significantly higher *net* profits to a dealership because new-car departments carry a much steeper overhead burden. (If a dealer didn't sell new cars, there'd be no need for a fancy showroom, a receptionist, and nicely dressed salespeople to explain a new vehicle's features. There'd also be a much smaller dealer advertising budget.)

With new-car prices sky-high, there will be continuing strong demand for late-model, lower-mileage used cars. If you've got one, you're driving a little gold mine. Car dealers are in the used-car gold-mining business, thanks to the twin factors of simple economics and simple new-car buyers.

THE SIMPLE ECONOMICS

New-car pricing is supercompetitive because every dealer has essentially the same merchandise to sell at the same price. The one you want is the same car, with the same sticker and dealer invoice price, at every dealer selling that nameplate. That makes it relatively easy for the smart consumer to get the lowest price by having dealers bid competitively in an apples-to-apples comparison.

By contrast, all used cars are different from one another, even when they're the same year, make and model. One's an apple, the other's an orange. With no standardized sticker prices or dealer invoice costs and no easy way to measure their condition, especially that of the important parts under the hood, it's more difficult for consumers to evaluate their true worth. That makes it relatively easy for car stores to sell every one of them at a profit.

THE SIMPLE NEW-CAR BUYER

The key to a dealer's used-car profit is the new-car buyer. Two out of three deals include a trade-in. And most people literally give away their trade-in, without understanding what they are really getting for it.

That's because they don't watch all the balls. Instead, they let the salesman confuse the issue by juggling the new-car sell price and the old-car buy price in a single package deal.

They may think they're getting a great deal because the trade-in allowance is $1,000 over the wholesale Kelley Blue Book listed price or some other impressive-sounding measurement. They don't realize that the juggler's deal combines that apparently attractive trade-in allowance with a much higher new-car price than they could have negotiated without a trade-in. He's simply taking money out of one of their pockets and putting it in the other. By the time they agree to the package, it's all mumbo jumbo to them, but at least part of it sounds terrific.

The car store then turns the trade-in into a nice little money machine:

• If it's in relatively good shape and the dealer needs it in his used-car inventory, he'll spend a couple of hundred dollars making it look great and retail it himself for a profit of $1,500 or more.

• If it's in relatively poor shape, or if he doesn't need it, he'll take a quick $300 to $700 profit by wholesaling it the next day to a used-car dealer. (Each year, new-car dealerships wholesale over 5 million used cars to other used-car dealers.) Alternatively, he'll send it to a used-car auction.

Either way, he'll probably make more money on that trade-in than on the new car he sold.

The bottom line is that customers with desirable used cars who buy this kind of trade-in allowance deal typically leave between $1,000 and $2,000 on the dealer's table.

If your car is an ugly hulk that barely wheezes onto the dealer's lot, you won't lose much by letting him take it off your hands. But if you have a clean, one-owner, average-miles-for-age vehicle that's mechanically sound, there are two ways to keep most of that money in *your* pocket:

• The best way is to *sell it yourself* at retail, as illustrated in chapter 11.

• The second-best way is to sell it to a dealer, but for its *true wholesale value,* as covered in chapter 10. And not just any dealer. . . .

SELL IT WHERE IT'S WANTED

What's the dumbest thing most folks do when they trade in their current car? That's easy. *They trade it to the wrong dealer.*

Here's an example. A Fighting Chance customer in Los Angeles was buying a new Ford Explorer. Her trade-in was a five-year-old Toyota Corolla in great shape with just 24,400 miles on the odometer—a very desirable used car. (Most folks in Los Angeles drive 24,400 miles in *one* year.) The Ford dealer's first offer was $3,500. She negotiated that up to $5,500, but still felt it was a lowball number. She called us for advice, and we asked her the obvious question: "If you wanted to *buy* that used Corolla, would you look for it first at a Ford dealership?"

"Of course not," she said. "It would look like an orphan there, like maybe there was something wrong with it and the Toyota dealer, who really knows the car, didn't want it."

"It's the Ford dealer who doesn't want it," we told her. "He just wants to steal it from you and wholesale it to the Toyota dealer down the street. So why not eliminate the middleman? Take it down to the Toyota store and sell it yourself." An hour later she had sold it to the Toyota dealer for $6,875—$1,375 more than the Ford dealer's best offer.

As a general rule, a desirable used car will always be worth more to a dealer who sells that make. That doesn't mean you'll never see a Toyota on a Ford dealer's used car lot. You will. But it's a more natural addition to a Toyota dealer's inventory. Used-car shoppers are like new-car shoppers; they know what they want, and they'll go first to a dealer who sells that nameplate. That used Corolla was a more attractive offering on a Toyota lot, and the higher price reflected that fact.

There's another reason why that Toyota dealership wanted that car. Remember, dealers sell about as many used cars as new each year, and they make more profit doing it. But most people buying a new Toyota, if they have anything to trade in, are trading either another nameplate or an older Toyota that belongs on an independent used-car lot. So if you're running the used-car side of a Toyota dealership, your biggest challenge isn't selling used cars, it's finding attractive used cars to sell.

If you're shopping for one nameplate but your trade-in is a relatively low-mileage, late-model car with a different nameplate, always check with the used-car side of two or three dealers who sell your current brand to see what they might pay for it.

Lots of this is just plain old common sense, but it's amazing how many adult brains shift into neutral during the new-car purchase process. Most folks trade in their old cars where they buy their new ones, no matter what makes they are.

Note, however, that there are three situations where this rule may not apply.

1. Many dealers own several different new-car franchises, often located near each other. If the Ford dealer in our example also had a Toyota store, he might have offered more for that used Corolla.

2. A dealer's current inventory mix affects his willingness to pay top wholesale dollar for a used car. If the Toyota dealer in our example had been loaded with Corollas of the same model year and condition, he too might have made a lowball offer, intending to wholesale the car himself to another dealer.

3. New-car dealers usually don't want older, high-mileage cars of the same brand, even those in relatively good condition. If the five-year-old Corolla in our example had had an odometer reading of 100,000 miles instead of 24,400, the Toyota dealer wouldn't have wanted it. Many new-car dealers won't stock used vehicles with over 80,000 miles. They may offer a trade-in value on them, but they'll quickly wholesale them to an independent used-car dealer, moving them down the "automotive food chain" to a buyer who can only afford an older, high-mileage car. Again, if you've got a car like that to trade, our advice is to eliminate the middleman and sell it to the used-car store yourself. At least shop it at one or two used-car stores to get a benchmark against which to judge the new-car dealer's trade-in offer.

One last caveat on this subject: *The way your state calculates the sales tax on new cars will affect your decision on whether to trade in your used car or sell it to another new- or used-car dealer or to an individual.* Most states tax the full purchase price when you buy a new car. But some states allow you to deduct your used car's trade-in value from the purchase price and pay tax only on the difference. Let's assume you live in one of those states and your local sales tax rate is 8 percent. You negotiate a $25,000 price on a new car. The dealer gives you a $10,000 trade-in allowance on your old car, which means you'll save $800 on sales tax (8 percent of $10,000). So you'd have to get more than $10,800 from another buyer to end up with more money in your wallet. (We are not sales tax experts for 50 states, and the tax laws can change over time. So check with your accountant or your state's sales taxing authority before deciding what to do.)

If your state allows you to subtract the trade-in value before computing sales tax, here's a trick worth trying that might let you have your cake and eat it, too. If another dealer offers you more for your trade-in than the dealer who's selling you the new car, ask each one if they'd be willing to work a "courtesy trade" or "courtesy transfer." In that arrangement, the dealer buying your trade would pay the higher amount he's offered you to the new-car dealer, and the new-car dealer would credit that higher trade-in value to your transaction, saving you additional sales tax dollars.

Before you talk trade-in turkey with any car dealer, you must master the next rule. *It's the single most important factor to remember if you're going to succeed in this competition.*

DIVIDE AND CONQUER, COMBINE AND BE CONQUERED

Most new-car shoppers leave a lot of money on the table because they let the salesman combine two elements that should never be combined: the selling price for the new vehicle and the buying price for their used vehicle. When they let him do that, they lose the ability to watch all the balls. As a result, they pay more for the new car than a smart buyer would have and receive less for the old car than a smart seller would have. And they never know what they paid for one or what they got paid for the other.

Write this a hundred times on the blackboard of your mind:

- **BUYING A NEW CAR IS ONE DEAL.**

- **SELLING AN OLD CAR IS ANOTHER.**

- **KEEP THEM SEPARATE AND YOU'LL WIN.**

- **COMBINE THEM AND YOU'LL LOSE.**

Now let's develop the knowledge you need to keep them separate and thereby keep control of the negotiation.

It's powerful pantomime.

The skilled salesman doesn't say a word as he checks out your trade-in. His hands do the talking, lingering over every little scratch or blemish—silently, but effectively reducing the vehicle's value . . . in your mind.

Don't attend his performance. Give him the keys and wait for his return. You'll have a punch line of your own: you know what it's worth.

10

The Wholesale Truth, and Nothing But

The only right price for your trade-in is its actual wholesale value. Unless you know that number and make the salesman aware that you do, you will get less than true wholesale, and the car store will make an extra profit selling your old car. (You will never get more than true wholesale. If they offer more, the difference is coming from your wallet, not theirs, in the form of a higher price on the new car or a higher interest rate on the financing, or both.)

Knowing your car's true wholesale value also helps you decide whether to trade it in or sell it yourself. Compare that value to the retail price you can expect to get from an individual, a subject covered in chapter 11. The difference will surprise you. If you decide to trade it despite this difference, at least you'll be doing it with your eyes open.

THE LAZY PERSON'S ROUTE TO USED-CAR PRICE ESTIMATES

Today, most folks start with the Internet when researching used-car prices. The publishers of those used-car pricing books have web sites where they provide estimates of both trade-in/wholesale and market/retail used-car values. The best-known sites are Kelley Blue Book (www.kbb.com), Edmunds (www.edmunds.com), and the National Automobile Dealer Association (www.nadaguides.com).

But don't take these numbers too seriously. You will often find substantial differences between these sources, which suggests that there may be no "right" number for your car. That's not surprising, since every used car is unique, based on its age, mileage, and condition. More important, these sites don't necessarily reflect the current wholesale climate for your car in your market.

Local conditions always affect values. For example, there's a town in Oregon where almost everyone drives a pickup, so there's always a glut of used trucks on the market there. But take the same truck 40 miles down the road to a larger, more-urban market and it's worth $1,500 to $2,000 more. There's no way to learn that from any web site.

Those little pricing books you can purchase in bookstores or find in libraries have similar limitations. The numbers for the same car can differ widely from book to book. And they'll give you a value for your vehicle that's supposed to be good for more geography than Marco Polo covered in all his travels. (The Western Edition of one we subscribed to covered Arizona, California, Colorado, Guam, Hawaii, Nevada, New Mexico, and Utah. How could it tell me what my car was worth in Long Beach, California?)

Another problem: the "retail editions" of many of the pricing books sold in bookstores and on newsstands give estimates of high and low retail prices, but no wholesale prices. That's because they don't want to offend automakers and dealers, from whom they get much of their information. Check your town's main-branch library, which may subscribe to a more helpful edition—the one that shows both wholesale and suggested retail values. Ask for either the Kelley Blue Book's Guide to Used Car Values or the National Automobile Dealers Association's Official Used Car Guide.

Despite their limitations, these web sites and pricing books are not bad starting places to get a "big picture" feel for values. They will tell you whether your car is in the $10,000 or $15,000 ballpark, but they won't tell you reliably whether it's worth $9,700 or $11,200. If that's good enough for you, you may stop reading this chapter now.

LOGICAL SECOND STEPS

If your used vehicle is no more than 5 years old and has less than 80,000 miles on the odometer, visit a few used-car lots at new-car dealerships that sell the same nameplate to check their asking prices for cars like yours. You can figure that there's at least a 20 percent profit built into the average used-car sticker price. Assume that the dealer probably put some money into those cars after buying them to replace worn tires, fix a dent, or just to make them look good on the lot. If they were trade-ins, he may have paid about 75 percent of the price on the window sticker. That's roughly what he'd offer you for your trade—assuming he wanted your used car for his inventory. (If any of the cars there are "factory-certified" used cars, you can assume there's an extra $1,000 premium for that certification in the asking price.)

Don't bother with this trip if you have an older trade-in or one with more than 80,000 miles on the odometer. New-car dealers don't want that car. They typically won't retail older, high-mileage cars themselves; they'll either send them to used-vehicle auctions or sell them to independent used-car dealers.

You can check used-vehicle asking prices for cars of all ages on the Internet. The most comprehensive web site for that purpose is probably www.autotrader.com.

The suggestions above will give you a rough idea of your used car's value, but discovering its true wholesale value today in your market will require additional time and effort.

THE ROUTE TO A BETTER ESTIMATE

There's an old saying: Nobody has a decision to make until somebody makes them an offer. Unfortunately, you won't find any offers on used-car lots or web sites or in pricing books. To get a number you can rely on, you need to turn up some real offers.

You can do that by playing a little game some morning or afternoon, shopping your used car at a few stores near home or work. You should do this when you're within about a week of negotiating for a new vehicle. (We're assuming that you've got a vehicle that someone might find attractive, not a heap ready for the wrecking yard.)

First, make sure your vehicle is clean and mechanically sound. Then, assuming your vehicle is less than 5 years old and has less that 80,000 miles on the odometer, phone a couple of dealerships that sell the make you own. As noted in chapter 9, a late-model car should bring the highest price at stores that sell that make, where it's a logical addition to the inventory. Ask to speak to the person who buys used cars. (Be sure to write down that person's name, with the correct spelling; our name is the only thing we enter and leave this world with, and most people respond more cordially to strangers who get their name right.) Tell him that you own a very clean, one-owner used car and then give details on the model, model year, and mileage. Say that you want to sell this vehicle because you're buying another one, and ask if he's interested in seeing it. If he's not, he probably has more cars of that model and year than he needs, and you've saved yourself a useless trip. If he is, tell him you'll be there within the hour to have him check out the car. After you've generated interest at two or three dealerships for your used car, drive to the first one, pull into the used-car side of the business, and ask for the person by name.

As he approaches, remind yourself that the average dealer sells about as many used cars as new cars, that used-car sales account for as much gross profit as new ones, and that a continuous supply of salable used cars is essential for the health of the business, whether new-vehicle sales are up or down. When consumer confidence is high and new-car sales are healthy, folks who would normally buy older used cars from independent dealers are likely to be trading up to the newer ones offered on franchised new-car dealers' lots. When consumer confidence is depressed and new-vehicle sales are down, more people opt for used cars, but there are fewer trade-ins of the late-model, low-mileage cars they'd like to buy. Since only two of three new-car transactions include a trade-in, and many of those are vehicles a dealership won't want for its own used-car department, every used-car manager needs additional sources of good used cars—especially the attractive one-owner cars that are his bread and butter. If you've got one, he is probably more interested in buying it than he wants you to know.

HERE'S THE SCRIPT

Tell him that you're planning to sell your car, you don't want the hassle of selling it yourself, you're visiting a few used-car dealers, and you'd like to know what he'd pay for it. If he asks why you're not trading it for another, say you're buying your sister's year-old Accord.

He'll take the car, check it out, and come back with a figure. Whatever number he gives, you should say nicely, "That sounds low to me. I got the impression from a couple of other dealers that it was worth more than that to a good used-car operation." Then bite your tongue and wait for him to say something.

If he says that's his final offer, you've learned what you came in for. Thank him for his time and drive to another store.

With most used-car managers, however, the first offer is typically a lowball opener to see how easy and uninformed you are. He might increase his initial offer right away. More likely, he'll ask what the other guys offered, or what you want for it.

FOLLOW THE BOUNCING BALL . . .

Remember that your objective is to find out how much higher he might go, so that you can put a realistic wholesale value on your car. Your answer to his question will depend on the "value ball park" your car is in. Here are some rough guidelines for answers that will help you get to a realistic number:

- If his offer is below $5,000, tell him that based on other dealers' comments, you believe the car is worth *at least $750 more.*

- If his offer is between $5,000 and $10,000, tell him that based on what you've heard elsewhere, you believe the car is worth *at least $1,000 more.*

You get the idea. If your car's value ball park is higher than these ranges, raise your response accordingly.

Most important, after you respond with a "bump," bite your tongue again! Don't say another word until he says something in return.

If he says your figure is way out of line, ask him if that means his first offer was his best offer. If he says your number is high, ask him how high he thinks it is.

Chances are, he'll counter with a better number than his opener. At this point, tell him (if it's true) that you're the only owner, you've got all the maintenance records, you just had the scheduled service done last month, and all it needed was new brake pads. He's not going to have to invest big bucks in fixing anything.

Then pick a number halfway between your last figure and his, tell him you think it should be worth that much to him, *and bite your tongue again.*

At this point, he might say it's not worth that much, that his last offer was his best one. Or he might agree with your new number and ask if you'd sell it to him for that price.

Your answer to either response should be, "I'll certainly consider it seriously. I'm going to make a decision within the next week. How long will your offer be good?" Make a quick note of the answer, tell him you'll get back to him in a few days, thank him for his time, and head for your next stop.

However the discussion ends, you've learned your car's true wholesale value to that used-car operation. Remember, however, that one used-car department might be fully stocked and the dealer may not want your car unless they can "steal" it from you at a lowball price and wholesale it to another dealer for a quick, easy profit. To get a reliable estimate, you must repeat the drill at one or two other dealerships selling that make.

If you've got an older, lower-value car with 80,000 miles or more on the odometer, few new-car dealers will want it for their inventory, no matter what make it is. You should use the same tactics to shop it at two or three big independent used-car-only stores to determine its wholesale value to them.

You'll spend half a day doing this, but it'll pay off when a new-car dealer gives you a lowball trade-in offer and you tell him that another dealer offered you $1,000 more! And that's the wholesale truth.

Private individuals represent the majority of the used-car market. They've sold over $57 billion in used cars annually without taking trades, providing warranties or service.

Right or wrong, buyers will pay more for a privately owned car. Why? Trust.

—President of a consignment consulting firm that applies the real estate sales concept to the used-car market (quoted in *Automotive News*)

11

Who Needs a Middleman?

The best way to avoid getting used by a new-car dealer is to avoid trading in a good used car. Instead, sell it yourself to an individual. It's more work, but it pays awfully well. The difference between wholesaling it to a car store and retailing it yourself can be $1,000 to $2,000 or more for a mid-priced car in good shape. (Generally, the better the condition, the bigger the spread between wholesale and retail.)

Why give that much money to a middleman when there's bona fide demand for what you've got to sell?

Lots of people would rather buy a clean, well-maintained, one-owner car from an individual than take a chance on something from a used-car dealer. In fact, over 50 percent of used-car sales are between private parties. These folks think they'll get a better car for less money. Also, they typically can get the maintenance records from the owner, and knowing how it's been treated gives them more confidence in its worth.

This preference may be strongest among *nonsmokers,* who now number seven out of ten U.S. adults. Many of them will even pay a premium for a nicotine-free vehicle.

To get a feel for retail prices of cars like yours, it's okay to start by checking the web sites and pricing books cited in chapter 10. *But remember, those sources know little or nothing about the value of your car in your market this month.* You need to do more homework.

REACHING OUT: LEARNING BY TALKING, NOT WALKING

Fortunately, you can do this homework on the phone. Check the ads in your weekend paper and in those used-car classifieds that seem to be everywhere. Call a few private sellers and ask about their cars—price, mileage, condition, equipment, type of driving done, and whether (a) they're the original owner, (b) they've got the service records, (c) they've permitted smoking in the car, and (d) the car has ever been in an accident. (Tell them you'd plan to have it checked by a mechanic who can tell.)

If they're asking $7,000 or more, find out how low they might really go by picking a number that's between $1,500 and $2,000 less and asking if they'd consider selling it for that price. If they refuse, bump the number in increments, starting with a couple of $500 bumps, followed by one or two $250 bumps, until you find a price they'd consider. Thank them and say you'll think about it.

Then mentally compare your car with theirs to see if you think yours is worth more or less. If the cars are roughly comparable except that they're smokers and you're not, yours should be worth at least $300 more to a nonsmoking buyer, no matter what year or model.

Next, call a few new-car stores that sell your make and ask for the used-car department. Tell them that you're looking for a good, clean used car that's the year, make, and model of the car you own.

If they have one, ask about the mileage, how it's equipped, the asking price, and (lastly) the color. If it's blue, tell them you want red or white and thank them. Don't give them your phone number.

If they don't have one, tell them that you'd prefer to buy from a reputable dealer than from an unknown private party, and ask what would be a fair price. When they quote a price and say they'll find one, say you'll think about it, but you want to talk to a few more dealers. Thank them, but don't give them your phone number.

If you don't get a satisfactory response by phone, visit a few dealers' lots some weekday morning around 8:00 A.M., when there are no salespeople there. Walk around and check the inventory for used cars like yours. Figure that realistic selling prices will be 10 to 15 percent below the retail asking prices on the window stickers.

This exercise will give you a good idea of what your car is worth at retail compared to other cars of the same year, make, and model.

Based on this research among private parties and used-car departments, you should be able to pick your expected price, the price you actually think you can get. Figure that this number is somewhere in the range between realistic dealer selling prices and the prices those private parties would "consider." Then choose a *slightly higher* number for your asking price, keeping it below the used-car department's asking price.

Next, have your car detailed to make it look beautiful inside and out, have the oil changed and all the other fluids brought to the right levels, and fix any obvious engine, brake, or wheel alignment problems that might shake a prospect's confidence during a test drive and kill a sale. Also make sure the radio, air conditioner, heater, defroster, lights, wipers, and turn signals work.

NOW YOU'RE THE CAR SALESMAN

Now you're ready to call your newspaper or contact an Internet site like www.autotrader.com to place a used-car classified ad that describes the good things about your car. The hot buttons (if they're true) are one nonsmoking owner, low mileage, very clean, and complete service record. The service record can be particularly reassuring to potential buyers, since many used-car swindlers buy high-mileage cars at auctions, roll back the odometers illegally, and then pose as private parties selling "pampered, one-owner cars."

Don't put a price in the ad. Just say, "MUST SELL," and add the hot buttons just listed, your phone number, and the best weekday and weekend hours to call. (Internet sites like www.autotrader.com require that you list an asking price.)

When prospects respond to those ads, repeat the asking price you picked, but make it clear that you've got some flexibility. If they ask for your rock-bottom number, tell them that you haven't established one. Say that some other people are interested in the car, that it's a one-owner car that's been reliable for you, that you're sure somebody is going to like it a lot, and that you're confident you'll be able to work out an agreeable price with that person. Then ask if they'd like directions to your place and about what time you should expect them.

If they like the car when they see it but make an offer that's well below your asking price, assume that's not their final offer. Counteroffer somewhere in between, but still above the price your research said you can expect to get.

To create a greater sense of urgency and value, try the old car salesman's trick: Say you've been offered $450 more by someone who's coming back in the morning. If they really want the car, chances are good they'll raise their offer when they hear that, and your excuse for taking it will be a bird in the hand.

If they like the car but instead of making an offer they ask what your rock-bottom number is, tell them you really don't want to sell the car for much less than your asking price, that you've done a lot of comparison shopping and know it's a fair price for a clean, one-owner vehicle like yours. Then counter by shaving a couple of hundred dollars off your asking price, but stay well above your expected price.

Always bite your tongue and let them react to your counteroffer before you say another word.

If they react negatively, ask them what they'd be willing to pay. If that's ridiculously low, reject it politely and thank them for coming, adding that it's clear they aren't that enthusiastic about the car and you're sure someone else will be. If their willing-to-pay number is not that bad but still below your expected price, counter with that price.

Somewhere in this kind of firm but flexible exchange, you'll get a price you'll find acceptable, one that's a lot better than any car store will give you.

A NOTE OF CAUTION

Unfortunately, we live in a hazardous world. One of the risks you face in selling your car yourself is that it could be *stolen* by a prospective "buyer" during a test drive. The thief may even leave another stolen car with you. (He may be trading up.)

Here are some thoughts on handling this potentially delicate situation:

- Ideally, you shouldn't let anyone test-drive your car unaccompanied.

- But be wary. You wouldn't get into a stranger's car alone, so why would you get into your car alone with a stranger? If you don't have a tall, powerful friend to accompany you, don't go. Most prospective buyers would rather test-drive a car without the owner along anyway.

- It's perfectly proper to ask a stranger for identification before permitting a test drive. Check a driver's license and a credit card and require that he leave one of those items with you until he returns. If he carries no identification or won't cooperate, tell him that you're sorry but you won't allow anyone to test-drive your car without seeing and retaining proper identification.

- Trust your instincts. If you've got any reservations about a person, politely decline the request for a test drive.

- Some serious buyers will want to have your car checked over by a mechanic—an inspection they will pay for. That's a reasonable request, and a sign that you've got an excellent prospect. Again, however, you must be wary. You need a security deposit important enough to guarantee their return—perhaps a wallet full of important identification papers and credit cards, or their current car and keys, after checking the registration information against their other identification data.

Some prospects may be offended by your caution, but if you ask them to put themselves in your place, most will say they'd handle the situation the same way.

TIE UP THE LOOSE ENDS NEATLY

In closing the deal, be sure to do these important things:

- Get a nonrefundable deposit in return for taking the car off the market.

- Ask the buyer to get a certified check made out to you for the full sales price and to meet you at your bank at a mutually convenient time to sign over the title. Don't give possession of the car until this is done.

- Write out a sales receipt, in duplicate, that says you've sold the car "as is" for the agreed amount, and include the buyer's name, address, and driver's license number, plus the date, time of day, and both signatures.

• Call your state's department of motor vehicles to learn how to release your liability for parking and/or traffic violations and civil litigation resulting from operation after the date of sale. Obtain and complete the required form, and mail it promptly.

• Inform your auto insurance agent that you no longer own the car. He will advise you whether to transfer, suspend, or cancel your coverage.

We haven't tried to touch every base in this sell-it-yourself lesson. We've focused primarily on the money issues. If you have questions and need more counsel, you should call the financial institution that has your auto loan, your auto insurance agent, your state's motor vehicle department, or your local auto club for more information.

Now let's look at the issue of financing. (If you're paying cash, you can skip to chapter 13.)

12

Auto
Financing
101

Always remember that everything that happens in a car store is designed to make money for that store. There's nothing wrong with that; it's our free enterprise system at work. And that same great system can work for you, too, if you take action at every step to keep it competitive. The first step is shopping for money, and the time to do it is *before* you visit any car stores.

DON'T GET REAR-ENDED

When you get down to negotiating a final deal, the salesman is going to want you to "buy" your financing money through his store. As indicated in chapter 7, that's an important source of his store's profit on the back end of the transaction.

That's when another interested party will get involved—the F&I (finance and insurance) manager. There is a lot of pressure on him to add profit to every deal. He usually gets a commission on anything you buy on the back end, including financing and the life and disability insurance he'll try to include in the transaction. In fact, some F&I managers make more money than any salesman in the store.

The dealership may arrange financing through a bank or finance company, or through the auto manufacturer's own finance subsidiary. These so-called captive companies, such as Ford Motor Credit or General Motors Acceptance Corporation, are very important sources of credit. (GMAC is the largest finance company in the country, with more than $100 billion in assets.) Depending on the automaker, its captive company typically handles between 30 and 60 percent of the consumer financing for its vehicles. It also finances dealer inventories. Nationally, captives provide about 40 percent of all new-car financing, roughly the same percentage accounted for by banks. Credit unions and independent finance companies account for the other 20 percent.

Understand, though, that no matter which company does the actual financing, the car store acts as a middleman and receives a commission or fee for its service. Most often, this income comes from a dealer finance reserve, which is the difference between the contract rate charged to the consumer and the retention rate earned by the bank or finance company.

As a rule of thumb, figure that a car store can *double* its gross profit on a sale if it arranges the financing. No wonder there's pressure there!

Depending on the deal with the lending institution, the car store's participation fee can amount to 5 percent or more of the loan. The longer the term and the higher the rate, the more interest you pay . . . and the more commission the car store receives.

Let's assume the dealer "buys" the money for an auto loan of $14,000 from a lending institution at 8.5 percent interest and "sells" it to you on a 48-month loan at 10.5 percent interest. Over a four-year period that little 2 percent spread will put a $645 profit in the dealer's pocket, nearly 5 percent of the loan amount.

SURPRISE: THE DEALER'S DEAL MAY BE A GOOD ONE

You may find that the financing available through the dealership is quite attractive. To stimulate sales, auto manufacturers frequently offer subsidized, lower-interest loans through their own finance companies—often as an alternative to a customer rebate or dealer cash incentive. (You don't get to "double dip." Customers get either a cash rebate or a below-market interest rate on loans as long as four or five years, but not both. Dealers get either the cash incentive or the cut-rate financing for the customer, but not both.)

Some automakers seldom use conventional incentives such as rebates or dealer cash because they feel they damage the image of their brands. But to boost sales of specific models, these same companies periodically offer 3.9 or 4.9 percent financing on 48-month loans when the going market rate is over 9 percent. Since the consumer doesn't perceive a reduced interest rate as a cut in the price of the car, the brand's image doesn't suffer.

Note, however, that dealers earn no commission on loans with super-low interest rates. If the captive finance company is paying 5 or 6 percent for money and loaning it to you for 3.9 or 4.9 percent, there's obviously no financing profit for automakers to share with their dealers. And sometimes, when there's an eye-popping rate as low as .9 or even zero percent, the dealer actually has to *contribute* money to get that financing for a customer.

Keep in mind, too, that manufacturers usually don't offer incentives *or* below-market interest rates on their hottest-selling models. They don't need to sweeten the deal when they're selling every one they can make, and dealers are stickier on prices when demand exceeds the supply. Conversely, the simple fact that incentives or below-market financing is offered for other models is a strong signal that they are not selling as well as the automakers would like, and that dealers will be more flexible on transaction prices.

Some manufacturers also have "recent college graduate" or "first-time buyer" financing programs to start building brand loyalty with a younger audience. The rates are typically higher than standard bank rates, but these programs are often geared to people who might not qualify for standard bank auto loans simply because they have little or no credit history.

So whether it's your first car or your twenty-first, the car store's current financing options are *always* worth checking out. But doesn't common sense say that you should be able to buy money cheaper if there's no middleman's commission for the financing entity to pay?

The only way to know whether the financing options the dealership presents are attractive is to shop competitively for money before you sit down in a negotiating session at the car store. Then you'll be able to compare the annualized percentage rates (APRs) charged under the different alternatives.

Unfortunately, many new-car buyers don't bother to check out their financing options before entering the F&I manager's den. The Consumer Bankers Association reports that about 80 percent of a bank's new-auto loans are originated indirectly, at dealerships, whereas only 20 percent result from buyers visiting the bank themselves to prequalify for a loan before they purchase a vehicle.

As a result, every year hundreds of thousands of car buyers who could have qualified for direct auto loans at lower rates end up paying a lot more money *to the same banks,* with the difference going to the car stores. Welcome to America, folks—the land where the average consumer is more interested in the convenience of one-stop shopping than in smart money management. Fortunately, you are not going to fall into that trap.

SHOPPING FOR MONEY: A PRIMER

As a first step, you should decide the highest monthly payment you can handle comfortably, *including auto insurance.* Call your insurance agent and tell him which vehicles you're considering. He'll be glad to tell you what your insurance will cost. (He works on commission, too.) He may even influence your final choice if you find that one alternative costs much less to insure than another.

Then decide on a down payment. If part or all of this will come from the sale of your current car, go through the steps in chapters 10 and 11 to learn what it's really worth under each of those scenarios.

CAUTION: DON'T DRIVE "UPSIDE DOWN"

As a general rule, we'd advise putting at least 20 percent down on any new vehicle and financing it over a maximum term of four years. If you can't handle those numbers without changing your lifestyle dramatically, you should buy a less expensive car. This advice may sound conservative, but it will help keep you from getting "upside down" when you want to sell or trade again.

You're upside down when the actual value of the vehicle is less than the principal you still owe on the loan. You've got negative equity in the car, and you'd literally have to pay someone to take it off your hands. Here's why it's easy to get upside down whenever you combine a small down payment with a long financing term (such as 10 percent down and a six-year loan):

- New cars are *terrible* investments. Knowledgeable people will tell you that, depending on the specific vehicle and the timing of your purchase, *most new cars or trucks depreciate from 15–20 percent to as much as 35–40 percent in the first few weeks you own them!* Only the most prestigious high-end luxury cars seem to hold their value significantly longer.

- Add the fact that your monthly payments will include more interest than principal until you get into the latter part of the payment schedule, and you can see how a car's value can go down much faster than your equity in it goes up.

This fact leaves you exposed to significant loss if your car is stolen or destroyed in an accident. Your insurance company will pay you the car's depreciated market value, but you may owe the bank or finance company much more. If you are unwilling to accept this risk, ask the lender about gap insurance, which covers the difference between the car's insured value and the amount you owe. This insurance could cost several hundred dollars over the term of the loan.

After you've decided whether to follow our 20 percent down, four-year rule or some other payment program, you're ready to contact some banks, your credit union, and other new-car financing sources including those you can find today on the Internet. (If you belong to a credit union, you should start there. Credit union rates on auto loans are typically at least 1 percent lower than bank rates. One reason: Credit unions usually don't provide a participation fee to car stores.)

REACHING OUT AGAIN

Start this process on the telephone by calling a bank loan officer about car loans. Say that you're starting to shop for a new vehicle, that you want to line up financing first, that your credit report is clean, and that you'd like some help in finding the "price ballpark" you should be shopping in. (We'll assume that you're following our 20 percent down, four-year guideline.)

First ask for the bank's annualized percentage rates on car loans. They will typically be higher for lower down payments and, sometimes, for longer payment schedules.

Tell the loan officer that you'd like to learn how large a loan you can afford if you put 20 percent down and finance a car over four years. Then take the total monthly payment you decided on, subtract one-sixth of the semiannual auto insurance premium, and ask how large a four-year loan you could pay off with the remainder.

Add to that loan amount the down payment you decided on previously, and you'll have the *maximum price* you can afford to pay under those terms. (Remember, that total must cover state and local sales taxes, license and title fees, and any other up-front costs. Since license fees can be substantial, you should call your state's licensing agency and ask for an estimate of the fee for a car in your price range.) Then consider whether it's reasonable to expect to buy any one of the vehicles you're interested in for that price or less, given what you'll learn in chapter 16 about what they cost the dealer.

If your maximum affordable price is a lot lower than the dealer's invoice cost, and there's no current consumer rebate offer or factory-to-dealer incentive program, the answer is probably no. That means you've got to lower your sights to a less expensive vehicle, find more down-payment money, or ignore the 20 percent down, four-year rule and risk getting "upside down."

HERE'S SOMETHING THAT MIGHT HELP

Before you make that call, use this amortization table to determine what the monthly payment would be for a three-, four-, or five-year loan.

As you can see, we've chosen annual percentage rates from .5 to 12.5 percent. This range covers the territory from automakers' highly subsidized below-market rates to sky-high levels that folks with good credit won't pay unless double-digit inflation returns. The dollar amounts in the table are the monthly payments per $1,000 borrowed. For example, assume you're borrowing $13,500 for four years at an annual percentage rate of 10.5. To calculate your monthly payment, go to the 10.5 percent column and find the payment per thousand for a four-year loan—$25.61. Multiplying that number by 13.5 (the number of thousands you're borrowing) gives you the monthly payment—$345.74.

MAKING THEM COMPETE

You should shop for a money deal as aggressively as you're going to shop for that auto deal. Financial institutions are in a competitive business, too. (They "book" only about two-thirds of the auto loans they approve.) Let them know you're shopping their competitors, and you'll borrow where you get the best terms.

It's worth the extra effort. Assume you borrow $15,000 on a four-year loan. If you can drop the interest rate just 1 percent by shopping competitively, you'll save over $300 in interest payments.

MONTHLY PAYMENTS FOR THREE-, FOUR-, AND 5-YEAR LOANS

Payment Factors per $1,000	Annual Percentage Rates				
	0.5	**1.0**	**1.5**	**2.0**	**2.5**
3-year loan	27.99	28.21	28.43	28.65	28.87
4-year loan	21.04	21.26	21.48	21.70	21.92
5-year loan	16.87	17.09	17.31	17.53	17.75
	3.0	**3.5**	**4.0**	**4.5**	**5.0**
3-year loan	29.09	29.31	29.53	29.75	29.98
4-year loan	22.14	22.36	22.58	22.81	23.03
5-year loan	17.97	18.20	18.42	18.65	18.88
	5.5	**6.0**	**6.5**	**7.0**	**7.5**
3-year loan	30.20	30.43	30.65	30.88	31.11
4-year loan	23.26	23.49	23.72	23.95	24.18
5-year loan	19.11	19.33	19.57	19.81	20.04
	8.0	**8.5**	**9.0**	**9.5**	**10.0**
3-year loan	31.34	31.57	31.80	32.04	32.27
4-year loan	24.42	24.65	24.89	25.13	25.37
5-year loan	20.28	20.52	20.76	21.01	21.25
	10.5	**11.0**	**11.5**	**12.0**	**12.5**
3-year loan	32.51	32.74	32.98	33.22	33.46
4-year loan	25.61	25.85	26.09	26.34	26.58
5-year loan	21.50	21.75	22.00	22.25	22.50

If your local bank quotes a rate higher than what you were quoted by a bank five miles away, tell the loan officer you'd prefer to do business in your neighborhood but his bank's rate is higher. Ask if that's absolutely the best he can do. He may have to get approval from another manager, but banks are in business to sell money, and you may find there's room to negotiate. It's also common for a bank to give a slightly lower rate if you have an account there and the monthly payment is deducted automatically.

You can do a lot of comparison shopping on the telephone. In many cities you can even arrange your loan by telephone, calling in your application and getting an answer within a day or two.

Note also that it is easy to shop for rates on the Internet. Visit any search engine and type "auto loans," and you'll find many alternatives.

Here are some more tips on financing.

1. Shop the Dealers Against the Financial Institutions

You should bargain aggressively to get the best interest rate from dealers. Usually they have some flexibility. After reviewing your credit application, the automakers' captive finance companies often give dealers a range of interest rates they can charge you, with a low and a high number.

Make the dealer compete with the best rate you've been able to find elsewhere, on or off the Internet. Here's how one Fighting Chance customer reported on his experience:

> I had a preapproved rate of 8.25 percent from a credit union. When the Chevy dealer's finance manager quoted 8.75 percent, I declined, stating the lower rate. He said he would match it. The next morning I called the credit union and told them I was going with GMAC. They said they would match GMAC or do better. I said I was tired of all the options, just give me your best rate. They gave me 7.85 percent, and GMAC could not match it.

2. Explore "the Non-Auto Auto Loan"

You may find, as *Fortune* suggested in one of its investor's guides, that "a home equity credit line is a cheap, tax-smart way to buy a new car." That's because interest is tax-deductible on home equity borrowings up to $100,000, whereas other personal loan interest (including interest on standard auto loans) is not. The Consumer Bankers Association reports that about 10 percent of home equity loans are used to finance autos.

Home equity loans and lines of credit come in many forms, with either fixed or variable interest rates, and with or without "origination points." In most cases, you'll probably pay a lower *effective rate* than you would for a regular car loan, simply because the interest is deductible.

For example, if you're in the 28 percent tax bracket and the loan's annual percentage rate is 6.0 percent, your net effective rate after taxes is only 4.32 percent. That may be significantly lower than any standard car loan rate you're likely to find. (We're not CPAs. You should check with your tax adviser for the best counsel.)

Another side to this that you should keep in mind is that with this type of financing, you'll be pledging *your home* as collateral. If there's any reason to be nervous about your ability to make those payments, you might sleep better with a standard auto loan, knowing that all they can repossess is your car, not your roof.

You should also note that Congress has become alarmed by a decline in the equity held by homeowners, caused in part by a sharp rise in tax-deductible home equity loans used for vacations and auto purchases. The lawmakers have asked the General Accounting Office to investigate equity borrowing. There's a possibility that Congress will move to curb these tax advantages sometime in the future. *This makes it mandatory that you check with the appropriate tax counselor before proceeding.*

3. Beware of the Credit Insurance Rip-off

Don't get pressured into buying credit life insurance as an add-on. You'll often find this item buried in the mouse type in your auto loan documents. These policies are very profitable to both the insurance companies and the sellers—financial institutions and auto dealers, who can earn commissions of 30 to 50 percent.

Money magazine reported that these policies pay out an average of only 38 cents in benefits for every dollar of premium, compared with 83 cents for the typical life insurance policy! And a spokesperson for the National Association of Insurance Commissioners has urged consumers to be particularly cautious of an insurer recommended by a *lender*, who is "going to be looking for the product with the highest commission, and that's usually the company that charges the highest premium."

By law, the purchase of credit life insurance cannot be a precondition for receiving a loan. Yet many people buy it. Ford Motor Credit Corporation reported that of the automobiles financed through a dealership, half of Ford's customers buy credit life insurance and 30 percent buy accident and health (disability) insurance. It's reasonable to project similar numbers for the other major auto manufacturers' captive credit operations.

If you feel you need any type of extra insurance coverage, discuss it with the agents you or your friends and relatives already deal with, and chances are you'll save a lot of money. Standard life and disability insurance policies are generally much better buys.

4. Remember that Finance Terms Are Less Favorable on Used-Car Loans Than on New-Car Loans

Financial institutions will lend a lower percentage of the purchase price for used cars, and they'll charge a somewhat higher interest rate. If you're considering a previously owned vehicle, it's even more important that you shop rates aggressively.

The bottom line: If you follow the steps we've suggested in this brief financing lesson, you'll be in a good position to determine whether the financing available at the car store is an attractive alternative for you or just a good deal for them.

A LITTLE TRAVELING MUSIC

We thought it would be appropriate to end this chapter with a song—one that F&I managers can sing to themselves on coffee breaks. So we've written these parody lyrics to the tune of that old standard, "Pennies from Heaven":

> Every time they finance here
> It's pennies from heaven.
> It's tough to keep my conscience clear
> With all these pennies from heaven.
> This really easy money just falls in my cup.
> You'd be amazed how quickly
> Those little pennies add up.
> All those banks and credit unions
> Think people are crazy,
> But we know one thing they don't:
> People are lazy.
> We give them one-stop shopping,
> They don't know that they pay.
> So there's pennies from heaven here every day.

A postal worker took his year-old car to a dealership in Providence, Rhode Island, for an oil change. To kill time while he was waiting, he browsed the showroom, admiring a fancy new sports car. Three salesmen converged on him.

Within minutes he found himself in the credit manager's office, loudly proclaiming that he wasn't in the market for anything new except oil. Before he knew it, he owned that sports car and a five-year payment schedule totaling $40,000.

He sued the dealership for engaging in deceptive trade practices. According to the Associated Press, his lawyer said, "I don't think he actually realized any paperwork had gone through. They made [him] feel empowered and enthusiastic about purchasing a new car. But the fact is [the dealership] took him for a ride and left him financially stranded."

13

The Fine Art of Shopping Without Buying

While you're working on determining what your car is worth, deciding whether to sell it at wholesale or retail, and getting your financial ducks in a row, you should also get to know some new cars well enough to narrow your choices to two or three finalists. You've been salivating over new-car ads for months. You know which models seem most appealing. Maybe you attended the annual automobile show when it came to town. You've devoured the model-year buyer's guides published by

Car and Driver and *Road and Track,* which usually appear on supermarket shelves in late fall. You've studied the annual new-car issues of *Money* magazine, *Kiplinger's Personal Finance Magazine, Consumer Reports,* and other sources for safety, economy, reliability, and insurance cost ratings.

Even with all this information, narrowing your choices may not be easy. Domestic and foreign manufacturers typically offer 500 to 600 passenger car models for sale in the United States each model year!

The real challenge, however, isn't the number of cars; it's the number of car salesmen. You need a safe and secure way to get through the test-driving and information-gathering stage without getting caught up in the juggler's act. Here's how to accomplish that and live to tell about it.

First review Psychology 101 in chapter 6, especially the part about projecting total emotional detachment. Then play the little game outlined next.

MAKE THIS AN AWAY GAME IF YOU CAN

If you live in an area that has several dealers for each major make, gather your information at car stores that are relatively farther from your home or office. That way, when you're ready to start serious negotiations with stores closer to home or work, you'll be an unknown quantity, without the implied commitments of previous visits. (The less a salesman knows about you, the less money he'll get from you.)

That doesn't necessarily mean you should ignore those more distant stores in your final negotiations. Indeed, you may drive a better bargain with them because they'll see you as business they normally wouldn't get. They may agree to a lower gross deal just because you're an out-of-town bird in hand. There are some advantages to buying the car locally where you'll have it serviced, but they are not worth paying an extra $500 or more.

Plan these trips by checking the dealer association's advertising in your newspaper, where you'll probably find the names and addresses of all the dealers for a given make in your metropolitan area. You may even find a map showing their relative locations. (Dealers love to put maps in their ads!)

You can also find dealers' names, addresses, and phone numbers on the Internet. Most dealers have web sites, which you can typically access from the automakers' web sites listed in appendix A. In addition, you can go to search engines such as Yahoo, type in "auto dealers," and get lists of dealers for the nameplates you're shopping.

Choose the stores you'll visit, grab a pen and a pad to take detailed notes, *leave your checkbook and your credit cards at home,* and jump in your car.

Your objective on this trip is to narrow your choices to a few specific cars that will meet your requirements and make you a happy driver for the next several years. Smile, this is going to be fun!

THE GAME PLAN

As you enter the showroom, walk briskly to one of the younger-looking, less experienced salesmen. Tell him you're just starting to look at new cars, and yes, you do plan to buy one soon. But no, you're not a candidate to buy one today under any circumstances. There are several makes you want to research and test-drive before making a decision.

You have no idea what you'll end up buying. It'll depend on a lot of (unspecified) things. But he's got a couple of cars that are on your list, and you'd like to test-drive them, learn about their features and benefits, and get some literature to review at home.

While you're in this tire-kicking stage, test-drive at least two different cars you like at each dealership. Make those test drives long enough to put the cars through most of the paces you'll require of them every day. And be sure to drive cars equipped the way you think you'll buy them. Don't test an automatic transmission if you want a stick shift, or the four-door sedan if you want the coupe.

Even if you love both cars, try not to show it. Remember that your behavior should say: A car is a car. I'm going to check them all out and buy the best deal.

When you're around that salesman, act undecided, uncommitted, even a little wishy-washy. For each car, comment on things you like and things you don't like. (If you like everything, invent a few things you don't like.) That will keep him from moving into his aggressive selling posture with the "if" questions designed to get verbal commitments, such as, "If I got you the right price, would you buy this car today?" When he asks that, your correct answer is, "Not today. As I told you, I'm just starting to narrow my choices. I've got more appointments to test-drive cars today and tomorrow, and I plan to keep them."

ANYTHING YOU SAY WILL BE USED AGAINST YOU

Remember, the one who asks the questions controls the conversation. So ask him all the things you need to know, such as, "What rustproofing warranty comes with the car?" and, "What specific direct consumer incentives is the factory offering this month on the cars you sell?" And one he probably won't answer in detail, "What specific factory-to-dealer cash incentives are in effect this month?"

But when he asks you questions, your stock answers should be, "I don't know," "I'm not sure," "I need to discuss it with my spouse," and "I'll have to think about that." When those get tired, answer a question with a question—for example, "How do most people answer that?"

In this little game, you'll get the information you need, but he'll get nothing concrete to move toward his objective of closing you before you leave. Remember, he's in a sell-it-now-or-never business, but you're in a don't-buy-it-now mode.

After test-driving cars you particularly like, write down the key information from the *manufacturer's* window sticker (not the dealer's separate sticker): the vehicle identification number, model number, and suggested retail price for the base car, plus the contents and prices of the optional factory equipment packages and other accessories.

Then thank the salesman for his time. Take his card, but don't give him your phone number or address. If he discovers that you live two gas stops from his store, he'll decide that it's now or never and try to chain you to a chair until you buy.

Above all, don't get roped into his office to talk about anything, including the weather. He's going to want you to sit down for a minute "just to see what it looks like on paper." Tell him politely that you're not ready to do that, and that you've got appointments to test-drive three other makes. Both statements will be true.

If you live in a smaller market without many dealers for the same make, you can't play the game exactly like this. But the essential rule still applies: *You want to get all the information you need while giving him none of the information he needs.*

NARROW THE FIELD, BUT NOT TOO MUCH

After a day or two, you should be able to narrow your choices to a few favorites. Try to keep at least two or three in the running. The big winners in this game will be those who maintain several options right down to the finish line. A single choice isn't an option, it's an obsession—one that's potentially very expensive.

SHAKE THE FAMILY TREE

One good way to open options is to consider "family relations," vehicles that have different brand names but are made by the same manufacturer on the same platform and are quite similar. The key differences are often in trim levels and suspension systems. For example, one might be aimed at older, more traditional buyers who value a cushy ride, another at younger auto enthusiasts who want tighter handling characteristics and more feel of the road. There also can be meaningful price differences.

For example, the Ford Taurus and the Mercury Sable are essentially similar vehicles at different price points. Ditto for the Chevrolet Trailblazer and the GMC Envoy.

At any time, there could also be hefty manufacturer incentives offered on some family members but not on others.

If you like one branch of a family tree, you may like another almost as well. And pricing and incentive differences may be meaningful enough to swing your choice to a vehicle you hadn't considered at the start.

Here is a list of "family relations," some of which are the products of joint ventures between automotive manufacturers (for example, GM and Toyota). While these relationships can change over time, with some older models discontinued and new ones added, automakers will always offer different vehicles that share common platforms as a way to produce cars more efficiently.

General Motors (and partners):

- Buick Century, Regal, and Pontiac Grand Prix

- Buick LeSabre and Pontiac Bonneville

- Buick Park Avenue and Cadillac Seville

- Buick Rendezvous and Pontiac Aztek

- Chevrolet Astro and GMC Safari vans

- Chevrolet Avalanche and Cadillac Escalade EXT

- Chevrolet Cavalier and Pontiac Sunfire

- Chevrolet Colorado pickups and GMC Canyon pickups

- Chevrolet Express and GMC Savana vans

- Chevrolet Impala sedan and Chevrolet Monte Carlo coupe

- Chevrolet Silverado pickups and GMC Sierra pickups

- Chevrolet Suburban, GMC Yukon XL, and Cadillac Escalade EXV

- Chevrolet Tahoe, GMC Yukon, and Cadillac Escalade
- Chevrolet Tracker and Suzuki Vitara
- Chevrolet Trailblazer, GMC Envoy, and Isuzu Ascender
- Chevrolet Venture and Pontiac Montana minivans
- Pontiac Grand AM and Oldsmobile Alero
- Pontiac Vibe and Toyota Matrix

Chrysler:

- Chrysler Concord, 300M, and Dodge Intrepid
- Chrysler Sebring and Dodge Stratus sedans and coupes
- Dodge Caravan and Chrysler Town & Country SWB minivans
- Dodge Grand Caravan and Chrysler Town & Country LWB minivans

Ford (and partners):

- Ford Crown Victoria and Mercury Grand Marquis
- Ford Escape and Mazda Tribute
- Ford Expedition and Lincoln Navigator
- Ford Explorer, Mercury Mountaineer, and Lincoln Aviator
- Ford Ranger pickups and Mazda B-Series pickups
- Ford Taurus and Mercury Sable
- Lincoln LS and Jaguar Type S

Others:

- Acura MDX and Honda Pilot
- Honda Accord V6 and Acura TL
- Nissan Maxima and Infiniti I35
- Nissan Pathfinder and Infiniti QX4

- Toyota 4Runner and Lexus GX 470

- Toyota Camry V6 XLE and Lexus ES 330

- Toyota Highlander and Lexus RX 330

- Toyota Land Cruiser and Lexus LX 470

CONSIDER THE BIG HIDDEN COST: DEPRECIATION

As you're assessing alternatives, remember that the most significant cost of car ownership isn't gas or maintenance or repairs or insurance. It's depreciation—the difference between what you pay to acquire it and what you'll get when you sell it as it moves down the automotive feeding chain. Some cars retain their value better than others, and you should factor these differences into your thinking.

Here's an example: Ford's Taurus and Honda's Accord are family sedans in the same general price range. Yet, the Automotive Lease Guide's residual value tables consistently show that the wholesale value of a three-year-old Taurus SE sedan will be about 31 percent of its original sticker price (the manufacturers' suggested retail price), whereas a three-year-old Accord LX will command about 54 percent of its sticker. Thus, if you negotiated the same price for each, you'd save about $100 a month over three years by choosing the Honda. As noted in chapter 3, nameplates with better quality and reliability scores tend to command higher prices as used vehicles.

COMPARE THE WARRANTIES

If several vehicles appeal to your eye, some may look better than others after you compare their basic bumper-to-bumper warranties. The industry standard is 36/36,000, which means that most parts of the car are covered for manufacturers' defects for 36 months or 36,000 miles, whichever comes first. (Typically, the battery, brakepads and tires are not covered by the basic warranty.)

If you check the warranty table in chapter 22, you'll note that some automakers offer better basic coverage than others. As an example, assume that you like the Honda Passport and its cousin, the Isuzu Rodeo, equally well. Honda's basic warranty is 36/36,000, but Isuzu's is 36/50,000. If you drive substantially more than 12,000 miles a year, that difference may tip the scales in Isuzu's favor.

CHECK THE COST OF REGULAR MAINTENANCE

Every new vehicle comes with a booklet that outlines the maintenance schedule recommended by the manufacturer. The booklet is free, but the service is expensive. (New-car dealers make most of their profits from parts and service, and that little booklet is a major source of their continuing prosperity, whether car sales are up or down.) As with insurance premiums, the cost of regularly scheduled maintenance can differ from one vehicle to another.

To get a handle on this, call the local dealerships for the models you're considering and ask to speak to a service adviser. (This is the person who meets customers as they drive in and writes up each service order.) Make this call in mid-afternoon, when most of his contact and follow-up with that day's customers is behind him. Tell him which car you're considering buying, and say you're interested in learning about the costs of recommended maintenance. Inquire about the mileage intervals for regular service in the first three years, and ask him to tell you the approximate costs for each visit.

IF YOU'VE GOT A QUESTION, CALL HOME

If you can't get all your important questions answered by people at a dealership, try calling the manufacturer. (You'll find a list of their phone numbers in appendix A.)

THE SMART SHOPPER'S TIEBREAKER

If you're having difficulty choosing a favorite, here's an idea that beats flipping a coin: Consider *renting* each finalist for a day or so on weekends, as a way to learn more than you can in those brief test drives. This will set you back a few dollars, but the rental cost pales in comparison to the financial and emotional cost of buying the wrong car.

You may have to make several calls to find what you want, but most popular domestic and import models can be rented. In fact, many dealers rent cars by the day.

However you narrow the field, remember to retain one or two fallback choices. At this stage, throwing away alternatives is throwing away leverage.

14

It's a marketing gimmick that dealers use, just like red tag sales, Labor Day sales, you name it. And if you say it's going to sweep the nation and it's going to all one-price dealerships, you're crazy. It's not going to happen. It's simply not going to last.
—Executive vice president of the Greater Los Angeles Motor Car Dealers Association (quoted in the *Long Beach Press-Telegram*)

"No-Dicker" Dealers and the Retail Revolution: Oasis or Mirage?

General Motors (GM) launched the small-car Saturn nameplate as an import fighter in the late 1980s. It arrived with a folksy, down-home ad campaign carrying the tag line, "A Different Kind of Company. A Different Kind of Car."

They could have added, "A Different Kind of Deal." Because the biggest difference between Saturn and the rest of the auto industry wasn't in the car, it was in the deal. *There wasn't any, and there still isn't any.* If you want a Saturn, you'll pay the full sticker price, even if the sales manager is your brother-in-law. The reason: *There's no competition between dealers for your business. And there isn't going to be any.*

THE KEY TO SATURN'S SUCCESS: ELIMINATING COMPETITIVE GEOGRAPHY

At its essence, Saturn isn't a car, it's an idea—one designed to extract the maximum amount of money from customers, while simultaneously using a neat bit of psychology to convince them that it's for their own good.

Starting with a clean sheet of paper, Saturn was able to give each dealer a large, exclusive sales territory. Because each market area has only one retail "owner," price competition is effectively eliminated between dealers. This exclusive selling territory could be one part of a huge market, like Los Angeles, or the entire metropolitan area of a smaller market, such as San Diego. In effect, GM took one of the most competitive retail businesses and made it noncompetitive for this brand.

As a result, the cold, hard fact is that the sticker price is the real price for a Saturn. *Think of it as a legal form of retail price-fixing.* It's also Saturn's policy not to offer rebates or other incentives—which saves GM anywhere from $500 to $1,500 per vehicle, depending on the competitive climate.

The bottom line for even the well-informed consumer: You'll pay at least $1,000 more for a Saturn than you would if Saturn had been, say, just another Chevrolet model instead of a separate GM division with an exclusive-territory dealer network. And the normal market forces of supply and demand will have no impact on transaction pricing.

The bottom line for dealers: They make a lot more money under this exclusive-territory pricing umbrella. With guaranteed front-end gross profits per sale of $1,000 to $1,500, Saturn is the most profitable small-car franchise by a country mile. Plenty of large-car franchises would gladly trade bottom lines with any Saturn store.

Ironically, Saturn's "no-dicker" sticker is a key ingredient in its success, because it eliminates the haggling over price. In the showroom, for a refreshing change, Saturn customers are treated like honored guests.

The salespeople simply help them fall in love with the car, tell them that the sticker price is fair, and (most important) assure them no one will get the car for less. No sales pressure is applied. In grateful response, Saturn buyers pay more than they would for comparable small cars sold by dealers willing to negotiate and factories willing to use incentives.

Saturn buyers *should* be treated like visiting royalty. They're paying the full sticker price! Think about it for ten seconds. If you called any dealer in the United States and told him you were on your way down to pay the sticker price for one of his cars, he'd probably send a chauffeur-driven limousine to pick you up, if only to keep you from stopping at another car store on the way. At that price, you'd have a wonderful sales experience anywhere. It seems almost un-American, doesn't it?

Who are these Saturn buyers? At a research industry gathering, we met one of the most influential automotive consumer researchers and asked him that question over lunch. His answer: "The cream puffs, the people who absolutely can't handle any kind of confrontation, however mild." He added, "Look at the folks they put in their commercials. They're not the most sophisticated shoppers, not people who will typically research dealer cost and incentive information and take a strong stance in a price negotiation. Saturn meets their needs perfectly by taking the anxiety out of the shopping process."

HAS SATURN CHANGED THE WAY PEOPLE BUY NEW CARS?

Not much. Saturn accounted for less than 2 percent of new-vehicle sales in 2002. Sales have stalled in the last several years because GM has been slow at refreshing the lineup with new models that turn people on.

There have even been years when Saturn sales were down instead of up. In that situation, GM and its dealers have found creative ways to be more competitive *and* still get the full sticker price for every car. GM will offer highly subsidized leases through General Motors Acceptance Corporation, with inflated residual values and below-market interest rates providing low monthly payments. (The consumer doesn't perceive an interest-rate cut as a cut in the price of the car, though it has the same effect.) For the dealers' part, they give inflated trade-in values that may be more than you can get elsewhere. So you *can* get a deal on a Saturn if you're shopping when sales are down, but you'll get it on the back end of the transaction. You'll still pay the full sticker price, and Saturn stores will remain among the most profitable dealerships.

The Saturn Wanna-bes

Before Saturn's initial sales year ended, it had become clear to the automotive establishment that Saturn's greatest achievement was getting American car buyers to pay the sticker price for every car, and that the key to pulling off this startling coup was the elimination of haggling over the price. Success in any field breeds imitation.

Other dealers, watching Saturn's apparently magical scenario unfold, decided to play follow the leader. They had seen the new religion, and they were converting—dumping their high-pressure sales forces and becoming one-price, no-dicker dealers.

That "fair" price would be somewhere between the sticker price and the dealer invoice price. It would be noted on a separate "civilized sticker" placed on each car, and there would be no bargaining. What you see is what you pay, and what everyone else pays.

There are now somewhere between a few hundred and just over a thousand no-dicker dealers—a small fraction of the 42,000-plus franchised new-car dealerships. Some make the switch in desperation, when sales are so poor they have nothing to lose. Others simply want to reap the short-term benefits of doing it first in their market, then plan to return to their old selling approach if several competitors adopt a no-dicker policy. And some see it as a long-term strategic move to give their store a unique appeal to the consumer segment that hates to negotiate prices.

Let's examine how this pricing transplant works, from both consumer and dealer perspectives.

FOR THE SHOPPER, THERE'S LESS THERE THAN MEETS THE EYE

As you might expect from the Saturn model, customers at other no-dicker stores pay higher transaction prices than customers at stores where prices are negotiable.

J.D. Power & Associates conducted a study of 24 dealerships that had adopted the system relatively early. The key finding, widely reported by the Associated Press, was that no-dicker dealers make more profit. (Otherwise, why do it?) Nine out of ten dealers reported increased sales since adopting the program. And half the dealers said their average gross profit per car had gone up; the other half split equally between those whose profits were the same and those with lower profits per sale.

A separate study—this one on *used-car* stores—produced similar findings. CNW Marketing Research surveyed 2,900 used-vehicle transactions. And they found that customers routinely paid more at dealerships that don't haggle than at those where there is give-and-take over price. For example, they paid:

- $481 more for a Ford Taurus

- $588 more for a Dodge Caravan

- $646 more for a Toyota Camry

- $694 more for a Ford F-150 pickup

- A whopping $937 more for a used Chevy Suburban

Now imagine yourself driving home smiling in that previously owned Chevy Suburban. You pull into your driveway. Your neighbor pulls into his, behind the wheel of the same vehicle. You compare notes and learn that he paid $937 less by haggling the price at a Chevy dealership down the street. Wouldn't that wreck your whole day?

Overall, these studies suggest that the no-dicker system does what it was designed to do: It gets the consumer to pay more, just as Saturn customers do. But Saturn customers at least have the satisfaction of knowing that no one will buy the same car for a lower price tomorrow, or next week.

Is that true for the other no-dicker stores? No. The J.D. Power & Associates study indicated that today's price is just that, and tomorrow's price is anybody's guess.

- The research showed that 33 percent of no-dicker new-car dealers changed their "civilized" prices as factory incentive programs changed.

- Another 29 percent of the dealers changed prices as their inventory conditions changed.

- 14 percent of dealers changed prices "when they needed to boost volume," another 14 percent changed them weekly, and 10 percent changed them every two or three days!

So buyers may enjoy the shopping experience, but they'll pay more for the car, and someone else may pay less for the same car tomorrow. And in most cases, they'll still have to dicker over their trade-in allowance and deal with the finance and insurance manager on financing and back-end options.

Does that sound like what you expected or hoped for when you heard about one-price, no-dicker dealers? We don't think so.

BEWARE OF CAR SALESMEN BEARING DOUGHNUTS

We decided to do our own research on the subject, and we concluded that one-price stores should be required to post "Buyer Beware" signs, just as cigarette packages carry mandatory warnings. Shopping incognito with a newspaper reporter, we walked into a big no-dicker Ford dealership, where there was coffee and doughnuts and absolutely no pressure. The salesman just walked us around the lot, where the price of every car was on the windshield. He said business was up 42 percent since the store switched to one-price selling—an amazing statistic, considering that this had to be one of the highest-priced Ford stores in the state. Its price on a midline Taurus was one the village idiot could have beaten by at least $1,000 with one phone call to any other Ford store in the city. Yet, business was up 42 percent! Clearly, the store's customers were lulled into lowering their guard by this "we're-on-your-side" selling approach that set them up for the big tumble, which they never even felt. One more triumph for American marketing ingenuity.

To avoid becoming the next victim, remember Bragg's Golden Rule: Whether it's Saturn or one of these Saturn wanna-bes, assume that the more pleasant the purchase experience, the more gold is being lifted from your wallet. Sadly, it's often true that the lower the pressure, the higher the price.

FOR THE DEALER, NO-DICKER IS NO NIRVANA

If car stores make more profit with no-dicker pricing, as both research and empirical evidence suggest, you might logically ask why so few dealers adopt this selling policy. These are the key reasons:

• In most large markets, there are several dealers for the same make. Chevrolet and Ford, for example, each have over 3,900 dealers nationally. When one adopts a no-dicker policy, he becomes a sitting duck for the others, who can cut prices selectively to steal his customers.

• The 80/20 Rule of Life still applies. Many dealers are reluctant to give up their shot at making a killing on the least knowledgeable 20 percent of buyers, the ones who probably provide 80 percent of the profits.

• In effect, one-price selling says to the customer, "Pay it or go somewhere else." That's not a message most dealers want to deliver. They'd rather make a small profit than lose the sale to a competitor.

• No-dicker is a better strategy for tough times, when sales are hardest to come by. When consumer confidence and sales traffic are strong, no-dicker makes less economic sense to dealers. As a spokesperson for the National Automobile Dealers Association said in response to questions about the no-dicker movement, "Dealers sell the way they do because it works. They are real wizards at local marketing, and they do what works."

• Finally, and most important, the bulk of dealers can't change to no-dicker successfully unless the customer changes, too. But the customer has been trained under the current system, the one dealers use "because it works." What are the chances of most shoppers buying a car at the first price offered? Slim indeed. After decades of 42,000 dealers shouting "shop us last" in their advertising, the cumulative impact has taught consumers that there will always be a better price down the street. As a result, research consistently shows that most new-car buyers prefer to negotiate prices.

As a former megadealer in Los Angeles said before he closed his last store, "People will shop you silly, and they should, too. Sooner or later, someone will sell you a car for the price you want."

The lesson for the smart shopper: *By definition, the no-dicker dealer's price will never be the best price.* If you make dealers compete for your business, as we recommend, the winner will never be a no-dicker dealer.

Eventually, most no-dicker dealers realize they've got a problem they can't solve: Without a Saturn-like umbrella of exclusive sales territories, they don't have a fail-safe formula. It's like grafting an eagle's wings onto a pigeon: That pigeon can soar, but without talons it can't catch fish.

We believe most new-car pricing will remain negotiable, for the simple reason that most folks prefer it that way and dealers that preclude that option will lose a lot of business. As one new-car dealer put it, "The no-dicker approach to car selling is not a positive. When competitors adopt that method, it helps us. Most Americans want to negotiate. They have a touch of the horse trader in them, and the only time they can test their trading skills is when they purchase a car."

Consumers are always going to seek out the best deal; if it's not in their city, they'll find it somewhere else. The dealers let the retail pricing genie out of the bottle a long time ago, and it will be very tough to put him back.

15

The Big Picture

An IBM sales representative in Milwaukee contracted with a dealer to buy a new Dodge Viper, Chrysler's limited-production sports car, for $2,500 over the suggested retail price. When the vehicle arrived, the dealer sued the customer to get out of the contract. According to the Wall Street Journal, *he thought he could sell it for as much as $20,000 over the sticker price! On learning of this embarrassing incident, Chrysler's executive vice president for sales and marketing lamented, "We have to change the entire culture of our franchise."*

A ny deal you make will be influenced by two things that have nothing to do with you: the overall state of the automobile market, and the specific supply and demand conditions for the vehicle you want.

Since the auto sales climate is one of the most overreported subjects in journalism, getting up to speed starts with simply keeping your eyes and ears open. As you think about new cars or trucks, pay attention to those monthly sales reports on the TV news, in your local paper, or in national media like the *Wall Street Journal* or *USA Today*. They'll give you a general feel for how eager dealers are to sell new vehicles.

What you really want to know, however, is how eager some specific manufacturers and dealers might be to sell the vehicles you're interested in buying.

THEIR WEAKNESS IS YOUR OPPORTUNITY

The retail automobile business is driven by momentum, in both the overall market and the fortunes of each specific make. Over a period of years the market runs in cycles, from hot to lukewarm to cold and back again. Within each cycle, there are winners and losers among both manufacturers and specific models. Some automakers watch their sales and market shares wither, while others develop the tough competitor's ability to weather any storm.

The smart shopper understands that these differences create buying opportunities, and that you should be able to negotiate a better deal with those who are most eager to sell.

LEARN HOW THEY'RE DOING

There is real power in knowing how the makes and models you are interested in are doing in the marketplace. Is their sales performance better or worse than their key competitors' and the total market's? Are their inventory levels relatively higher? As a general rule, dealers selling makes that are doing less well, with higher inventories, will be more willing to deal aggressively on price than those selling makes with relatively better sales and lower inventories. Automakers with poor sales are also more likely to offer customer and/or dealer incentives.

For perspective, industrywide inventory levels tend to fluctuate throughout the year in a range from roughly a 55-day supply to about a 75-day supply. For most manufacturers a two-month supply is an ideal target, providing the vast majority of buyers with sufficient color and equipment choices. Inventories higher than that usually increase costs much more than they do sales. Whenever they approach the three-month level, you can bet that the costs of financing that supply are hurting both the manufacturers and their dealers. Those makes should be more vulnerable to smart, informed shoppers.

Here's a comparison of two vehicles to illustrate the point:

• One car's sales are running 38 percent below previous annual levels. The average dealer is selling just one each month. And on the first of the month, there was a whopping 120-day supply in inventory.

- A directly competitive car of another make has sales 5 percent ahead of last year's level. The average dealer sells 15 each month. And there was a 42-day supply in inventory on the first of the month.

Given the relative sales and inventory positions of these two vehicles, which dealers are likely to be more flexible on price? The ones selling the first car, naturally.

Where can you find the information you need to understand the current status of the makes and models you are considering? Visit a large public library and ask to see the most recent issues of *Automotive News,* the industry's weekly newspaper. Many big libraries subscribe to this publication, which prints the most recent sales and inventory data in successive issues each month, by make and model.

It's also helpful to know the number of franchised dealers for each make, as shown in this table. These numbers tend to remain relatively constant. In bad times, some dealers go out of business; in good times, manufacturers add a few franchises. (Note, however, that GM, Ford, and Chrysler have a long-term objective of eliminating smaller dealerships and consolidating others.)

This information enables you to analyze sales figures in order to determine how many of each model the average dealer sells each month.

Make	Number of Dealers	Make	Number of Dealers
Acura	261	Land Rover	148
Audi	259	Lexus	200
BMW	340	Lincoln	1,376
Buick	2,766	Mazda	708
Cadillac	1,488	Mercedes-Benz	317
Chevrolet	4,180	Mercury	2,005
Chrysler	2,942	Mitsubishi	637
Dodge	3,077	Nissan	1,067
Ford	3,927	Pontiac	2,807
GMC	2,237	Porsche	192
Honda	1,005	Saab	217
Hyundai	604	Saturn	440
Infiniti	162	Subaru	588
Isuzu	477	Suzuki	440
Jaguar	160	Toyota	1,203
Jeep	2,822	Volkswagen	606
Kia	638	Volvo	341

That knowledge will often strengthen your confidence by confirming that it's a lot easier for you to find someone who wants to sell one than for them to find someone who wants to buy one.

When you're ready for serious negotiating, you should know that there is an easier way to get the current sales and inventory picture for the makes and models you are considering, along with the data on the current dealer invoice price of the vehicles and an up-to-date listing of manufacturers' incentives. See chapter 24 for details.

16

Dealer Cost:

What We

Can Learn

(and What

We Can't)

It happened at a convention of the National Automobile Dealers Association in Dallas. The president of Chevrolet's Dealer Council got up and asked his cohorts to sell one more Chevy a week, even if they made no profit on it.

Why? Because that would mean another 250,000 Chevys sold each year, giving GM billions more for new-product programs over the next few years. (And you thought those guys had no heart.)

O f all the insights we've gained from Fighting Chance customers, this is the most important: *Most dealers agree to several slim-profit deals each month with customers who have done their homework and know how to use it.*

What's a slim-profit deal? For a popular mid-priced family sedan, just a few hundred dollars over the dealer invoice price, not counting incentives (which would reduce the price further). For a high-end luxury import, from $1,500 to $3,000 over invoice.

Why do dealers who make a killing with some customers agree to slim-profit deals with others? For four key reasons:

1. First and foremost, they're in a sales-driven, ego-driven business. At the end of each month, the first question anyone asks is, "How many cars did we sell?" not, "How much profit did we make on each deal?" By definition, almost any sale is a good sale.

2. Frequently, a dealer's future supply is based on his current sales performance. It's called "turn and earn." Most dealers are terminal optimists, and they want to be sure their vehicle allocation will always be sufficient to support their dreams. In this business, an extra sale today means an extra sale tomorrow.

3. Once they understand that you're a knowledgeable shopper who will negotiate a slim-profit deal, they'd rather take the slim profit than give the sale to a competitor. Selling one more car this month and making a modest profit always beats not selling it and making no profit.

4. Finally, since they make the bulk of their profits from parts and service, they want that vehicle out on the road, where it will generate a steady income stream. (Parts and service account for less than 15 percent of the average dealership's gross sales, but about 50 percent of its net profits.)

To negotiate a slim-profit deal, you should start by learning as much as possible about what your vehicle is going to cost the dealer.

Virtually all automotive information sources we've seen imply that it's possible to learn the dealer's true "dead cost" for any vehicle. *You need to understand from the outset that that's not true.* Only the owner of each dealership knows his or her real dead cost. That's because there are several nontraditional ways that auto manufacturers are putting cash in dealers' pockets today that are not reported anywhere and that no one, on or off the Internet, can tell you about. We will describe these kinds of programs later in this chapter.

If that's the bad news, the good news is that you don't need complete information on the dealer's dead cost to get the best deal available on the vehicle you want. If you take our advice, you will learn as much as possible about dealer cost and how your vehicle is selling in the marketplace, and then make dealers bid competitively for your business. We'll tell you exactly how to do that in the upcoming chapters.

Let's focus now on what we can learn about dealer cost.

THE STARTING POINT: DEALER INVOICE PRICE

The dealer invoice price is the actual price billed by the factory, the "invoice" the dealer must pay when the vehicle is delivered to his lot. (Typically, the dealer pays the manufacturer with money he borrows under his "flooring plan" credit arrangement with a bank or finance company or with the auto manufacturer's finance subsidiary. He pays the lender interest until the car is sold, then repays the loan.)

To determine this figure, you need a printout of dealer invoice prices for the specific vehicles you're considering. To get familiar with the kind of information contained on a printout, turn to appendix B and look at the simplified pricing data we've created for a fictitious car and manufacturer, the All-American Speedster, built by the All-American Motor Corporation.

Our simplified printout for the All-American Speedster contains the following information:

• The dealer invoice price and the manufacturer's suggested retail price (MSRP), which is the price you'll see on the sticker attached to the window of each new car or truck. Note that the list shows pricing for all available body styles and trim levels, from the least expensive low-end Speedster model to the most expensive high-end model.

• Just below the initial price table, a complete listing of all the standard equipment items included in the base price of each trim level.

• Dealer invoice and retail price information for all available factory-installed optional equipment and accessories, including those sold as packages and groups.

• The factory code number, in the column on the far left. This is the manufacturer's computer code, the number by which each model or accessory is ordered or identified, just as it appears on the window sticker of a new car or truck.

It's important to have a printout covering all the configurations a manufacturer offers for a given vehicle. Without the complete picture, you can't make price/value comparisons between different trim levels. For example, a higher trim level frequently represents a better value, because it includes standard equipment in the base price that would be treated as extra-cost options in a lower trim level.

BUILDING YOUR WORKSHEET

Once you have current pricing printouts for the vehicles you're interested in, you can determine the dealer invoice cost for the specific models you want, outfitted with the exact optional accessories and equipment you choose. To illustrate how easy this is, we'll build a simple worksheet using the pricing data we've created for our fictitious car—the All-American Speedster.

• Let's assume you're interested in a Speedster wagon. You don't want the lowest trim level (A), but you can't justify spending more than $3,000 extra for the highest trim level (AAA) because you really don't need things like luxury cloth upholstery and a tachometer. So you settle on the middle trim level (AA, factory code S87), with a sticker (MSRP) price of $15,200 and a dealer invoice price of $13,000. Note that we have entered these numbers on the new-vehicle worksheet shown below.

• Looking at the preferred equipment packages available for the AA wagon, you're attracted by factory code 444B, which includes air conditioning, rear window defroster, AM/FM stereo radio-with-cassette, power door locks, power windows, and cruise control. The package price is less

NEW-VEHICLE WORKSHEET

Factory Code #	Model and Optional Equipment	Dealer Invoice Price	Suggested Retail Price
S87	All-American Speedster AA 4-door wagon	$13,000	$15,200
444B	Preferred equipment package (air conditioner, rear window defroster, power door locks, power driver seat, power windows, cruise control, AM/FM/cassette, P205/65R15 SBR blackwall tires)	1,500	1,800
947	3.8-liter V-6 engine upgrade	470	560
314	Rear-facing third seat	130	160
	Subtotal	15,100	17,720
	Add: Destination Charges	+500	+500
	Total	15,600	18,220

than the items would cost separately. The retail price is $1,800; the dealer invoice price is $1,500. We have added these numbers to the worksheet.

• You'd also like to have a more powerful engine than the standard 3.0-liter V-6. Looking at the equipment and accessories list, you see that you can add a 3.8-liter V-6 (factory code 947). Sticker price: $560; invoice: $470. These numbers are also placed on the worksheet.

• The only other item you want is a rear-facing third seat (factory code 314). This adds $130 invoice, $160 retail, to our worksheet.

• We must also add the $500 destination (freight) charge. Note that there is no markup on freight; the dealer simply charges the buyer what the manufacturer charges him. Note also that the sticker price does not include sales taxes or license and title fees.

• Adding the subtotals in the two columns, we find that there's a difference of $2,620 between the suggested retail price ($18,220) and the dealer invoice price ($15,600). We'll discuss in chapter 19 exactly how to use this information in the negotiation process. For now, let's just say that the $2,620 difference between the dealer's cost and the retail price allows significant room for price improvement—in your direction.

SOURCES OF DEALER INVOICE PRICING DATA

There are several sources of dealer invoice pricing available to new-car shoppers.

• Many Internet web sites provide this data. The most popular are Kelley Blue Book (www.kbb.com) and Edmunds (www.edmunds.com).

• There are several pricing books you can buy in bookstores and on newsstands. But beware, those books are not published every week or every month, and new-car pricing can change frequently. As an example, General Motors (GM), Ford, and Chrysler increased prices on most of their vehicles six to eight times during the 2003 model year to help pay for sky-high incentives and cut-rate financing. If you trust any of those books, you may not have the current numbers.

• Complete dealer invoice pricing for the vehicles you're shopping is also available as part of our Fighting Chance information package, described in chapter 24. We get weekly updates and typically have price changes as quickly as any other source.

THE MONRONEY DOCTRINE

That sticker on the window of every new car is known in car-store jargon as "the Monroney," after Oklahoma's Democratic Senator A.S. "Mike" Monroney, the lawmaker who sponsored the 1958 bill that mandated its presence. (If you refer to it as "the Monroney" when you talk with a dealer, he will know you're not someone who just fell off a turnip truck.)

Monroney's federal law requires that label to include the make, model, and identification number of the vehicle; its suggested retail price and the retail price of all factory-installed options not included in the base price; and the amount charged to the dealer for delivery to his store.

It's a federal crime to remove or alter that sticker before the vehicle is ultimately delivered to the purchaser. This effectively prevents car stores from replacing the original with a higher-priced sticker if a manufacturer raises the price on subsequent shipments of the same vehicle.

DEALER HOLDBACK (THE MONEY NO ONE TALKS ABOUT)

The second piece of this cost puzzle is called "dealer holdback," and no one talks about it. It's something no dealer wants you to know. Chances are, dealers don't even discuss it with their salesmen because it's the last thing they want them thinking about. For most makes, both domestics and imports, holdback is one of the most significant ways manufacturers put money back into dealers' pockets. It is *not* an incentive, and it applies to every vehicle sold with that nameplate.

Holdback is a specific percentage of a vehicle's price that is built into the original factory invoice price the dealer pays, held back by the manufacturer for awhile, and then credited back to the dealer's account after the vehicles are sold, typically quarterly. For example, GM and Chrysler each hold back an amount equal to 3 percent of the total retail sticker price (the manufacturers' suggested retail price [MSRP]), excluding the destination charge. While this percentage may seem relatively small, the dollars involved can be significant because even a midpriced new vehicle costs so much today.

For example, a Dodge dealer could take a sedan with a $20,000 sticker, sell it at his invoice price, and still make almost $600 from holdback. And a Cadillac dealer could unload a $40,000 luxury car at invoice and receive a holdback credit from GM close to $1,200.

In effect, holdback is a discount to the dealer that reduces the cost of the vehicle below an inflated dealer invoice price. Think of it as boomerang bucks: It's money he sends the factory when he pays the original invoice, but it eventually comes back to him.

Because the dealer pays it out up front, he treats it as if it were a cost item, instead of the profit item it really represents when he gets it back from the factory. Since it's a hidden item, it's excluded from the sales transaction. That means he doesn't have to pay a sales commission on it, and it's not on the table for a buyer to negotiate away.

Holdback was instituted in the early 1960s, we understand, as a way to ensure that dealers would have money on hand to pay Uncle Sam at tax time. While that may be one of several benefits to a dealer, holdback clearly benefits manufacturers as well. They've got use of that money, interest free, until the next quarterly payment. (In return, they give the dealer an extra couple of weeks to pay for cars received.) And if a dealer owes them money he won't or can't pay, they've always got a chunk of his cash on hand to cover some of that debt.

Dealers typically don't share holdback with their salespeople or their customers. Trying to beat them out of this money can make them angry; they count on it to pay basic overhead expenses. But telling them you know about it helps you keep them in their cage, making it more difficult for them to claim they aren't making money on your transaction. In effect, it gives you firmer ground on which to stand.

There's an accounting aspect of holdback that you should understand. Frequently, a dealer won't have the exact car you want, but he'll get it from another dealer's inventory. In this situation, the holdback will be credited to the dealer who originally purchased the car, not the selling dealer. But don't let the dealer use this fact as an excuse to go for a higher price. Dealers buy and sell cars with each other all the time, a practice that enables all dealers to operate more efficiently, with lower inventories. Your dealer may lose the holdback on your deal, but next week he'll earn the holdback on a car sold by some other dealer. It tends to even out over time.

The practice of holdback started with the domestic nameplates, but has spread to most import brands. Holdback percentages can differ substantially from one automaker or nameplate to another. Based on the best inside information available, here are the holdback numbers by manufacturer:

• All GM and Chrysler nameplates hold back 3 percent of the full sticker price (MSRP), excluding the destination charge.

• All Ford nameplates except Lincoln hold back 3 percent of the full sticker price (MSRP), excluding the destination charge. Lincoln's holdback is 2 percent of the full sticker price (MSRP), excluding the destination charge. In addition, the Ford Motor Corporation has certification programs in which top-rated dealers earn extra holdback dollars. Top-rated Ford "Blue Oval" dealers and Mercury "Advantage" dealers receive additional holdback of 1.25 percent of the sticker price (MSRP), excluding the destination charge. And top-rated Lincoln "Premier" dealers get an extra 2.5 percent of the sticker price, excluding the destination charge.

• Isuzu, Saab, Subaru, and Volkswagen hold back 3 percent of the full sticker price (MSRP). Isuzu also gives dealers another 1 percent of the total MSRP as a "floor planning allowance" to help pay interest carrying charges on their inventory.

• Others hold back a percentage of the base sticker price (MSRP), excluding the destination charge and the price of any additional option packages and accessories. Honda's holdback is 3 percent of the base sticker price. Lexus, Mazda, and Suzuki hold back 2 percent of the base MSRP.

• Mitsubishi dealers get 2 percent of the base sticker price in holdback, plus another 2 percent of the base MSRP as a floor planning allowance.

• Acura dealers receive 2 percent of the base sticker price (MSRP) in holdback, plus another 1.5 percent as a floor planning allowance.

• Infiniti and Toyota dealers get 2 percent of the base MSRP in holdback, plus another 1 percent as a floor planning allowance (which Toyota calls "wholesale financial reserve").

• Volvo's holdback is 1 percent of the base sticker price (MSRP).

• Some nameplates figure holdback as a percentage of the total invoice price, including the destination charge and the invoice price of any additional option packages and accessories. Mercedes-Benz dealers get 3 percent of the total invoice price and Nissan dealers, 2.75 percent. But Hyundai's holdback is 2.6 percent of the total invoice price, *excluding* the destination charge.

• A few manufacturers hold back a percentage of the base dealer invoice price, excluding the destination charge and the price of any additional option packages and accessories. Porsche and Kia hold back 3 percent, and Jaguar, 2 percent.

• Audi, BMW, and Land Rover have no holdback.

These holdback percentages may differ from some you'll find on the Internet. We get our data from the people at CarBargains, a national new-car shopping service described in chapter 20. Since their people are in constant contact with dealers for all makes, we believe their information is the best available. Holdback policies can change over time. The Fighting Chance information package covered in chapter 24 always gives you the most current holdback information.

We'll discuss in chapter 19 exactly how you should use your knowledge of holdback. Since it can't really be used as a negotiating chip, we don't recommend making a subtraction for holdback in any document you share with dealers. Instead, you will let them know you are aware of it, making your point without making them angry.

STRAIGHT TALK ABOUT INCENTIVES: WHAT TO EXPECT AND WHAT NOT TO EXPECT

When Chrysler hired Joe Garagiola in the late 1970s to stand up on television and say, "Buy a car, get a check," he changed the fundamentals of new-car marketing forever. Enticing buyers with direct cash rebates opened a Pandora's Box that no one can close.

The number of incentive dollars spent per vehicle tends to rise and fall somewhat with changing market conditions. But as one industry analyst put it, "Incentive programs are like hard drugs; once you get on, it's hard to get off." The consumer has been trained to expect incentives, and fierce competitive pressure will keep them around as long as there's excess production capacity.

As noted in chapter 3, incentive spending has increased dramatically in recent years, frequently reaching the level of thousands of dollars per vehicle for domestic nameplates, though significantly less for the European and Japanese makes. Incentives can be very attractive and stimulate sales, but remember that *you,* the car buyer, are paying for them. The cost of incentives is built into the price of the car, just as the cost of the tires is.

Some vehicles rarely have incentives because they sell well without them, but they are in the minority. In today's competitive auto market, more than half of new vehicles seem to need incentives. So whenever you see an incentive, think of it as a blinking neon sign that says, "This car is going to be easy to deal on. If it were selling better, it wouldn't need this incentive."

Some incentive programs are directed at consumers, others at dealers. Let's examine both.

MANUFACTURER-TO-CUSTOMER OFFERS

There are three types of customer incentives: cash rebates, low-interest financing, and subsidized leases.

• **Cash Rebates**—Automakers offer cash rebates directly to customers when they buy specific cars within certain time periods. These offers are widely advertised. No dealer would lie to you about a rebate. He can't get his hands on that money until you sign a paper authorizing the manufacturer to credit those dollars to the dealer's account as part of your payment. Automakers seldom send rebate checks to customers these days because almost everyone elects to use the rebate as a down payment against the purchase price.

Note that most states tax the full sales price before deducting the rebate (and often before any trade-in allowance is subtracted). You should check your state's tax laws, but no dealer would steal "bogus" sales tax money from you. If a dealer were caught doing that, your attorney general would be on that dealership like ugly on a baboon.

• **Low-Interest Financing**—Auto manufacturers frequently offer cut-rate, below-market financing to qualified buyers. This low-rate financing is sometimes offered in addition to a cash rebate, but it is usually an alternative to a rebate. In effect, the automakers transfer the rebate money to their captive finance subsidiaries (General Motors Acceptance Corporation, Ford Motor Credit, Toyota Motor Credit, etc.), which use it to "buy down" the annual percentage rate to a level below the going market rate. This financing can be very attractive, but it is normally based on the top customer credit tier, and not all consumers will qualify for this rate.

When choosing between a rebate and low-interest financing, it's helpful to run the alternative numbers on a financial calculator to determine which alternative would be best for you. You will find several on the Internet. One is at www.edmunds.com. Scroll to the bottom of the home page, click on "Search," then scroll to the bottom of the next page and type "calculators" in the search box. On the next page select "Financial Calculators." After skimming the text on the page that appears next, click on the "Calculators" link.

• **Subsidized Leases**—Automakers can also offer special lease programs, where they take what would otherwise be rebate dollars and shift them to their captive finance companies. This money is typically used to (a) inflate the *residual value* above the actual worth of the car at the end of the lease and/or (b) reduce the interest rate, which is expressed as a *money factor,* to a level below the current market rate. Alternately, this subsidy may be subtracted from the negotiated price of the car, reducing the *capitalized cost.* Any of these actions will make leasing more attractive by lowering the monthly lease payment. (If this sounds like "boomfog" to you, don't worry. Leasing is explained completely in chapter 21.)

Before leaving this section, we should add that there are some direct-to-consumer offers that are not publicized broadly because they apply to only a small percentage of new-car buyers. Since the cost is born by the automakers, dealers will readily tell you about them if you ask. They fall into four categories:

1. Recent College Graduate Offers—Some automakers offer additional rebates to recent college graduates on the purchase or lease of a new car or truck, typically $400 to $500. These offers are usually from Ford, GM, or Chrysler, though you may occasionally find similar offers from import makes. They make good business sense. If a company can sell you an entry-level vehicle, it probably has a better chance of attracting you to its higher-priced models in later years. (Over 30,000 people take advantage of Ford's program each year.) If you've graduated from college or graduate school in the last year or two, or if you'll graduate within the next year, you should ask about these programs. In some cases, you may have to finance through the automaker's finance subsidiary to qualify.

2. Discounts for Commercial Users—If you're buying a truck that will be registered to a business, you may be eligible for a commercial discount from some manufacturers, usually around $300 but sometimes more.

3. Customer Loyalty Discounts—Another kind of offer worth asking about is a discount for people who own or lease a car of the same make, or people who have *ever* owned a car of the same make. The domestic nameplates offer this additional incentive frequently as they fight their war of attrition against the imports. Some of the smaller import brands also make these offers, since a good percentage of their sales comes from previous customers. As one Fighting Chance customer reported to us, "When I called Saab's 800 number to ask for information, they sent me a coupon good for $750 if I purchased a new Saab by the end of the month." If you're shopping for a make you've owned before, it's always a good idea to make the phone call and ask the question.

4. Discounts for Military Personnel—We live in a troubled world, one where our armed forces regularly put their lives on the line in foreign lands. To show appreciation for what they do, some automakers offer bonus cash of $500 or more to active military personnel, National Guard, Coast Guard, reservists, and military retirees.

MANUFACTURER-TO-DEALER OFFERS

As noted above, the first element determining the dealer's "dead cost" for your vehicle is the dealer invoice price, and the second is dealer holdback. There's a third and final piece to this puzzle, but this is where the trail gets difficult to track because we can't see all the footprints.

Have you ever watched late-night television and wondered how so many dealers can shout about "prices below dealer invoice," implying that they're selling them for less than they paid? What they're trying to do, in dealer jargon, is "create a sense of urgency" that will get you off your couch and into their showrooms. The best way to do that, apparently, is to convince you that they're almost giving those things away.

But how can dealers sell cars and trucks for less than they cost? The answer, of course, is that they can't. At least they can't for long and stay in business, and who wants to buy a car from a dealer who's about to go out of business?

So, when they spend all those ad dollars implying that that's what they're doing, are they telling us less than the whole truth, or even misleading us? The answer lies somewhere between yes and no. Yes, because a dealer can sell cars all day long for less than he paid for them and still make money. And no, he can't sell cars for less than they cost him without losing money.

Yes, the dealer invoice cost is what he paid for the car. It's the bill he got from the manufacturer, the invoice he had to pay when the auto arrived. But what he paid for the car is not what it ends up costing him, because there are several ways manufacturers put money back into his pocket through factory-to-dealer incentive programs.

There are two classes of factory-to-dealer incentives: traditional dealer cash and what we will call undisclosed incentives—undisclosed to everyone except individual dealers.

• **Traditional Dealer Cash**—In these programs, automakers give dealers a specific cash payment for every vehicle sold within a given time period. Most of the time there will be either a customer incentive or a dealer incentive; in rare instances, a vehicle may have both. Sometimes, these incentives are advertised, but often they are not. It is usually possible to learn about these traditional dealer cash offers through published incentive reports.

As a general rule, Detroit concentrates the bulk of its incentive activity on direct customer rebates and cut-rate financing, while the Europeans favor factory-to-dealer cash. Some Japanese companies lean toward consumer offers,while others lean toward dealer incentives. But it's not uncommon for a manufacturer to have rebates on some cars and dealer cash on others, or rebates in some regions and dealer cash in others. Sometimes, the dealers in each market get their choice of either a rebate or a dealer cash program.

• **Undisclosed Dealer Cash**—This is where the hunt for the true dead cost of your car hits a wall. Because today virtually all automakers are rewarding dealers in ways that aren't revealed outside the dealer community—ways other than holdback and traditional "sell one, get $XXX" sales incentives. Most of these programs are tailored to objectives set for each individual dealership and are not tied directly to your transaction. And no source can report them because they will differ from one dealer to another, depending on a dealership's performance against its targets.

Think about it this way. Assume you owned a store selling television sets and everyone who walked in knew exactly what you paid for them and used that information to get you to sell for little or no profit. Surely, you'd eventually go to Sony, Toshiba, and Mitsubishi and say, "We're getting killed here. You'd better find other ways to put money in our pockets, or you won't have retail stores to sell your products."

That's what's been happening in the retail automobile business. Here's how a couple of these programs work:

• BMW has no holdback and Volvo's holdback is just 1 percent of the base sticker price (MSRP). But their dealers can earn additional cash incentives approaching $1,000 or more for every car sold by reaching their individual customer satisfaction index targets, based on questionnaire responses from both sales and service customers. Of course, there's no way for anyone to know whether any given dealership is earning $1,000, $500, $100, or nothing. We believe other manufacturers are motivating dealers in similar ways to improve the way they treat customers, but no one can attach a dollar figure to any individual dealer.

- In another incentive format, automakers set specific sales targets for each dealer, stretching over several weeks or months, and they'll pay an additional $XXX per vehicle if the dealer beats the target by X percent, $YYY if he beats it by Y percent, and $ZZZ if he beats it by Z percent. These targets may include all cars or be geared to specific product segments, such as sport utility vehicles. Again, there's no way to know where any dealer stands vs. his target, so there's no specific dollar number we could use as a negotiating chip even if we knew a program like this existed.

ADDITIONAL REALITY CHECK: MORE CAVEATS

After years of studying incentive reports, we've come to some other conclusions we should share with you, so that you can gear your expectations to reality.

No report picks up every incentive offer. Many automakers don't run the same incentives everywhere, because they gear them to the needs of each market. There are always regional offers that you wouldn't learn about or be affected by unless you lived in those markets. The available reports, including *CarDeals,* have long-standing, reliable sources, including many dealers. But there may be one deal in Hartford and another in New Haven. No single report blankets this country with enough spies to ferret out all the different regional and local rebate, dealer cash, and low-cost financing offers.

For example, one winter BMW dealers in the Northeast couldn't give away convertibles, but Florida dealers couldn't get enough. So in February, BMW gave its snowbelt dealers an extra $2,000 for each convertible sold. This offer didn't show up in any incentive report; we learned about it from Fighting Chance customers.

Don't expect to see incentives on all vehicles. As noted earlier, no manufacturer needs to put incentives on vehicles that sell well without them. This doesn't necessarily mean that you can't deal aggressively on the price of these vehicles. It just means the automakers don't have sweaty palms over sales. (On the hottest sellers, of course, where demand exceeds supply, you'll pay the full sticker price or more.)

You'll seldom find incentives on all-new models during their first several months on the market. That would be an admission of failure from the start, a signal that the vehicle was overpriced. And some low-volume and specialty vehicles never have incentives. There are some cars whose sales average only one or two per month per dealer. When demand is that low, incentives don't help much. The implicit assumption is that the few customers who want the vehicle are so committed to the product that incentives aren't required, and those that don't want it won't be won over by a rebate, no matter how high it is.

Some automakers avoid traditional incentives like the plague because they believe they damage the brand image. As an example, we seldom see rebates or dealer cash on current Honda models, though the company has used model-year-end dealer cash offers to move out last year's cars. The strategic thinking is that it's crazy to spend $500 million on advertising to convince us to buy their cars because they're so wonderful, then spend another $300 million to convince us to buy them because they're so cheap. The company believes those actions work at cross-purposes, and it's right.

Does that mean Honda doesn't occasionally spend promotional dollars to boost sales of certain models? Of course not. But instead of offering rebates, the company will put that incentive money into subsidized financing for purchases or leases through its captive finance company, Honda Motor Credit Corporation. For example, Honda might spend $1,000 to offer five-year financing at a rate that's well below the market interest rate, saving the customer at least $1,000 in interest charges over the term of the loan. Why will Honda do that, but not offer a $1,000 rebate? Because the average consumer doesn't perceive a cut in the interest rate as a cut in the price of the car, so the brand's image doesn't suffer.

Does Honda ever use *undisclosed* dealer cash programs to increase sales? We believe it does on certain models. Every year, the Accord battles the Toyota Camry for sales supremacy in the midsize family sedan segment. And every year, significant numbers of Fighting Chance customers report buying Accords for prices well below the dealer invoice, when there apparently are no rebates or traditional dealer cash incentives. Clearly, Honda is rewarding dealers for those sales in ways that are not made public.

Many luxury makes focus their finance deals on leasing, which accounts for a major percentage of their sales. In lieu of rebates or dealer cash, they simply transfer the same amounts of money to their captive finance subsidiaries, which use it to increase the vehicle's residual value and/or reduce the lease's interest rate—both of which reduce your monthly payments.

Note that if *CarDeals* or another incentive report shows a dealer cash incentive on a vehicle, the dealer usually doesn't get that cash if it's a subsidized lease through the automaker's finance subsidiary. But you will get the benefit of that money in the form of lower monthly payments. In this situation, the automaker is buying the car back from the dealer at the agreed-on transaction price and applying that money to the back end of the lease, jacking up the residual value and/or reducing the interest rate.

If, however, the lease is through a bank or other third-party financial institution, the dealer will get that factory cash, since he's selling the car to someone other than the automaker's captive finance subsidiary. In this instance, you can use that cash on the front end of the lease, negotiating a lower capitalized cost. From your perspective, it doesn't matter whether the capitalized cost is $1,000 lower or the residual value is $1,000 higher; the effect on your monthly payment is the same. (For more insight on leasing, see chapter 21.)

Living Proof: Vehicle Options Can Be Valuable

There may be a very tangible benefit in keeping more than one car on your wish list—particularly if you're shopping for a vehicle that's one of the "family relations" in chapter 13. Because the maker of one car may be offering a substantial consumer or dealer incentive, while the maker of a similar car offers less or none at all. This difference may be just what it takes to make one car the best choice for you.

To illustrate, let's assume that you were interested in a Toyota Matrix, which is virtually a "twin" of the Pontiac Vibe. Both are assembled by the same people on the same basic platform in the same plant and should have equal quality and reliability. But since the Pontiac brand projects a weaker quality image than the Toyota nameplate, Pontiac needs bigger incentives to move its cars. It would not be unusual for there to be a $1,500 rebate on the Vibe, but little or no incentive on the Matrix. If that were the case, the Vibe could be the smarter choice for you.

If you've got your heart set on just one vehicle, and it isn't covered by a current program, you should consider waiting a month or two. New programs start all the time. Remember, though, that many better-selling cars and trucks almost never have incentives.

SOURCES OF INFORMATION ON INCENTIVES

Okay, so we can't get perfect information on incentives that will reveal the dealer's dead cost. But there are sources that can tell us much of what we want to know, and we should use them.

- Many Internet web sites provide incentive data. Among them: Kelley Blue Book (www.kbb.com) and Intellichoice (www.intellichoice.com). We've found that the best site is Edmunds (www.edmunds.com), which seems to do a better job of turning up traditional dealer cash incentives. Edmunds also provides incentives by zip code, but that information isn't always correct. And these Internet sources frequently don't agree with each other.

• *Automotive News,* the industry's trade paper, publishes a weekly listing of national customer and dealer cash incentives. It may be available in your local library.

• The biweekly *CarDeals* report that's included in our Fighting Chance information package is the best hard-copy publication we've found. It covers the national customer and traditional dealer cash incentives well, typically listing many more offers than *Automotive News.* (You can view a sample of a typical *CarDeals* report in a portable document file [PDF] format on our web site, www.fightingchance.com.)

• Believe it or not, the best information sources for customer incentives in your market are probably the dealers there who sell the nameplates you're shopping. Since the automakers pay the costs of these offers, they should readily disclose them to you. Call two or three local dealers, ask to speak to the finance manager, tell him you're considering one of the vehicles his dealership sells, and ask him what customer rebates, special financing, or leasing programs the manufacturer is offering on that car.

YOU CAN WIN IN THIS IMPERFECT WORLD

If you're troubled by the lack of complete information on dealer incentive programs, don't shoot the messenger. We don't invent the news, we just report it. And from day to day, we are probably closer to that news than anyone else.

More important, don't despair. If you take our advice in chapter 19 and make dealers bid competitively for your business, these secret cash incentives will almost always be reflected in the price proposals you receive, because dealers earning extra cash from these programs will be in a position to make lower bids.

You can take comfort from this fact: The retail automobile market is so competitive that in most cases, dealers are forced to pass these undisclosed incentives along to their price-conscious customers. There are always a few dealers in every market who price aggressively, forcing the others to follow suit. In a price competition, if a dealer is unwilling to include his dealer incentives in the bid, he won't even participate because he knows the other dealers will.

Virtually all dealer cash should end up in your pocket, based on this rationale: The dealer was willing to sell you that car for a certain profit before that extra cash was there. He should be willing to sell you that same car for the same profit after that extra cash is there. The purpose of dealer cash isn't to make him richer on your deal. It's to make him more competitive on price so that he can sell more cars. More cars sold means more cars needing parts and service, and as you'll recall, that's where he earns most of his profit.

We live in a world where we can never learn everything we'd like to know. In the final analysis, every dealer has to make a profit to stay in business, and that's neither illegal nor immoral. Your objective shouldn't be to beat them out of every last nickel, but to get a deal you can feel good about, based on the best information available in the real world. That information, imperfect as it may be, still provides powerful leverage in your price negotiation. And those who use it to make dealers bid competitively will get much better deals than those who don't.

ADDITIONAL DEALER COST ITEMS

There are two other cost items you can expect to hear about before you complete a deal. One is for advertising, the other is for processing documents.

Dealer Advertising Association Charge

All manufacturers require their dealers to participate in the regional dealer group advertising effort in their markets. (These are the commercials inviting you to "Visit your southern California Toyota dealers," not the ones promoting an individual dealer's store.) The dealers form an advertising committee, and they assess every dealer a certain dollar amount for each vehicle sold. This is typically 1 to 3 percent of the invoice price, depending on the media costs in the market and how often the dealers need to run advertising. The charge is usually several hundred dollars per car, and it's included in the dealer's version of the invoice price. (On a Toyota dealer's invoice, for example, it might appear as "Toyota Dealer Association" or "TDA.") This charge is not included in the dealer invoice prices you will find in books or on the Internet because the amounts will differ from market to market, and there are hundreds of television markets. When the dealer claims that your invoice price is too low, this advertising charge will usually be the main reason.

Is this a legitimate charge for the buyer? We believe it is. Don't we pay for the advertising of everything we buy? When other retailers run ads to attract us, aren't we paying for those ads when we respond by visiting their stores? Of course we are; the cost of advertising is built into the price of the products we buy there. The only difference is that the car store treats the advertising as a separate charge that's added to the final bill.

Some automotive web sites and books will tell you to refuse this charge. And every few months, a Fighting Chance customer will tell us he did just that and that the dealer waived the charge because he needed to make the sale. But these reports are rare, and in most cases the customer had to walk away from several dealers before finding one so accommodating. In our view, these other sources are giving dated advice. Today, virtually all dealers are demanding that customers pay this group advertising expense. Occasionally, a dealer may not want to risk losing a sale over it, but most dealers will let you walk if you refuse to pay it—especially if you've already negotiated a slim-profit price on the new vehicle. If a dealer doesn't mention an advertising fee, this may be a sign that you're paying much more than you should for a car. (Some luxury-car dealers don't discuss this cost as a separate charge, but you'll be paying it; it's just built into the hefty gross profit in the deal.)

Document Processing Fees

Many dealers will charge a documentation fee. Of course, they can't sell anyone a car without processing some documents and sending messengers with paperwork to and from your state's motor vehicle department. You could argue that's their cost of doing business, not yours. Frankly, it's not worth much of an argument unless the fee is unreasonably high. We won't dig in our heels over $25 to $50.

But sometimes this fee is several hundred dollars. In this situation, consider this number in the context of the rest of the deal. If you're buying the car for ten cents over the dealer invoice, or well below the invoice, then figure that all but about $50 of that charge is profit, and maybe it's okay if they make a buck or two on your $20,000 purchase. But if they're getting a decent profit, then want several hundred dollars to process documents, ask for a job there processing documents.

The way to avoid exorbitant charges like this is to make dealers compete for your business. The one who charges an arm and a leg for paperwork is unlikely to be the low bidder.

Many that are first shall be last;
and the last shall be first.
                    —Matthew 19:30

17

Timing Is Money

Success in any serious endeavor can have a lot to do with being in the right place at the right time. For the new car buyer, timing is money. There are so many timing-related issues in the auto shopping process that we've prepared a separate chapter to focus your attention on all of them. In this race, getting there last often beats getting there first. Here are some specific illustrations of how the turtle beats the hare.

IF YOU'RE LATE, YOU'RE RIGHT ON TIME

As it says in the Bible, "There is a time to every purpose under heaven."

• The time to kick tires and take test drives and do research is during the first three weeks of the month.

• The time for serious negotiation is during the last week of the month—ideally the last few days. Auto dealerships are sales-driven organizations that live or die from month to month based on their performance against specific objectives. Auto manufacturers report sales monthly, and they focus their dealers on the same time frame, using sales targets, incentives, or just plain fear to motivate them. The dealers pass along the targets, the incentives, and the fear to their sales managers and salespeople.

Optimism rules early in the month; they all think they'll reach their goals. But as they enter that final week, dealers that aren't on target get more anxious to sell . . . and more flexible on transaction prices. Fighting Chance customers regularly report getting the lowest price proposals on the last few days of the month, with sales managers acknowledging that they wouldn't have made those deals if they hadn't needed them to close the period on a positive note.

Incentive programs typically follow a month-to-month pattern.

• Customer incentives (cash rebates, cut-rate financing, and subsidized leases) almost always end on the last day of the month. They're designed to provide a sense of urgency, to give dealers a rationale for getting you off your couch and into a car store "because this all ends next Tuesday." What they don't tell you is that it starts again the next Wednesday. A vehicle either needs incentives to boost sales or it doesn't. If there's a customer incentive on it this month, chances are good there will be one next month.

• Both traditional and undisclosed dealer cash incentive programs may stretch over two or more months, but they are geared to finish at the end of a month. A dealer may need to sell just a few more cars to reach one of those secret sales plateaus that will give him more money on all the other cars sold during the promotion period. In that situation, he may be willing to sell those cars for prices well below his actual cost.

This makes the end of the month the best time to buy. If your old car just died or was totaled in an accident, you may need to move sooner. But if this is not the case, don't even think about negotiating before the last few days of the month.

If it's late in the fall, remember that dealers also have yearly sales goals. Some of the smartest shoppers always buy their new cars during the last few days of December, between Christmas and New Year's Eve. Dealers can get very aggressive then, hoping to punctuate the end of the year with a big sales flourish.

There's one more reason dealers are often willing to sell cars at the end of a month for little or no profit, or even at a loss. It's called "turn-and-earn," which means, "Sell one and we'll send you another one." For popular cars that sell well, automakers frequently base future allocations on current sales results. So if it's the end of a month and some dealerships haven't reached their turn-and-earn sales target on a popular car, they might sell a few at bargain-basement prices just to guarantee their future supply of that top seller.

THE END OF THE LINE CAN BE A GOOD PLACE TO STAND

Many people like to buy at the end of the model year, during those year-end closeout sales. The new models are about to arrive, and they've got to make space for them. (For the purpose of measuring sales, the industry designates October through September as its model year.)

One reason prices are friendlier at the end of the model year is that most automakers allocate money to help their dealers sell those year-end leftovers. (They won't get heavy orders for new models if dealers are loaded with last year's cars.) This money usually comes in the form of standard incentives, either customer rebates or traditional factory-to-dealer cash. Even vehicles that normally don't get incentives may have them in the July–September quarter.

In the past, two automakers, General Motors (GM) and Ford, regularly provided a "carryover allowance" to move out year-end leftovers. That allowance was 5 percent of the sticker price (the manufacturers' suggested retail price), which they credited to dealers for every previous year's vehicle sold after the new model of the same vehicle arrived in the showroom. On a vehicle with a $20,000 sticker price, that 5 percent represented an additional $1,000 for you to bargain for. The allowance generally covered all vehicles, but sometimes it excluded hot-selling models in relatively short supply, especially if the new models had only minor changes.

But in recent years, carryover has been dropped by GM and Ford. Now they simply put much higher incentives on year-end models, as other automakers do.

A Key Closeout Issue: Slim Pickings

One problem with waiting until the end of the model year to shop for your dream car is that you may not be able to find it then. Most automakers stop assembling the current year's models in June and start producing the next year's models in July, to be shipped after Labor Day. As a result, you may have trouble locating the particular color-and-equipment combination you want, especially if new car sales have been strong.

Sometimes year-end pickings can be slim in a down market. If sales have been depressed for months, both manufacturers and their dealers may write off a model year when it's only half over. Dealers get very selective with their orders as the current year's production winds down, and the factories structure their build-out plans to allow dealers to maintain lean inventories of only the fastest-moving models. They're both hoping to end the old-model year without a glut of leftovers, so they can focus all their resources on the new-model launch in the fall.

If you plan to shop for an end-of-year bargain, you'll have more to choose from if there are two or three finalists you'd be equally happy to drive home. If you've got your heart set on one model, try to have an open mind on color and equipment.

The Other Side of the Year-End Coin

Don't be blinded by those apparently great year-end clearance deals. Savvy buyers understand that they are a mixed blessing. There's a reason automakers put bigger incentives on last year's cars each summer, in anticipation of the new models' arrival: *They're worth considerably less then.* Indeed, it's proper to question whether those incentives are large enough to make the leftovers a smart buy.

The culprit is depreciation. Any new car—even the new year's model—is worth a lot less the moment the wheels leave the dealer's lot as you drive it home. That's just a fact of life in the new-car business. If you want an asset that appreciates, buy common stock, not common cars.

Similarly, the incentives on year-end closeouts don't begin to cover a vehicle's precipitous drop in value after the new models are introduced. The day the new models arrived, that old model became last year's car. A year later, when next year's models come out, it'll be a two-year-old model. If you have to sell it then, you will have taken a two-year depreciation hit in one year, no matter how much TLC you've lavished on it. And if there have been extensive styling changes in the new model, that older, out-of-style car may depreciate even faster than normal because there's a much prettier successor on the highway.

So the first question to ask yourself is how long you plan to keep the car. If you plan to drive it till the wheels fall off, depreciation really isn't an issue; whether you buy the leftover model or the new-year model, it won't have much value when you're done with it. In that scenario, the leftover is probably the smart buy, since anything you save at the time of purchase is a real saving.

But most new-car buyers don't keep cars forever; they trade them for another new car after a few years. If you're shopping for a midpriced car, you can figure that five years from now the new-year's model will be worth at least $1,000 more than last year's leftover, assuming the same mileage and condition for both.

Another issue to consider is the year-to-year inflation in auto prices. Buying last year's leftover makes more sense when prices are increasing 5 percent or more a year ($1,000 or more on a $20,000 car) than when yearly price hikes are just 1 or 2 percent. The dollar-yen relationship plays a major role in this. When the yen is surging against the dollar, as it did in the late 1980s and early 1990s, the Japanese repatriate fewer and fewer yen for each dollar earned here, so they have to raise prices continuously just to stay even. (That's why the sticker price of the Lexus LS 400 went from $35,000 at its introduction to over $50,000 a few years later.) Those Japanese price hikes provide a nice umbrella under which Detroit can raise its prices aggressively. But when the dollar is surging against the yen, as it did in the late 1990s, the reverse is true. The Japanese take home more yen for the same dollar, and there's no pressure on them to raise prices. In some cases, they can even *reduce* them. Which puts a lid on Detroit's ability to raise prices.

In making this decision, your reference point should be the most current model, not the leftover. First determine what you'd have to pay for the new one; then see how much you can save by buying last year's version. *Our rough rule of thumb: On any midpriced car, if you can't save at least $1,500 by buying the leftover, it's usually smarter to buy the newer model— unless you plan to drive it until it's virtually worthless.*

The moral of the story is that year-end is a great time to buy a leftover bargain, as long as you don't have to sell it in a year or two. You should plan to keep that car for several years to ride out the negative effect of the car's lower real value when it was purchased. And when you eventually trade it, you should do it for another year-end closeout model, so you don't get stuck selling low and buying high.

GETTING THERE FIRST CAN BE AN EXPENSIVE TRIP

Remember the Mazda MX-5 Miata. (This is a warning, not a question.)

The Miata was introduced with rave reviews, with a sticker price o $13,800 and just enough cars to reach from your kitchen to your dining room, end to end. Mazda dealers loved it! Many put their additional dealer markup stickers on every one and doubled or tripled their gross profit per car. And the newspapers were still full of consumers' buy-and-sell offers a prices from $20,000. Talk about being in new-car heat!

Ten months after the Miata arrived, you could buy one for a few hun dred dollars over the dealer invoice price and have just as much fun driving it as the folks who had paid an extra $5,000 or $10,000 when it was intro duced. You just couldn't be the first on your block to own one.

Supply and Demand: It's the Law

Whatever the item, if more people want it than can get it, those who get it will pay for the privilege. World Series tickets, Super Bowl hotel rooms, the first 2,000 Mazda Miatas . . . you name it.

With most all-new vehicles, there is an initial period of sales excite ment, usually three to six months, when dealers are just order-takers, not salesmen, and supply is chasing demand. That's when folks who've been postponing their purchase in anticipation of the new car come in, most of them willing to pay dearly to be among the first to own one. The hotter the car, the longer that period lasts. Eventually, the initial excitement dissi pates, supply and demand come into their normal long-term relationship and dealers become more flexible on transaction prices.

You will sometimes find dealers adding "additional dealer markup" or "additional market value" stickers to the windows of cars that are ex tremely hot and in short supply. When Volkswagen introduced the new Beetle, dealers were getting just two per week, but could sell ten. Taking advantage of this situation, they put stickers on every car with an addi tional markup of $3,000 or more. And some foolish people were actually paying $3,000 over the full sticker price to own the first one on their block.

If you're after a hot car, the ability to postpone gratification can save you a lot of money. Check periodically to see whether dealers have devel oped any price flexibility. The best way to assess the supply situation in your market is to stop at a few dealerships on your way to work, at 7:30 or 8:00 A.M., when there are no salespeople around to bother you. Check the inventory on their lots. If there are just a few, there's a message there. If there are many, there's a different, more encouraging message. When you begin to see more than a few regularly, and some of the same cars are there from visit to visit, you may assume the leverage is shifting from the seller to the buyer.

The law of supply and demand can also work against the car buyer at the beginning of the model year, though usually less dramatically than in the case of a hot new car like the Miata or the reincarnated Volkswagen Beetle. From October through December, when a new-year model can be in relatively short supply, the dealer may not accept the same price he will later in the year, when the only things standing in line are the cars on his lot.

Bugs Aren't Just on Windshields

There's another reason to avoid a brand-new model in the early months of production: bugs. Even in this era of dramatically improved product quality, it frequently takes auto manufacturers several months or more to get the hang of making glitch-free products.

Glitches are more likely to happen on vehicles with domestic nameplates than on imports. As an example, consider the vexing little problems that plagued GM's Saturn in its first year: there were recalls for defective seats and for a corrosive engine coolant, and early buyers complained about noisy, vibrating engines.

Saturn was launched with great ballyhoo, following a $5 billion capital investment and seven years of meticulous planning. Yet, many say that what Saturn did best in its first year was to correct problems with great consumer and public relations sensitivity.

By Saturn's second year, the bugs had been eliminated and the Saturn buyer could anticipate a glitch-free vehicle. But Saturn's early pratfalls illustrate that even a company determined to get it right can stumble coming out of the blocks. The wise buyer will always count to ten before purchasing a brand-new vehicle.

A CROWDED SHOWROOM IS A BAD PLACE TO BE

If you take our advice in chapter 19, once you've decided which vehicle you want, you won't go anywhere near a car store to do your negotiating. You'll get a number of dealers to play *your* game by making it a competitive bidding process. But whether or not you take that advice, you should avoid contacting dealers around a weekend. That's when they're crowded with other shoppers. The impression they want to project then is that there's a feeding frenzy for the car you want, so you'd better get it while you can— at a price you won't like.

Your chances of striking a terrific deal are enhanced dramatically when you're not just another face in the crowd. However you decide to negotiate, plan to do it in the middle of the week (Tuesday, Wednesday, or Thursday), when almost no one else is car shopping. The middle of a blizzard or a deluge is also good timing. And car stores can be particularly accommodating in January and February, when most people are paying off holiday bills and not thinking of buying new cars and trucks.

AT TENT SALES, YOU GET GREAT DEALS ON CAMELS, NOT CARS

The timing elements to ignore are the corny sales events dealers love to advertise. In car salesman lingo, their purpose is always to create a sense of urgency and to get prospects into their showrooms by implying that this gigantic tent sale is the opportunity of a lifetime . . . and when it's over, it's over. Sure it is. Until the following month's red tag sale, or the midnight madness sale, or the President's Day sale, or the overstock clearance sale.

The transaction prices at most of these phony events are no lower than they were before the sale. They are probably higher, because those ads attract gullible people who believe that a car dealer's advertised sale is as real as a department store's advertised sale. Unless the ads feature some very specific offer, such as a manufacturer's below-market financing program, the only real opportunities are for salesmen to take advantage of folks who fall for the come-on. So if there's a midsummer heat wave in your town and the "beat-the-heat" sale ads promise free air conditioning with every car sold, you should extend your antennae fully. For a midpriced vehicle, that air conditioner costs the dealer more than his profit on a typical sale to a knowledgeable buyer. Unless it's supplied free by the manufacturer, assume that you're paying for any "free" equipment. If the dealer giveth, the dealer also taketh away.

> *THE STRONGEST OF WARRIORS ARE THESE TWO: TIME AND PATIENCE.*
> —LEO TOLSTOY, *WAR AND PEACE*

TIME IS ALWAYS ON YOUR SIDE, NOT THEIRS

In a waiting game, the loser will be the one who needs the deal the most. The sooner you need to have a new car, the more it's going to cost. If that's today, or this weekend, you'd better have a Brink's truck for a trade-in. A loaded Brink's truck. But if you can wait them out, the time will come when they'll want a sale even more than you want a new car—particularly in the cold, hard glare of the end of another month. Sometimes, just one more sale—even a slim-profit sale—can be very important to a dealer.

All it takes is time, a luxury car dealers seldom have. If you've got it, use it.

18

A great price on something you don't want or need is not a great bargain.
—W. James Bragg

The Option

Game

T he *Random House Webster's College Dictionary* defines "option" as "the power or right of choosing." "Optional" is also defined as meaning "not required."

Auto manufacturers and their dealers have a different dictionary. Theirs defines "option" as "any additional equipment or accessories they can stick on a new vehicle that will maximize the profitability of the automaker and the car store."

FACTORY OPTIONS: WILL THEY BUILD IT THE WAY YOU WANT IT?

Automakers publish pricing schedules which imply that you can configure your vehicle however you wish, but that's not true. They can't efficiently produce more than a limited number of configurations. To maximize profits, they tend to load those configurations with equipment packages and accessories that you may not need or want. For example, it can be next to impossible to find a relatively spartan base model—especially one with a manual transmission.

Complicating the picture, some automakers will ship certain configurations to some areas, but not to others. A Fighting Chance customer in Seattle wanted a Camry equipped a certain way, but no dealer in Washington, Oregon, or Idaho could order that car from Toyota. He found that Las Vegas dealers could, but decided it was cheaper and easier to pay for equipment he didn't want in Seattle than to spend the money and time traveling to and from Nevada.

You need to understand the basic configurations that are shipped to your area, so that you can gear your expectations to reality. You can accomplish this when you visit car stores to do your test driving. Walk around dealers' lots to check the stickers on models similar to the one you want. And ask the salespeople if they can get a vehicle equipped to your specifications.

If a dealer doesn't have the color and equipment combination you want in his current stock or on order, he can run a computer search of the inventory of all the dealers in the same sales territory, which in some cases can cover several states. If that search turns up your ideal car or one almost like it, he can buy it from the other dealer or trade a similar-cost vehicle for it. He will ask you for a good-faith deposit before getting the car, probably about $500. That's reasonable, considering that you're asking him to add that extra car to his inventory for you.

It's also reasonable for you to demand some assurance that the car will be acceptable to you when it arrives. Ask the dealer for the current mileage on the odometer and a complete list of the equipment shown on the manufacturer's window sticker. Make sure he understands that you don't like unpleasant surprises and that you won't buy the car if the equipment turns out to be different or if the car isn't in perfect condition. (Put that $500 good-faith deposit on a credit card if you can; then, if there's a last-minute problem, you'll have the option of refusing to pay the charge when your monthly bill arrives.)

If the car has to be trucked in from a dealership a considerable distance away, you should expect to pay that extra cost. To avoid any misunderstanding, be sure to discuss this issue before you instruct the dealer to get the car for you. Remember, too, that the dealer who purchased the car initially is the one who gets the factory holdback dollars on the vehicle.

INDIVIDUAL FACTORY ORDERS: THE SOLUTION TO THE OPTION GAME?

As you may know, domestic vehicles can be special-ordered from the manufacturers. This is an excellent way to get one equipped exactly to your specifications, assuming they'll build it that way. And perhaps there is something special about having one built just for you.

Special orders are placed most often by buyers of full-sized pickup trucks. These vehicles come in a mind-boggling array of configurations: half-ton, three-quarter-ton, and one-ton models; regular cab, extended cab/club cab, quad cab, and crew cab; two-wheel and four-wheel drive; short and long bed; V-6, V-8, V-10, and diesel engines; and a long list of trim levels, equipment groups, and optional accessories. A dealer would need hundreds of trucks in inventory to stock just one of each possible configuration.

Any dealer would be happy to take your factory order for a car or truck. You won't pay more than you'd pay for one on his lot, in fact, you might even pay less. It's an easy sale, and he'll never pay interest carrying charges to inventory your car because you'll own it the day it arrives.

In most cases, a dealer will want a deposit from you as "earnest money," probably about $1,000. That's a reasonable request. You've asked him to commit for a vehicle he wouldn't necessarily purchase for his regular inventory, and he wants some assurance that you're going to fulfill your end of the bargain. Mostly, he wants to be sure you don't go down the street and try to beat the deal at another dealership.

Sometimes, a factory order can save you money if you're shopping for a vehicle that's in short supply and you don't need it immediately. There are always a few hot all-new models where supply trails demand. And whenever a dealer gets fewer units of a vehicle than he can sell, he will demand—and get—higher prices.

Many Fighting Chance customers report buying all-new vehicles in short supply for a few hundred dollars over the dealer invoice by placing a special order. Dealers understand that no vehicle stays hot forever and that the initial sales excitement subsides eventually. They'd rather take a slim profit on a factory order that won't arrive for a couple of months than turn down a sale. Most important, they can save their slim inventory for the idiot who'll walk in after you and pay the sticker price or more for that all-new vehicle.

The Caveats

Special ordering has many advantages, but there are some potential downside issues you should consider as well.

- For openers, it's likely to take six to eight weeks or more to get delivery. A lot of things can happen to your current car in that time—none of them good—that may cause the dealer to lower his offer for your trade-in.

- You'll usually have to place your order before the first of May if you want the current year's model. Automakers need at least two months' lead time, and the production switch over to the next year's model usually occurs in July.

- You may not be able to predict a realistic delivery date, especially if you order in the second half of the model year. When sales are slower, manufacturers periodically shut down selected factories for a week or more to avoid excess inventory buildup. The plants selected may include the one that makes your car.

- In the worst-case scenario, the United Auto Workers might go on strike, which might add two weeks or two months to the timetable, and you'd be thumbing a ride to work.

- Typically, only the domestic automakers will actually build a vehicle to your individual specifications. You can "order" an import make, but that just means the dealer will add your car to the order he places periodically for his own inventory. In general, your ability to customize a vehicle is more limited because import models don't offer as many different configurations, trim levels, and options as General Motors (GM), Ford, and Chrysler products. And you face a longer lead time if the model is made in Europe or Japan.

- You may not be able to take advantage of the current incentive offers with a factory-ordered car. Both the consumer rebate and low-cost financing programs and the traditional factory-to-dealer cash programs require that you take delivery by a certain date. The incentives that apply to your vehicle will be those in place when it's delivered, not when it's ordered.

(But we understand that the Chrysler group—Chrysler, Dodge, and Jeep—will allow you to apply either one, whichever is higher.)

- You may not have price protection on your order. The domestic name plates tend to raise prices regularly. (GM, Ford, and Chrysler raised the price of 2003 models six to seven times throughout the model year.) In most cases, dealers (and customers) must pay the price that's in effect when the vehicle arrives, not the one in place at the time of the order. If you're placing a factory order, be sure to discuss this with the dealer so that you won't be surprised when it happens.

- Finally, you may have a better shot at negotiating an attractive price on a car that is in a dealer's stock than on a special-ordered car. He's paying floor plan interest to keep that car in inventory, so he's highly motivated to get it off his lot and into your garage.

Here's how to estimate how long a car has been in a dealer's inventory. Look for the federally mandated manufacturer's sticker or plate, which shows the month and year of manufacture. It also carries these words: "This vehicle conforms to all applicable federal motor vehicle safety, bumper and theft prevention standards in effect on the date of manufacture shown above." It's usually placed inside the jamb of the driver's door, but may also be under the hood—on the fire wall between the engine and passenger compartments—or on one of the wheel wells.

If the date of manufacture is more than four months ago, you may assume the dealer is particularly anxious to sell that vehicle and might accept a lower price than he would for a car that just arrived on his lot.

BACK-END DEALER OPTIONS: JUST SAY NO

It's bad enough that the automakers load their cars with expensive options, whether you want them or not. But then the car stores pile on, adding their own high-profit dealer options on the back end. You'll find them hung all over the vehicles on some dealers' lots. That doesn't mean you have to buy them.

Your first clue that something's up is the other sticker on the window. It's often designed to look just like the Monroney, complete with an illustration of that little gas pump. It's not; *it's the car store's sticker.* There's often more profit potential on that sticker than on the basic car itself, but most of the items there won't add a dime's worth of value or utility. Let's replay a few of "the greatest hits."

"The Mop 'n Glow"

This group includes things like "rust-preventive undercoating," "fabric guard protection spray," "paint sealant," "sound shield," decorative striping, mud flaps, and deluxe floor mats. This strange entourage frequently masquerades under important-sounding names like "Optional Environmental Protection Package."

This little protection package can carry a retail price from $300 to as much as $1,000 or more. Its cost to the car store is peanuts—typically under $100. You need this stuff like a moose needs a hat rack!

• Let's start with "rust-preventive undercoating." Today's new vehicles carry very substantial anticorrosion warranties from just about all manufacturers. Most typically cover 5 to 7 years, or 100,000 miles, whichever comes first. (Check the coverage for your vehicle in chapter 22.) Probably the best argument against buying dealer rustproofing is that many factories recommend against it! Here's a quote from a GM warranty:

Some after-manufacture rustproofing may create a potential environment which reduces the corrosion resistance designed and built into your vehicle. Depending upon application technique, [it] could result in damage or failure of some electrical or mechanical systems of your vehicle. Repairs to correct damage or malfunctions caused by after-manufacture rustproofing are not covered under any of your GM new vehicle warranties.

Any questions?

• "Fabric guard protection spray": You call this Scotchgard. A fourteen-ounce can of 3M's Scotchgard sells for a few dollars in your supermarket and covers 14 to 21 square feet of fabric. Three cans should do the trick.

• "Paint sealant": Today's automotive paint jobs are technological wonders compared to 25 years ago, when additional protection may have been beneficial. The primary thing it benefits now is the size of the dealer's bank account.

The bottom line: Tell them to leave the Mop 'n Glow in aisle 9 in the supermarket, where it belongs. If they won't throw in the $79.95 cost of the total package for free or find you a car without it, find another dealer who will. (In fact, you'd rather buy a car without it.)

Here's one more option you should avoid: The car store's logo, either drilled into or glued onto the back end of your new car. Tell them you won't accept delivery of any vehicle with the dealer's advertising attached to it. The exception to this rule is a license plate frame bearing the dealer's name, which you can remove easily.

ADM, ADP, AND AMV

Printed boldly on the "other sticker," these acronyms represent the most arrogant form of customer-fleecing. They stand for "additional dealer markup," "additional dealer profit," and "additional market value," respectively. They used to be added to any car in relatively high demand and short supply, particularly imports.

In today's tough sales climate, most car stores have dropped these extra charges, but they're not extinct. You'll still find them on the hottest-selling, all-new vehicles at some stores—typically in the first several months of the introductory period, when the demand often outstrips the supply and there's a waiting list of buyers. These added markups can range from $1,000 to $3,000 or more. In that situation, when many people are willing to pay anything to have the first one on their block, the buyer has no leverage. If you're shopping for a hot new car that's selling for more than its sticker price, you can either take a number, get in line, and pay the bandits what they ask, or wait a few months for that initial sales excitement to dissipate. It always does. Eventually, supply and demand reach their normal long-term relationship, and transaction prices become more flexible.

If you see ADM, ADP, or AMV stickers on other cars, ignore them. Their purpose is to establish an artificially higher asking price from which to start negotiating with uninformed car buyers. You will find dealers moving off those above–manufacturers' suggested retail price stickers as soon as they realize that you know too much.

People who have no weakness are terrible; there is no way of taking advantage of them.

—Anatole France

19

Just Do It!

You've done all your homework. You've decided either to sell your old car yourself at retail or to a dealer at wholesale, and you've learned its true wholesale value. You've decided how much you can spend, including insurance, and you've researched financing alternatives. You've taken your test drives and chosen your vehicle. You've prepared work sheets showing the manufacturer's suggested retail price (MSRP) and the dealer invoice price for the vehicle, equipped the way you want it. You know about dealer holdback on the car. And you're aware of any current consumer incentives or traditional dealer cash incentives.

Before you do anything, review these key principles from chapter 6:

- Economics 101—You are shopping for a commodity. You will always get a better price on a commodity if you make suppliers compete. So you're not going to walk into any car stores to negotiate the price. Only a fool would do that.

- Geography 101—You're going to cast a wide net by contacting several dealers, many of whom may not be in your local area.

- Timing 101—You're going to negotiate on the last few days of the month. Only a fool would negotiate at any other time.

- Reality 101—It's a lot easier for you to find someone who wants to sell a new vehicle than for them to find someone who wants to buy one. That means you're in charge. They will play your game, not vice versa.

OUR FAVORITE NEGOTIATING TOOL: THE "FAX ATTACK"

Several years ago, a Fighting Chance customer in Colorado Springs, Colorado, reported that his family had faxed a number of dealers requesting price quotes and received several attractive offers on the vehicle they wanted. All they did was answer phone calls to get the price proposals from dealers who were bidding for their business. The first calls came before the last fax was sent. This customer said, "It was as easy as ordering a pizza."

Reading that report, we said to ourselves, "Duh! Why didn't we think of that? These things are commodities. Why would anyone waste time walking into car stores to negotiate the price? Why shouldn't everyone do this?" From that day onward, we have recommended the "fax attack" negotiation method to all Fighting Chance customers, and, based on the feedback we receive, estimate that over 90 percent of them use it. We've had over 60,000 customers and are adding about 10,000 a year. That's a tiny drop in the ocean of new car buyers, who number over 35,000 per day in a typical sales year. But it's a sample size that's more than large enough to illustrate that this idea works.

How the Fax Attack Works

Faxing works for any vehicle in good supply, whether you're buying or leasing. It's equally effective at the $70,000 luxury level, as well as at the

$10,000 entry level. If you fax fifteen to twenty dealers, you'll usually get responses from about half of them, much of it within the first few hours. And you'll be sitting in the comfort of your home or office while they play your game, instead of in the discomfort of a car store, playing their game.

The fax attack tends to separate out the dealers who will make better deals at that time. Some want to sell in quantity; others want to maximize the profit per sale. Dealers move in and out of these classifications, depending on market conditions and their current sales, inventory, and incentive positions. *There are no dealers who always give the best or worst deals.* The dealer who will give you the best deal this week may offer the worst deal or not even participate in the bidding next week because his situation has changed.

Faxing also turns up both traditional and undisclosed dealer cash incentives. As noted in chapter 16, today many dealer incentives are truly secret because they are geared to each individual dealer's performance against either (a) his customer satisfaction index (CSI) or (b) his ability to beat specific sales targets by certain escalating percentages to earn increasing bonus amounts per vehicle sold. Even if we knew these programs were in place when we were shopping, we couldn't use that information effectively as a negotiating chip because there'd be no way to tell where any dealer stood in relation to these targets.

This argues for casting a wide net via the fax attack, which should turn up better prices from dealers who are performing at higher levels against their targets. Dealers know they won't win your business without including that dealer cash in the bid because their competitors will include it. A dealer may even sell at well below his bottom-line cost if that sale will help him reach a "sales plateau" that will deliver more cash for all the other cars previously sold.

Given the feedback we get from Fighting Chance customers, there is solid evidence that the fax attack works. The 2003 Honda Accord is a perfect example. Consistent with Honda's incentive philosophy, there were no rebates or traditional dealer cash on this car during the entire model year. But fully 60 percent of the Accord transactions reported to us by customers were *below* the dealer invoice price, ranging from just under invoice to a whopping $987 below invoice. The most anyone reported paying was $600 over invoice. And almost all of those deals came from the fax attack.

This feedback represents evidence that Honda uses undisclosed dealer cash incentive programs to accomplish certain objectives. In this instance, the 2003 Accord was in a knock-down, drag-out battle with the Toyota Camry to be the best-selling passenger car in the country, and it is clear that Honda dealers were getting secret cash to help Honda win that competition.

There is also anecdotal evidence that Honda dealers get rewarded for making customers happy. Two examples:

• A Fighting Chance customer who bought an Accord for $151 *below* invoice reported: "The dealership had the #1 CSI ranking in Northern California and they wanted to keep it. I used another dealer's low bid from the 'fax attack' as a negotiating tool, and this dealer went $250 *below* that number, asking only that I give his dealership a 100% rating on the CSI survey. He was ready to sell at almost any price to keep that #1 CSI rating!"

• Another customer negotiated a similar Accord deal at a different dealership. But as she was signing the paperwork in the finance manager's office, he tried to pressure her into buying everything from an extended warranty to credit life insurance. That experience was so unpleasant that she gave the dealership low marks on the questionnaire she received by mail a month later. Ten days later, she got an angry phone call from the sales manager at the dealership saying, "We gave you a great deal, why did you do that to us?" She told him, of course. The relevant question here is, "Why would the sales manager make that angry call if her poor rating on that questionnaire didn't cost his dealership something it wanted?" Maybe it was money, maybe a better allocation of hot-selling new vehicles.

If Honda uses secret dealer incentives like these, it's safe to assume that most other automakers do. The fax attack is a powerful negotiating tool that encourages dealers to include this cash in their price proposals.

Will the fax attack work on every vehicle? No. If you want a hot, all-new car in short supply, forget faxing unless you tell them you're willing to wait several months for delivery. When dealers are selling every car they can get at or above the full sticker price, they will ignore your fax. (And no one puts incentives on hot new cars.)

What's the "Right Price" for Your Car?

We get questions like this all the time. People want to know what they should pay for the car they want. They want to know if a dealer's price proposal is the "right" price. They want to know what their car is selling for in their market. As you might guess from what you've read so far, there is no "right" price for any car in any market.

There is no significant difference in selling prices between one market and another. The average sale price on an Accord is about the same in Portland, Maine, as it is in Portland, Oregon. But there's a great deal of difference between the prices dealers will sell for in the same market. It is not unusual to have a $1,000 to $2,000 difference in a competitive bidding.

We are amused when we see a "True Market Value" number for each new vehicle on the Edmunds web site. Edmunds states, "The TMV is what you need to know to negotiate a fair price, the most important piece of your car pricing research. It's the average price that other consumers are paying for this vehicle." Now, why would you want to pay the average price that other consumers are paying, when more than half of the people included in that average probably don't have a clue about how to shop smart for a new car?

Consider this example: In 2002, when the all-new Lexus ES 300 was available, the transaction reports we received from Fighting Chance customers ranged from $1,700 to $2,300 over invoice. Edmunds would probably say the true market value was $2,000. But what about the folks who paid less than that by getting Lexus dealers to bid competitively? Should they simply have rolled over and offered $2,000? What about the Las Vegas, Nevada, woman who paid just $69 over invoice to the low bidder, a dealer in southern California who delivered the car to her doorstep? And the Plano, Texas, couple who got their car for $86 *below* invoice by making dealers compete? Should they have offered $2,000 more?

Note that Edmunds doesn't recommend that you get dealers to bid competitively for your business. If you spend a little time on that web site, you will see why: it's loaded with advertising paid for by auto companies and their car dealers. Edmunds doesn't tell you how to get the best deal because those advertisers don't want you to get the best deal.

The "right" price for your car is the best price you can get today in your market. You'll get that price by making dealers compete. Based on the experience of tens of thousands of our customers, the fax attack is an excellent way to do that. And you'll often be surprised at how low that price can be.

HOW TO MAKE FAXING WORK FOR YOU

The fax attack is a five-step process over a two- to three-day period: (1) identifying the people you'll contact; (2) preparing and sending the fax; (3) fielding the responses; (4) getting back to the participants after all the bids are in; and (5) finalizing the deal to avoid last-minute surprises.

Identifying the Dealer Contacts

Your objective should be to contact at least fifteen dealers. On average about half will respond. Locating fifteen dealers near you is relatively eas if you're shopping for a domestic nameplate, since most of them have 2,00 to 4,000 franchised stores. By contrast, the luxury imports have 400 o fewer dealers.

If you're shopping for a popular vehicle in short supply, a manual trans mission (which represents only a small percentage of sales and invento ries), or a full-sized pickup with tight configuration specifications tha might not be easy to find, fax more than fifteen dealers because the re sponse rate will be lower.

Define your faxing territory as anywhere you can drive in two or thre hours. If there are only a few dealers within that driving radius, expand you geography. Broaden your search to the entire state or surrounding states Remote dealers can be very willing to deal, viewing you as business the wouldn't otherwise get. (For example, a Texas customer who couldn't ge local dealers to deal on a Lexus LS 430 faxed dealers in Florida and save over $3,000.)

To identify dealers near you, go to the "dealer locator" on the manufac turer's web site and get the names and phone numbers of fifteen dealership ideally more. (Automakers' website addresses are listed in appendix A. Since only about 50 percent will respond, the more faxes you send, the be ter off you'll be. If a dealer locator gives you only the nearest two or thre dealers, try several more times, telling the locator each time that you live i a different surrounding town or city. If the locator asks for zip codes, go t zipfind.net or zipinfo.com, where you can get zip codes for any town or cit in the country. (Note: You'll find links to dealers' web sites on these deale locators. Many dealers list current inventory on their sites, so you can iden tify those with vehicles you'd consider and refer to them in your fax.)

Call each dealership and ask for the name of the sales manager or th fleet manager and the fax number closest to him or her, which will ofte differ from the dealership's general fax number. Most stores will have flee managers, but some may not. The sales manager is an equally good con tact. Getting names and numbers is usually not a problem. (Be sure to ge the correct spelling of the person's name.) If the operator asks why yo want this information, say that you're going to fax them an offer on a ca If they connect you to the manager, ask for the fax number and say you'r going to give them a shot at selling you a car.

Why sales or fleet managers? They have the authority to make th slim-profit deals. If you entered a busy showroom on a weekend with th

Fighting Chance information package and spoke above a whisper, you'd be treated like the Ebola virus and whisked behind a closed door. And you'd probably be talking to a sales or fleet manager, who typically deals with shoppers who know too much.

It's important that you do this right. If you simply send a generic fax to "Fleet Manager" or "Sales Manager" at the fax number you find on the automaker's "dealer locator," you are wasting your time and will typically receive little or no response. Chances are they have several fax machines, and that manager may work far from the fax number listed or even in a different building. And faxes without a person's name may be perceived as electronic junk mail and trashed.

If you're shopping for a luxury nameplate, include dealerships in less-affluent surrounding markets or more remote areas of larger markets. They don't see the fat-cat traffic that others do, and they delight in beating the big-city dealers out of a deal (For example, in southern California the deal is often better in hot-and-dusty Bakersfield or smoggy Riverside than in Beverly Hills, Santa Monica, Newport Beach, or La Jolla, where the high-rollers live.)

Will e-mailing work as well as faxing? Although many Fighting Chance customers have reported good results from an e-mail attack, we prefer faxing for two key reasons: (1) The best person to contact is the sales or fleet manager. Is he or she into e-mail? Maybe, maybe not. (To find out, ask for e-mail addresses when you call to ask for names.) (2) An e-mail approach may go to the Internet salesperson, who may have the authority to give you the same deal he or she gives everyone else, but no authority to go below that number. By contrast, the sales or fleet managers are more likely to be no-nonsense veterans of the car wars who have the authority to be more flexible on pricing.

Creating and Sending Your Fax

• Address the fax to the sales or fleet managers by name, title, and dealership.

• Start by telling them which model year and model you are shopping for and say you are ready to buy by the end of the month. Add that you are contacting several dealers and will buy where you get the best price.

If it's true, tell them that you haven't worked with any salespeople at their store. Don't fax dealers where you've spent significant time test driving with salespeople, whose business cards you probably still have. You will contact those people after the others respond.

If their store is one where you'd plan to have your car serviced, tell them that. This will enhance your position, since most of their net profits come from parts and service. But only make that promise where it's true. Those stores will typically be close to your home or work location. A dealer an hour or two away won't believe it and will question whether you're a straight shooter.

- Then show them how you'd like the vehicle configured, outlining it in a table like the one for the fictitious All-American Speedster on page 238. Include columns for the code numbers, descriptions, and invoice and retail prices, as that table does. Start with the base price of the car, add any options and accessories that don't come as standard equipment, and include the destination charge.

- Below the table, tell them your color preferences and say that you don't want add-ons such as additional undercoating, paint sealant, or fabric protection. Remember, however, that many automakers ship only certain configurations. They also like to ship "loaded" vehicles, so finding one without equipment you don't want may be difficult. If those sales or fleet managers think you're looking for a needle in a haystack, they may not respond if they don't have that needle. Remember, you're trying to start a dialogue with several dealers. If you've got some flexibility, your response rate will be better. So, assuming it's true, say that if they don't have a vehicle with your specifications, you'd consider one that's reasonably close—adding that if they can't find something close, you'd be willing to have them order one for you.

- Check the holdback information in chapter 16. If your vehicle has holdback, tell them that you are aware that the dealership will earn $XXX in holdback from the sale, based on the holdback percentages shown for that nameplate in that chapter (e.g., 3 percent of MSRP, excluding the destination charge for Chevrolet, 3 percent of total MSRP for Mercedes, etc.).

- If you discover through a reliable source that there's a traditional dealer cash incentive (e.g., "sell one and get an extra $500"), say that you understand that money is there and you'd expect it to be reflected in their price proposals. But if there's a rebate, there's no need to mention it. No dealer will lie to you about it. It will be credited to you when you sign it over to the dealership as part of your payment.

- If you learn that sales of the vehicle you want have been down recently, telling them you know that will enhance your bargaining position. You can find monthly sales figures by model in *Automotive News,* the industry's weekly trade paper, which may be available in a library near you. That data is also included in our Fighting Chance information package, described in detail in chapter 24.

• Add that you are aware that the dealer invoice numbers in the table don't include the cost of their mandatory participation in the regional dealer advertising association. Ask them to tell you that cost.

You don't make an offer. The buyer *never* makes an offer in a competitive bidding situation. You're not bidding for their business, you're asking them to bid for yours. Think of this as a poker game. You want to see their cards first. When you make an offer, three things can happen, and none of them are good: (1) if you offer so little that it appears you're trying to beat them out of every last dime, you'll get little or no response; (2) if everyone accepts your offer, you've offered too much; and (3) when you make an offer, you're telling them that that price is good enough for you, and you're ignoring the possibility that someone might offer you a much better deal.

You'll almost always get the best deal simply by saying, "I'm ready to buy, here's what I know, I'm contacting several dealers, and I'll buy where I get the best price." This approach usually "smokes out" a better price than any offer you'd make.

• Don't mention a trade-in in the fax. This complicates the transaction and will reduce your response. (A Fighting Chance customer told dealers what he expected to get for his trade-in and got no responses to his fax.) Discuss the trade-in only after you've established the new-vehicle price. Dealers will not tell you what they'll pay for it without seeing it, anyway.

• Don't require that they send you written bids. Demanding only fax or e-mail price proposals will reduce your response rate dramatically. You're going to buy from only one dealer, and he'll be glad to put it in writing if you ask.

• Tell them you look forward to hearing from them soon, and give them several ways to contact you (daytime and evening phone numbers, fax number, e-mail address, etc.). Most will want to pick up the phone and call you.

If you're planning to lease, send a similar fax, stating up front that you're ready to lease by the end of the month, you're contacting several dealers, and you're going to lease where you get the best deal. Add that you're a knowledgeable consumer who understands leasing and you're not going to discuss monthly payments until you've established the price of the vehicle—just as if you were buying it.

The middle of the fax should follow most of the flow mentioned above—outlining your vehicle specifications, discussing holdback, etc. Be sure to tell them the lease terms you're seeking (e.g., 3 years, 15,000 miles per year, and gap insurance included).

Regarding the elements of the lease, tell them you expect a competitive money factor and residual value and you know how to do the lease arithmetic. (See chapter 21 for everything you need to know about leasing.) You will also need to know details of other costs (lease acquisition and disposition fees and sales tax) and the amount of the drive-off check required (first payment, security deposit, vehicle registration fees, etc.).

If you're considering more than one vehicle, choose just one for the fax attack. Shopping for two or more nameplates concurrently will eventually kill this approach. Salespeople want to respond to folks who want to buy what they have to sell. If you choose another nameplate, they'll feel they've wasted their time and eventually decide not to answer a fax attack. So try for your favorite alternative first. If you can't get a good deal on that one, go for number two.

• You don't need to own a fax machine to send these faxes. Stores such as Office Depot, Staples, UPS, and Kinko's will send them for about a dollar a page. Look for them in the "Fax Transmission Service" section of the Yellow Pages in your phone book.

• Send your fax on a Tuesday or Wednesday morning in the last week of the month. The process takes up to three days to complete, and you don't want it to run into the weekend, when car stores are loaded with shoppers and most dealers will ignore your fax. (Almost no one shops for a car in the middle of the week.) If the month ends on Friday, Saturday, or Sunday, fax on the previous Tuesday. If it ends on Monday, Tuesday, Wednesday, or Thursday, fax on the previous Wednesday.

Exceptions to the end-of-month rule: Fax at your first midweek opportunity (a) if your car was totaled or has died and you're riding your bike to work or renting a car, or (b) if you're shopping for a "leftover" at the end of the model year, when supplies are dwindling and you may not find the one you want if you don't move quickly.

- Most of your responses will come in the first 24 hours; some might arrive before the last fax is transmitted. But you'll often get one or more responses the second day, perhaps from a manager who was off the previous day. (We avoid faxing on Monday; after working all weekend, many managers may take that day off.)

- Never fax at night. Your nighttime fax may get sandwiched between other longer off-hour faxes and go unnoticed.

- After faxing, be available to answer calls. Try to avoid telephone tag, which will frustrate your dealer contacts and make the process more difficult for you. If you can't take calls easily during the day, leave a message like this on your answer machine: "Hello, this is Casey Smith. I can't take your call now, but if you're responding to my fax about a new car, I am anxious to talk to you. Please leave your name, your dealership's name, your phone number, and what hours you'll be there. I will definitely return your call as soon as I can, and I won't make a deal until we've had a chance to talk."

Fielding the Responses

- You will usually hear from about half of the dealers you contact.

The person who calls you may not be the one you faxed; it might be a salesperson or the Internet sales manager. Don't let this upset you; it's not something you can control. But you are still *in control,* they are playing your game, and the only important issue is the price of the car.

- As dealers respond, thank them for calling and ask them where they stand on that price. If they say they'll sell the car for "X dollars over or under invoice," ask what their invoice is. It will usually be higher than your numbers because it will include their regional group advertising charge. Ask what that charge is.

If there's a customer rebate or a traditional dealer cash incentive that you know about, ask whether they've subtracted that incentive to get to the price they've quoted. (When assessing the bids, you want to be sure you're comparing apples with apples.) Ask if there are any other charges, such as "documentation fees" or "dealer prep." Then ask for the out-the-door price, including the sales tax and the registration fee.

- If a dealer responds by asking how much you want to pay, say, "I'm sorry, but I'm not going to play that game. Other dealers are quoting me a price. I've promised to tell everyone where they stand before making a final decision. If you don't want to quote a price, that's your decision, but you're not going to sell me a car. Thanks for calling."

- If someone says, "Call me after you've got all the bids and give me a chance to beat them," say, "I won't do that. You want to take advantage of this process without participating in it, and that's not fair. I *will* call to tell every participant where he stands, but if you won't give me a price proposal now, you won't sell me a car."

- If you're asked whether you've got a trade-in, say that you're not going to talk about a trade-in until you nail down the price of the new car.

- If you're considering dealer financing, ask what interest rates the automaker is offering to customers with excellent credit. And if you'll be leasing, ask about the residual value and money factor the automaker's captive financing company is placing on your vehicle.

- If you plan to buy an extended warranty, this is a good opportunity to ask each respondent about the various policies the manufacturer offers. Focus your questions on: (a) the time and mileage terms (e.g., 5 years/ 75,000 miles, 6 years/100,000 miles, etc.), (b) the things that are and are not covered, and (c) whether or not there's a deductible dollar amount for each occurrence. When you've picked the warranty that sounds best for you, ask the dealer for his best price. As you'll learn in chapter 22, warranty prices are negotiable, and you'll get the best price by making dealers compete.

- After you've got all the information you need from each contact, thank him again for responding, say that you're hearing from other dealers, and you expect to get all the responses within the first two days. Tell them you'll call them back either the next afternoon or the following morning to tell them where they stand.

Round Two: Getting Back to the Bidders

- Make your follow-up calls, starting with the high end and ending with the low bidder. (Don't bother calling dealerships that haven't responded; you'll usually be wasting your time.) Thank them again for participating. Then say, "My best offer was $XX,XXX, so I guess that's the one I'll take," and bite your tongue. Don't lie about the offer, and don't tell them where it came from, because it's none of their business.

Sometimes your follow-up "courtesy call" will initiate another round of bidding that nets you an even lower price. If someone offers to beat your best Round One offer by XXX dollars, thank him, tell him there are still some initial respondents you haven't called, and promise you'll call back once more before making a final decision. You'll then have a new, lower bid to report to the others.

If a dealer tells you he will meet the low price, but only if you show him the other store's proposal on paper, tell him to take a long walk off a short pier. He's telling you he doesn't believe you, and you're not buying a car from a dealer who calls you a liar.

• If the store where you did your test driving is close to home or work and one you'd probably go to for service, those are good reasons to consider buying there. When you're reasonably sure you've turned up the lowest price proposal from the stores you've faxed, phone the salesperson whose business card you have and say, "I was in to test drive a couple of weeks ago. I've been shopping price, and the best offer I've received is $XX,XXX. I'm just calling to see where your dealership stands. I plan to have it serviced there, and I'd prefer to buy it there, but I won't pay a big premium." Then bite your tongue and let the salesperson decide how to respond. He may decide not to play. But chances are he will, and you're not going to drive two hours each way to save $100 or $200, right?

Finalizing the Deal to Avoid Surprises

When you've decided which offer to accept, call your contact person at that dealership and say:

• "Okay, it looks like we've got a deal. But before I drive over there, I want your assurance that you've got the car, with the exact color and equipment I want." If it's not there, ask when it will be there.

• Next, say, "I also need to understand all the financial aspects of this transaction. I don't like surprises, so I don't want to get there and find there's something about dollars that you haven't told me. So let's pretend I'm going to walk in with a cashier's check for the 'out-the-door' total. What is that total, and what are the pieces? The price of the car is $XX,XXX right? What's the sales tax? And what's the cost of registering the car in this state? Anything else in that number?"

If you have this straightforward conversation, you probably don't need to request anything in writing, though that would not be an unreasonable request. At this stage of the game, they want to make you a happy customer. A month or so after your purchase, you will typically receive a questionnaire asking about your experience with the selling dealer. If you give them nothing but high marks, there's money and/or other goodies in it for them. It's rare for us to hear of unpleasant customer experiences after a deal has been agreed to.

• Whether you're buying or leasing, if you plan to finance through the dealership ask if they can fax you the application and have you fax back the completed forms to speed up the process and avoid an extra trip to the dealership. If you're leasing, ask for all the relevant numbers and be sure you can do the arithmetic and come to the same monthly payment they're quoting.

• If you're considering using your current car as a trade-in, this is the time to mention it. They'll want to inspect it, of course, before quoting you a price. When you arrive at the dealership, they'll take your car and come back with an offer, which you can counter, based on the homework you've done on the car's true wholesale value. If they won't pay you that number, or something close to it, take it to one of those places that will.

• One more request you should make, especially if the winning dealer is some distance away: Before you drive over to pick up the car, tell them you'd like them to inspect it as if it were their own, then call you and confirm it's in perfect condition for delivery. In addition, make it clear that you will inspect the car yourself when you arrive. (See chapter 23 for a checklist of things to go over while they still own the car, before you give them the final check and sign the delivery receipt.)

• If they require a deposit to hold the car for you, use a credit card if possible. If there are any last-minute problems and you refuse delivery, they won't really have any of your money. You can simply refuse to pay that charge when the monthly statement arrives.

- When you arrive at the dealership to sign the papers and pick up the car, read every word of the sales agreement before you sign it. Make sure all the blanks are filled in. And be sure someone with proper authority signs it for the dealership before you do. (If the salesman's signature isn't binding, you don't have a firm deal.)

Assuming there are no last-minute glitches, the deal is done!

20

There is no substitute for hard work.
—Thomas Alva Edison

We won't say Edison was wrong. But, considering all the better mousetraps he invented, surely he knew there was more than one way to catch a mouse.

Other Ways
to Do It

The problem with doing something right is that somebody's got to do it.

We recognize that at least a few of you are sitting there feeling that this task may require more time and effort than you can give it, wondering if there aren't easier ways to accomplish the objective. You may even be wishing that someone else could do it for you.

As you might expect, we think you should practice what we preach.

We're convinced that you can negotiate the best deal yourself, using the "fax attack" to make dealers bid competitively for your business.

But, yes, there are other ways to buy or lease new cars and trucks, whether you do it yourself or assign the task to someone else. Here are a few you should consider.

GETTING BIDS BY PHONE

In this approach, you'll be making it a competition by calling a few dealers, telling them what you want, and asking for their price.

For the fax attack, we recommend contacting at least fifteen dealers because, on average, only half will respond. But for this phone attack, you should restrict the number to three or four—ideally those near your home or workplace, where you are likely to have the car serviced. They will probably ask you how many dealers you're calling, and they'll be more likely to respond in a timely and positive way if they don't think you're conducting a statewide lottery for your business. And playing "phone tag" with fifteen car stores would be much too cumbersome, lengthening the negotiation process substantially. Getting bids by phone will be quicker and somewhat easier than using the fax attack, but it may not turn up as low a price because you'll be canvassing fewer dealers.

To best prepare for these phone calls, you should check out the dealers' inventories to see if they have any cars that fit your specifications. You can do that by visiting dealers' lots between 7:00 and 8:00 A.M. on a weekday morning, when there will be no salespeople around to bother you. If you find any vehicles there that you'd buy, write down the seventeen-figure vehicle identification number on the manufacturer's window stickers. (You can also check inventories on dealers' web sites, where many car stores list their unsold models.) In addition, you should prepare a two-column work sheet showing dealer invoice and suggested retail prices for the car you want, including all the equipment packages and optional accessories and the destination charge.

Call those three or four dealerships on a midweek morning in the last week of the month, following the timing guidelines on page 152 in chapter 19. (Never call on weekends, when car stores are loaded with shoppers.) Ask the name of the new-vehicle sales manager and write it down. (The fleet manager is an equally good contact if the sales manager is not there.) When you get through to him, introduce yourself and tell him you're going to buy a car by the end of the month and you're calling just three (or four) car stores near you to give them a shot at winning your business. You'll buy where you get the best price. Also say that this will be a house sale because you haven't worked with any salesperson at his store (if that's true), so he knows that he won't have to pay a sales commission on the deal. (If you have spent time with a salesperson there, tell him. That knowledge will help him avoid a potential personnel problem.)

It will enhance your bargaining position if you can say that he has one or two vehicles on his lot that you'd be happy to drive home if the price were right. If it's true, tell him you also plan to get all your regular servicing done at his store. (Remember, car stores earn the bulk of their net profits from parts and service.) Tell him that you'd love to see his dealership's name on your license plate frame.

Give him the specs on the car you want and tell him you've done your homework. You know the dealer invoice price. You know about their holdback (if there is any). You know about any rebates or traditional factory-to-dealer cash incentives. (Be specific.) You know how that model's sales have been going (if you do). (Be very specific if sales are down.) Offer to fax him your work sheet if he'd like to see it. Also say that you're aware that his version of the invoice will include a charge for the local dealer advertising association.

Repeat that you're contacting just three (or four) dealers, that you'll call them all back and let them know where they stand, and that you're going to make a decision within the next 24 hours. Then ask him for a price.

You will complete this process just as you would if you were using the fax attack to get competitive bids. (Review that advice in chapter 19.)

This approach can work as well for leasing as for buying. Follow the general conversation flow outlined above, but say up front that you're planning to lease a new car by the end of the month. Add that you don't want to discuss monthly payments until you've settled on the price of the vehicle. Once you've established the capitalized cost, tell him you expect a competitive money factor and residual value, and you understand leasing and can do the monthly payment arithmetic. You'll want to know details of any other costs (dealer advertising association charge, lease acquisition fee, lease-end disposition fee, sales taxes, etc.) before you sign, and also the amount of the drive-off check required (first payment, security deposit, registration fees, etc.). He will quickly realize that you've done your homework. (See chapter 21 for a thorough primer on leasing.)

There are still some dealers who refuse to make deals over the phone. They want to get you on their turf, in the showroom, where they think they'll have the advantage. But consumers are finding more time-efficient ways to shop for everything, and dealers who won't do business over the phone are losing sales to those who will.

THE INTERNET CAR-BUYING SERVICES

Today, consumers can shop for and purchase almost anything on the web, including new vehicles from individual car dealers and national buying and referral services. The best-known online referral services are probably Auto-by-Tel (www.autobytel.com) and Cars Direct (www.carsdirect.com), but you'll find many others if you go to any major search engine and type "new-car buying services."

Checking the price proposals of online buying services is easy to do. As we've said to many Fighting Chance customers, we'd buy a car from O.J. Simpson if the price were right, but first we'd determine the lowest price we could get through competitive bidding as a basis for comparison. Many customers have reported getting good deals from these sources. Many others, however, have reported beating the online quotes, often by several hundred dollars. (It's also not uncommon to hear that some dealers who call will refuse to quote a price on the phone, demanding instead that you visit their stores in person.)

One problem with these online buying and referral services is that *in many cases there's no competition between dealers for your business.* When you give the service your name, address, and phone number and the specs on the car you want, it forwards the information to just one dealer, who has paid a substantial monthly fee for the exclusive right to all leads from your area or zip code. That dealer may or may not offer you a great deal.

But a deal isn't a great deal until it's a done deal. An online dealer may quote you a great price on the phone, as a way to get you into his store, then renege on the first price and charge much more. For example, a Fighting Chance customer used the AutoAdvantage online referral service and got a bid of $1,000 over invoice on a Toyota Sienna minivan from a dealer an hour's drive from her home. When she got to the store to complete the deal, the sales manager told her the price would be $2,000 over invoice. We frequently hear stories like this about all kinds of referral services, not just those online.

As you ponder this option, remember that no matter what medium you use to negotiate with dealers, the only relevant issue is the price. To know whether it's good or bad before you agree to it, you still have to do your homework. And even in cyberspace, you have to shop dealers against each other to get the best deal.

The dealers from those online buying services can be sitting ducks, just like other "no-dicker" dealers. They close only about 20 percent of the deals they quote, which suggests that their prices aren't that great. Once you have a price quote from an online dealer, use it as the place to start negotiating with other dealers near your home or work—the ones you'd probably rather buy from anyway. You may find that they'll match or beat any online deal.

CARBARGAINS—A GREAT WAY TO HAVE SOMEONE DO IT FOR YOU

If you like the idea of having someone else do the hard part (negotiating for you), there's a special service you should know about. It's called Car-Bargains, and it's offered by the Center for the Study of Services (CSS), a nonprofit consumer service organization in Washington, D.C. (The CSS publishes *CarDeals,* our source of detailed information on manufacturers' current consumer and traditional dealer incentive programs.)

CarBargains is a systematic process in which the CSS gets dealers in your market to bid competitively against each other to sell you the car you want. Here's how it works.

You call CarBargains toll-free at (800) 475-7283 and tell them the make, model, and style of the car or truck you wish to buy or lease. If you're buying, they'll charge your credit card $190 for the service; if you're leasing, the charge is $335. (This book will be in circulation for years, and any prices quoted herein can change over time. Always call for current prices.)

CarBargains then contacts dealers with its own version of the fax attack. Within about two weeks (time may vary depending on their workload), they will get at least five dealers in your area—including any specific dealer you request—to bid blind against each other for your business. Each dealer commits to a selling price that's a specific dollar amount above or below the factory invoice price. The bids are then confirmed in writing.

The participating dealers know that they're in a competition and that it will take a low bid to win. They know that CarBargains has a real customer, since anyone who has paid for this service is almost certain to buy a vehicle very soon from one of them. Dealers are also aware that the CSS knows the market and will get prices from out-of-area dealers who will deliver locally if local dealers' prices aren't good enough.

The CSS launched CarBargains in March 1991 and has helped over

25,000 people save money on new cars and trucks via competitive bidding. In addition to their own data on current transaction prices, they use a solid base of inside information to remind dealers of current factors that give them room to cut prices. Traditional factory-to-dealer incentive programs and manufacturers' holdback could come into play in the bidding, depending on each dealer's specific sales and inventory situation. This is also a house sale for the dealer, with no salesman's commission to pay.

When the bids are in, the CSS sends you a report containing a specific price quote sheet for each dealer, showing exactly how far above or below the invoice cost the dealer has agreed to sell the vehicle. The report also includes the name of the manager responsible for this commitment. Each dealer's bid must include all the costs involved, including any advertising association fees, processing fees, or other miscellaneous charges. You'll have no last-minute surprises.

Their report will also include a printout showing the dealer invoice price for the base vehicle and for all factory-installed options and equipment packages. You can add the invoice prices for the vehicle and the options you want, then add (or subtract) the amount of the dealer's agreed markup (or markdown). Thus, you'll know the price you'll pay before you leave home.

You'll contact one of the dealerships (presumably the lowest bidder), identify yourself as a CarBargains client, select the specific vehicle you want, and see the manager listed on the quote sheet to purchase the car at the price to which the dealer has already agreed. The bidding dealers will honor their commitments; they know they won't get future opportunities to bid if they don't.

Important note: The CSS can get bids anywhere in the country and has no ties to any specific dealers. They are scrupulously honest; for instance, there are always a few hot vehicles dealers won't bid on competitively, and in those cases, CarBargains will tell you they can't help you. The only income the CSS derives from the bidding process comes from the consumers who order the service, which is something many car-buying intermediaries cannot say.

The CSS believes that CarBargains frequently results in "the lowest price a dealer will allow," simply because he perceives it as a one-shot, out-of-the-blue opportunity for an incremental sale that he wouldn't normally get. CarBargains has performed very well in several consumer tests against other car-buying services—including those conducted by *ABC News 20/20, Motor Trend,* and *Money* magazine. *Money* reported, "We had correspondents in five cities comparison shop three Internet buyers (Auto-by-tel, AutoVantage and CarPoint) vs. CarBargains. The result: In nine out of ten comparisons, the lowest CarBargains bid beat the lowest Internet bid, even after adding the CarBargains service fee."

This strikes us as an attractive, reasonably priced alternative for people who can't or don't want to negotiate for themselves.

AUTOMOBILE BROKERS AND OTHER MIDDLEMEN

You have lots of other options if you're willing to pay someone else to do your car shopping. There are buying services, auto brokers, and buyers' agents who will do it for you. These people charge you a fee for their service— sometimes (if you can believe it) as little as $50 or $100, sometimes a lot more. They negotiate a price that's supposed to be much lower than you could get without their help, since they move a lot of metal for dealers.

As you surely know by now, we are convinced that you can do the job very well by yourself, if you have the right information and use it effectively in a competitive bidding process. If we didn't believe that, this book wouldn't exist.

Whether you do it yourself or hire someone else to do it, there's only one relevant question: How good is the deal? The answer will be based on the total price you pay for the car, including the cost of the helper. We believe in most instances the helper's deal won't be that terrific. The major reason for employing any helper should be simply to avoid doing it yourself. You should decide what that's worth to you, but don't go into it assuming you're going to save a bundle, compared to doing it yourself.

In our view, the most attractive helpers are those who work only for you and are compensated only by you. We'd place the CarBargains service at the top of that list because they charge a relatively low fee and you are their only source of income. A growing number of independent buyers' agents are worth considering; they also work only for you and get paid only by you. Their fees are typically higher than that charged by CarBargains, but at least you know whose side they're on.

Then there is the automobile broker, who may charge you $100 or less for his service. But how cheap is that service, and how much does he really save you? Let's consider the low service fee. How do the numbers work for him? Remember, he's got to communicate with you, negotiate with one or more dealers, and coordinate the paperwork and delivery, which he frequently does himself. All this for only $100?

Assume he sells a car every working day, about 250 a year, giving him a gross income of $25,000, before phone bills. No way, José! Assume he sells 2 a day, 500 a year, giving him a $50,000 gross. Maybe, but it still seems very skimpy for the work involved.

You won't be surprised to learn that most brokers have another source of income from the deals they make. Brokers are typically in cahoots with dealers and get a silent, undisclosed commission that is often several times the size of the fee they charge the customer. Of course, all of that money ultimately comes from the customer's pocket because it's built into the price he pays. This leaves open the question of how much they really save knowledgeable, disciplined shoppers, who might negotiate equally good or better deals on their own.

As one broker reported in a feature story in *Automotive News,* he "sells" 300 to 500 vehicles in an average year, and makes "anywhere from $70 or $80 to more than $1,000 per transaction, depending on the vehicle *and the deal he can cut with a dealer.*" And while all brokers contacted said they always pass along any factory-to-consumer incentives, the factory-to-dealer incentives are a different story. As one put it, "We don't get too involved with the dealer's business, we (just) supply them with the audience."

Let's return to the one relevant question: How good is the deal? Assume the car is a popular midpriced sedan. If the broker gets a $100 fee from you and another $200 to $300 from the dealer, you're starting off $300 to $400 in the hole. And remember, the dealer still wants to make a profit on the sale—at least as much as he's paying the broker, and probably more. So how good can the broker's deal possibly be—especially considering that Fighting Chance customers routinely report negotiating their own deals on popular midpriced sedans from a few hundred dollars over invoice to well below invoice?

When you're dealing with a broker, you may simply be trading one car salesman for another. He may have an alliance with the dealer that increases his compensation as the overall profit increases. Our sources tell us these kickback alliances are common and that many buyers can expect surprises like unwanted add-on options—for example, dealer-applied paint sealant that "lists for $750 but will cost you only $225" (and probably costs the dealer only $50). As we noted in chapter 18, you need paint sealant like a moose needs a hat rack.

Whenever a negotiator gets the bulk of his income from the firm he's negotiating with, there's an inherent conflict of interest. The broker tells you he's working on your behalf, but he's much more dependent on his long-term relationships with specific car dealers. Indeed, he's much more concerned with the dealers' satisfaction than with yours; he may never see you again, but he's got to go back and do business with those dealers the next day.

Many car-buying services operate much like brokers. They charge you a modest fee, positioning themselves as consumer champions, but have a "sweetheart network" of dealers who are a major source of their income. Some disclose this, but many don't.

In sum, you must draw your own conclusions about these hired guns. Maybe some of them are terrific, but others are not. The proof will always be in the result. In most cases, however, we'd bet that you can negotiate a better deal yourself, if you're willing to put in the effort.

Even if you're not, we believe that an alternative like CarBargains is likely to save you more money than any broker. Why? Chances are, that broker is dealing mainly with one dealer for each make. (Concentrating his business is the key reason he can get good prices, right?) That means, by definition, there's little or no price competition between dealers for your business. And in the retail auto business it's the competitive aspect that enables a buyer to take advantage of price flexibility, which may change dramatically from dealer to dealer . . . and from week to week.

AFFILIATION REFERRALS

The same principle applies to those fleet purchase referral services that are offered by all kinds of affinity groups, including Price Club, your state's automobile club affiliate, and credit unions. They all claim they'll set you up with a nearby participating dealer whose fleet or sales manager will give you a terrific price.

One problem: He's not competing against anyone for your business. That dealer paid for the privilege of being on that referral list. He doesn't want to compete with anyone, which means that you will pay more for the privilege of buying from him—including the dollars he had to pay to the organization that referred you to him. (Surely, most folks are not naive enough to believe that the Auto Club and Price Club and their credit unions get nothing in return from those dealers they recommend.)

Another problem: All members of your affinity group must be offered the same price. Imagine the furor that would ensue if different members of a credit union paid different prices for the same vehicle at the dealership recommended by that credit union's referral program! Then ask yourself this question: "If I'm smart enough not to pay Edmunds True Market

Value price, which is the average price paid by everyone in the country, why would I pay the same price every other automobile club, Price Club, or credit union member pays?"

If we've said it once . . . whether you're negotiating for yourself or having someone else do it for you, the key to getting the best deal will always be having several dealers compete against each other for your business.

21

Unfortunately, buyers are not really wise on leasing right now. . . . If you are willing to pay $250 a month, I can make a lot of money on you. If you haven't compared me with other dealers on the details, I can probably really take advantage of you . . . if I were that kind of guy.
—General manager of a large import-make dealership, quoted in *Kiplinger's Personal Finance* magazine

The Leasing Alternative: Breaking the Language Barrier

Retail auto leasing is here to stay, and it's big. Pick up any paper. Half the car ads are pushing leases, and not just at the luxury end of the spectrum, where leased vehicles have traditionally accounted for over half of new-car sales. What's happened?

What's happened is that the prices of new cars have skyrocketed, and the automakers and their dealers have found leasing to be an effective way to combat monthly-payment creep. Leasing enables consumers to drive more car for the same monthly payment, or the same car for a lower payment. Addressing the Consumer Bankers Association's Automobile Finance Conference, the chairman of Ford Motor Credit said, "Leasing will become as big as the auto industry wants it to be." Leasing accounted for about 35 to 40 percent of new-car and -truck sales from the late 1990s through most of 2001. But after September 11, 2001, when General Motors led the way with sky-high cash incentives and zero percent financing over four or five years, the monthly car payment for purchasing got much closer to that for leasing. The result: many consumers who previously couldn't afford to buy, switched gears, and leasing fell below 30 percent of sales. As the competitive winds keep shifting in the retail auto marketplace, you can expect the pendulum to swing back and forth between buying and leasing.

WHY DEALERS LOVE LEASING

Leasing is popular among dealers for several reasons, all of which have to do with profit.

• First, it generates quicker customer returns to the dealership, since the average lease term of three to four years is shorter than the average new-car loan of five to six years.

• Second, because dealers know exactly when a lessee will need another new car, they have a tremendous advantage over other dealers in the market. They can start contacting the prospect months before the end of the lease.

• Third, leasing leads to higher customer retention. Research shows that about 80 percent of leasing customers return to the same store when they're in the market for their next vehicle. That's more than double the percentage of regular purchasers who return to the same dealerships.

• Leasing also provides dealers with a predictable supply of relatively low-mileage, one-owner cars—the bread and butter of a profitable used-car operation.

• *Most important, leasing frequently gives dealers an opportunity to make more profit than they'd earn on a straight sale of the same vehicle.* That's because most consumers don't understand leasing well enough to negotiate the terms effectively.

Here are two examples that illustrate the last point.

A friend faxed us the figures for his three-year lease. It was a done deal, but he wanted our opinion anyway. The details, presented in full on the dealer's summary sheet, showed a capitalized cost of $18,457. Terrific, except for one thing: The full sticker price of the car was $18,302. This friend had "negotiated" a lease in which the price he paid for the car was above the manufacturer's suggested retail price! We told him it was okay, that if he was comfortable with the monthly payment, he should relax and enjoy his new car. But what we were thinking was, "If he were *buying* that car, and he paid the sticker price, would he fax a copy of the sticker and ask what we thought of the deal?"

A student at one of our smart car buyers' seminars came up after the class with two contracts in hand—one for a purchase that didn't happen, the other for a lease of the same car. She had first agreed to buy the car for a net price of $9,500, after subtracting the value of her trade-in. When she arrived the next day with a $9,500 cashier's check, she mentioned to the salesman that she was a real estate salesperson who would use the car for business. Learning this, he said, "You shouldn't buy this car, you should lease it. That way, you'll get more favorable tax treatment." (Why would anyone take tax advice from a car salesman?) She agreed and quickly signed a five-year lease on the car. The lease contract showed the capitalized cost: $13,500! They had added $4,000 to the price of the car and made it a five-year term to keep the payments down. Is it just a coincidence that *leasing* rhymes with *fleecing?*

Unfortunately, we hear stories like these regularly. Many people are paying the full sticker price or more for leased cars. They don't realize what's been done to them because they don't understand leasing. They only understand monthly payments, and the monthly payment on the worst lease deal can be a lot friendlier than the monthly payment on the best purchase deal.

As these two instances illustrate, simply disclosing capitalized costs in leasing contracts doesn't protect the uninformed consumer. In both cases, the paperwork clearly spelled out the size of the rip-off by stating the capitalized cost. But those numbers meant nothing to people who didn't know that the capitalized cost was the price they were paying for the car. And the dealers laughed all the way to the bank.

Many car salesmen will say to you, "What do you care what the price of the car is? You're not buying it, you're leasing it." Nice try, guys, but no cigar. The lion's share of every lease payment you make will pay for depreciation, which is the difference between the price you pay for the car and its value at the end of the lease. And whether you pay the full sticker price or $2,000 less, the value at the end will be the same.

We'll give you all the information you need to avoid a leasing rip-off. But the first question to address is whether leasing represents a viable option for you. Let's examine the issues you should consider.

THE PLACE TO LOOK IS IN THE MIRROR

Leasing can make a lot of sense for some people and be a poor choice for others. Start by asking yourself these questions:

- Do you like to trade cars with reasonable frequency, at least every three or four years?

- Do you value the image you project by always driving a late-model vehicle?

- Would you like to drive a more expensive car than you can afford to buy? Or would you like to drive the same car for a lower monthly payment?

- Do you drive an average of less than 15,000 miles a year?

- Would you rather take the cash you'd use for a down payment and put it into an investment that appreciates?

- Conversely, are you someone who can afford to make the monthly payments but doesn't have enough cash for a significant down payment?

- Are you in the early part of your career and needing the reliability of a new car, but not yet able to afford the monthly payment required for a purchase?

- Do you need one kind of vehicle now but know you'll need another kind in two or three years?

- Are you more intrigued with the concept of paying only for vehicle usage than with the psychic rewards some people get from vehicle ownership?

- Would you like to always be driving a car that's covered by the automaker's initial bumper-to-bumper warranty?

- Are you willing to make monthly car payments indefinitely?

- Do you own a business that will be making those payments?

If you answered yes to many or most of these, you're a candidate for leasing. Leasing is a viable option for people who trade often and drive a moderate number of miles each year, especially if they can write off most of the payments as a business expense. It also makes sense for folks who want to minimize their monthly car payments.

If you answered no to most of these initial questions, ask yourself a few more:

- Do you hate making car payments?

- Do you look forward to Car Payment Freedom Day, when you've made your last payment and you get the title certificate from the lender?

- Do you buy new cars infrequently, typically keeping them five years or more?

- Are you someone who likes to squeeze the last drop of value from every dollar you spend?

- Is keeping up with the Joneses relatively unimportant to you?

- Are you someone for whom pride of ownership of a car or truck is important?

- Do you drive significantly more than 15,000 miles a year?

- Do you have enough cash to make a down payment of 20 percent or more on the vehicle you want, and can you afford the monthly payments on a four-year auto loan?

If you answered yes to most of these and no to most of the previous group, you're not a good candidate for leasing.

If you're a candidate for leasing, you'll be pleased to know that you can almost always lease a better car than you could buy with the same monthly payment, and do it with little or no down payment. And frequently, auto-makers' subsidies reduce lease payments further by offering below-market interest rates and inflated residual values that reduce the depreciation you'll pay for.

If you're not a candidate for leasing, you'll take comfort in the flip side of this fact: The average car loses 65 to 70 percent of its value in the first five years. As depressing as that is, it does say that the average car retains 30 to 35 percent of its value after five years . . . which is 30 to 35 percent more value than you'll ever retain if you always lease your cars.

Although monthly lease payments are almost always lower than the monthly payments for a purchase with conventional financing, leasing is always more expensive than buying in the long run because lessees never own their vehicle. The only way to squeeze every drop of value from the money you spend on a car is to drive it until the wheels fall off. If you pay for a car in four years and use it for eight years, you'll be driving relatively cheap transportation during the last half of its life. And you'll spend much less for the use of a car than someone who leases several vehicles sequentially over the same period. On the downside, you'll pay the psychic cost of driving a somewhat older car than your less frugal neighbors, the Joneses.

Here's another aspect worth considering: In a sense, people who lease a car for three or four years have a much wider range of vehicle choices because their time frame is so short.

If you're planning to buy a car and own it for five years or longer, your analysis has to be fairly pragmatic because your objective is a successful long-term ownership experience. You'll be projecting your automotive needs over a lengthy time span and narrowing your choices based on those needs. You'll probably carefully weigh ratings of initial quality and long-term reliability. And the emotional component of the decision will take on additional meaning, because this is going to be *your car* for a long time. In a small way, this is like marriage, and most of us are going to be very picky in deciding which car to buy.

By contrast, choosing a car to lease is more like picking a partner for a brief fling. Long-term needs aren't an issue; you get to shuffle the new-car deck and deal again in three or four years. Long-term reliability isn't an issue; it's covered by a bumper-to-bumper warranty for most, if not all, of the lease term. If there's a problem, it's their problem, not yours. And the emotional component has less meaning because *it's not your car,* it's really just a Hertz car that you're renting for awhile. All of which leaves you open to almost any vehicle, because there's no serious penalty for making a mistake.

If you've already decided that leasing is not for you, you should skip to the next chapter. But anyone considering leasing should pay close attention to this next point.

AUTO LEASE ADS ARE FINE-PRINT HEAVEN

Let the buyer beware: Mouse type was invented for car leases. You'll need a magnifying glass to read the ads, and you'd better use one. Here are some actual fine-print examples (the italics are ours):

- "Lease based on total MSRP including destination charge."

- "Optional equipment not included in monthly payment."

- "Mileage charge of $.20 per mile over 15,000 miles/year."

- "Monthly payment based on *10% down payment*."

- "Customer responsible at signing for first monthly payment, insurance, taxes, title and registration fees, *plus $450 documentation fee.*"

- "Prices may vary based on dealer contribution."

- "$7,079 *dealer/customer* capitalized cost reduction due at lease signing."

- "$350 disposition fee due at lease end *if vehicle is returned.*"

- "Non-refundable prepaid rental reduction of $1,350 (cap reduction) required."

If leases seem more complex than standard auto loans, it's primarily because the language of leasing is so different from that of buying. And both new-car dealers and independent leasing companies can use that extra layer of "boomfog" to take advantage of leasing prospects.

LEASING BASICS DEMYSTIFIED

If you like the idea of leasing but are put off by the language barrier, relax. Although leasing has more aspects to consider than conventional financing, it is neither mysterious nor hard to understand. A straightforward walk through the basics should convince you that it's a relatively simple concept that gets tangled in its own underwear by the terminology.

The Simple Concept

Think of leasing as long-term car rental. When you sign a lease, you agree to make a specific monthly payment for a specific number of months in return for use of the car during that period.

In lease language, you are the **lessee,** and the company that leases you the car is the **lessor.** The lessor is typically not a dealer but a separate financing company that buys the car from a dealer and then leases it to you. This could be one of hundreds of independent leasing companies, a national, regional, or local bank, or an auto manufacturer's captive finance subsidiary, such as GMAC or Toyota Motor Credit Corporation.

What You Pay For

The monthly payments you make to the leasing company cover two basic elements:

1. You're paying for the estimated depreciation in the vehicle's value over the term of your lease. You're not paying for the whole car; you're paying only for the part of its value that you use. That's why the monthly payment will be lower than a standard auto loan payment.

2. You're paying an interest charge. Often called a lease fee or a lease rate, it's the equivalent of a bank's interest charges on an auto loan. You're paying interest on the depreciation, which you are financing and paying off over the term of the lease, just as you would pay off the principal of a conventional car loan. You're also paying interest on the balance of the car's value—what it will be worth at the end of the lease term. That's because the leasing company has to pay the dealer for the whole car, not just the depreciation. Otherwise, you couldn't drive it home. In effect, you're borrowing that lease-end value and driving it around for a few years.

In the language of leasing, the amount of depreciation that you pay for is determined by the difference between two components: the capitalized cost and the residual value. Here's the simple equation:

Depreciation = Capitalized Cost – Residual Value

• The "capitalized cost" (or cap cost) is the starting point for calculating a lease payment. The cap cost is the equivalent of the negotiated "purchase price" paid when you buy a car. It is the price the leasing company pays the dealer for the vehicle. It includes the agreed upon price of your vehicle as well as any other start-up charges you wish to finance by "rolling them into the lease" and paying for them monthly instead of up front. These charges could include the lease acquisition fee, gap insurance premiums, title and registration fees, and sales taxes, depending on how and when your state collects them. If you are trading in a vehicle that's not fully paid for, the amount of your loan pay-off may also be rolled into the capitalized cost of your lease.

Your cap cost will be reduced by the amount of any down payment, trade-in allowance, or manufacturer-to-customer rebate. These adjustments are called "cap cost reductions." (Note, however, that in most states you will typically be charged sales tax on these cap cost reductions.) After all the additions and deductions are made, the final cap cost is called the "adjusted cap cost." Think of it as the equivalent of the amount financed in a standard auto purchase contract.

• The "residual value," sometimes referred to as the "lease-end value," is an estimate of the car's value at the end of the lease period, stated as a percentage of the vehicle's original sticker price (the manufacturers' suggested retail price). This percentage is established by the leasing company, the financing entity that will own the vehicle, and it is not negotiable.

Roughly 75 percent of your monthly lease payment is based on the difference between the adjusted capitalized cost and the residual value placed on your vehicle by the lessor. Projected depreciation accounts for the vast bulk of this number. If you think about this for more than five seconds, you'll recognize that the higher the capitalized cost and the lower the residual value, the more depreciation you'll pay for and the higher your payments will be. And, of course, vice versa.

• The "lease rate" or "lease fee" is the interest rate the leasing company charges you to finance the lease. It is also typically not negotiable, and is stated as a "money factor," a decimal number used to calculate the interest part of the monthly lease payment. This interest is often referred to as a "rent charge" or "lease charge." (To convert a money factor to an approximate interest rate, multiply by 24. For example, a money factor of .003125 times 24 equals .075, or 7.5 percent. We'll discuss this in more detail later in the chapter.) The higher the money factor, the higher the payment. And, of course, vice versa.

Keep It Closed

Virtually all leases today are closed-end agreements, which is the only kind you should consider. That means you'll know all the financial requirements from the start. At the end of the lease term, you'll return the car and walk away with no additional obligation. The residual value of the vehicle is predetermined; if the car is worth less, that's the lessor's problem, not yours, as long as you've taken reasonably good care of it.

Keep It Repaired

Because the residual value estimate assumes you'll return the car in good shape, you'll pay the cost of fixing anything beyond normal wear and tear. The better leases contain guidelines for acceptable damage, but some definitions can be fuzzy. Ford does a pretty good job of defining what's acceptable and what is not. For example, Ford tells customers these items are normal wear and tear:

- Dings

- Minor dents

- Small scratches

- Stone chips in the paint finish

- Reduced tread on tires

By Ford's definition, these items represent excess wear and tear:

- Broken or missing parts

- Dented body panels or trim

- Damaged fabric

- Cracked or broken glass

- Poor-quality repairs

- Unsightly alterations

- Tire/wheel damage or less than one-eighth of an inch of tire tread remaining

- Mechanical and electrical malfunctions

As you can see, there is room for subjective interpretation on several items in each category. To be safe, assume that you should take better care of a leased car than you would of your own, and that "unacceptable damage" means anything you'd repair or replace if it were yours. A dented fender. A broken antenna. An automatic window that won't go up and down. If anything needs fixing, have the work done before you return the car at the end of the lease term. It will cost you much more if the lessor has it done.

Down Payments

One of the selling points of a lease is that you don't need to come up with a down payment. You will, however, have to write a **drive-off check** in order to get the car keys. This typically covers the first month's payment, a lease acquisition fee, the first year's vehicle registration fee, sales taxes depending on your state, and a refundable security deposit equal to about one monthly payment. (The security deposit is usually waived the second time you lease from the same lessor.) For most cars this drive-off check will be $1,000 to $1,500.

But there are lots of exceptions, especially in the most attractive leases. You'll note that the ads for many of those low-payment lease deals have fine print that says something like: "Estimated monthly payment is based on suggested retail price, with a nonrefundable prepaid 10 percent capital cost reduction"—otherwise known as a *down payment*. This **cap reduction** pays part of the depreciation charge in advance. Even when no cap reduction is required, some folks might decide to make one to reduce their monthly payments, perhaps by using the proceeds from selling or trading in their old car.

Advance Payment Leases

Some leases offer the option of a single large payment up front that covers all costs for the term of the lease, with no monthly payments thereafter. Such a payment avoids the interest charge for depreciation and prepays the interest on the residual value. These leases tend to be for luxury cars, probably because only luxury-car buyers can write a check that large.

The Purchase Option

You'll have the option to purchase the vehicle for its residual value at the end of the lease term. Going in, you want the highest possible residual value. The higher the residual, the lower the depreciation and the lower your monthly payment. (As we'll discuss shortly, the automakers often subsidize leases by using incentive dollars to establish artificially high residuals.)

Of course, an inflated residual value works against you if you plan to buy the car at the end of the lease. But you can't have it both ways; it's "pay me now, or pay me later." If that **buyout price** is above the street value of the car, you're not going to pay it . . . and neither is the dealer. In that situation, the leasing company's alternative is to send the car to a wholesale auction, where some dealer will buy it for a price well below the residual value. So if you want the car, make the leasing company a realistic offer, as you would for any used car. In theory, everything is negotiable in this business, and they may take less if the residual is out of line with reality.

There is a way to get a low residual/buyout price. Simply have the company write the lease for 25,000 or 30,000 miles/year instead of the standard 12,000 or 15,000. The residual will be artificially lowered to a much friendlier buyout price, but your monthly lease payments will be sky-high. That will make sense only for people who can write off those payments as a business expense. Before doing this, talk to your accountant to make sure you won't be waving a red flag at the IRS.

Always check a leased car's street value before you turn it in. This rarely happens today, but it's possible for a vehicle to be worth *more* than its residual value at lease-end. If it is, and if your next car will be the same make, the dealer may convert some or all of that extra value into a price concession on your new car. Alternatively, you may want to buy your leased vehicle and re-sell it yourself for a quick profit. Note, however, that your state may allow only a brief time period before requiring that you pay the sales tax on the purchase. That means you'll want to have the next buyer lined up before you buy the car.

Excess Mileage Charges

The lease contract will specify a **mileage allowance,** and a penalty for exceeding it. Typical terms: 12,000 or 15,000 miles a year over the term of the lease, and a penalty of 15 to 25 cents per excess mile. If you know you'll exceed the limits, lessors will sell you extra miles at the beginning of the term for a somewhat lower rate, and you'll pay for them with a somewhat higher monthly payment. (But you may not get your money back if you don't use those extra miles.)

Since the terms of most leases are negotiable, you may find you can get the lessor to waive the mileage restriction, reduce the penalty charge, or increase the yearly mileage allowance. This is generally not easy to accomplish, but it's worth trying.

There's a happy flip side to this issue. If you drive only 5,000 to 10,000 miles a year, you may qualify for a low-mileage discount from some leasing companies, since your car will have a higher value at the end of the lease.

The Lease Term

Most automakers are offering lease terms of three to four years for three reasons: (1) the payments on a two-year lease are too high for most people; (2) lessees will be back relatively soon for another new car; and (3) dealers need a steady supply of off-lease cars with 36,000 to 50,000 miles on the odometer to support their profitable used-car business. What's the best lease term for most people? One that's no longer than the length of the original bumper-to-bumper factory warranty, so you'll never have to face a big repair bill.

Don't sign a lease for a term that's longer than you're sure you'll keep the car. Every lease has an "early termination clause," and it's a painful end to consider. Once you've signed that lease, you've agreed to pay a significant amount of money over several years. When you terminate early, you must pay the entire liability all at once. That will typically include: (a) a $250 to $400 disposition fee, (b) any past-due payments, (c) the remaining depreciation due under the lease, and, in some leases, (d) an early termination penalty. Add it all up, and the total may come close to the sum of all the remaining monthly lease payments.

No leasing company will let itself get stuck with a year-old car from a three-year lease contract. That's because you're making level monthly payments over the lease term, but the car doesn't depreciate at a level rate. The biggest depreciation hit occurs in that first year, and one year of payments doesn't begin to cover the actual loss in value. Before you sign any lease agreement, be sure you understand your liabilities in the event of early termination.

Closing the Gap

What happens if your leased car is stolen or damaged beyond repair (totaled) in a wreck? All lessors treat a stolen or wrecked car as a form of early termination. Your insurance company pays them the car's market value, but that number can be a lot lower than the amount you still owe on the lease. It's not smart to leave yourself open to this financial risk.

Many auto manufacturers' captive finance companies—such as GMAC, Ford Motor Credit Corporation, and Nissan Motors Acceptance Corporation—shield their customers from losses if a leased vehicle is stolen or wrecked, paying any difference between the insurance payoff and the lease balance and allowing the customer to get a new car. To cover potential losses, they provide their own **gap insurance,** either by self-insuring or by paying a modest premium for each vehicle leased (probably under $50 per vehicle). They build this cost into your monthly payment.

Whether you're leasing from one of the captive companies or from an independent leasing outfit, you should ask about *and get* gap insurance. If it's not built into the lease agreement, treat it as a bargaining point and ask the company to provide it at no cost. (They may not agree, but it's worth a try.) Gap insurance shouldn't add more than a few dollars to your monthly lease payment. For example, a credit union in California charges only $102 for a policy covering a three-year lease term. But beware of rip-offs. One large independent leasing company quoted a $100 per month premium on a five-year lease of a luxury car! Clearly, the dealer was an accomplice in this larceny, and the biggest gap was between the price and the value of that insurance. If anyone tries to pull this on you, walk out and lease somewhere else.

Basic Auto Insurance Costs

You may have to pay more to insure your leased car. Leasing companies tend to require higher limits than many people normally carry. Check this out early and factor it into your cost projection.

Credit Requirements

Most financing companies have higher standards of creditworthiness for leases than for conventional auto loans. If your credit history is spotty, you may not be approved for a lease, or the company may require a significant down payment and charge you a higher interest rate.

Sales Taxes

Most states treat leasing like any other purchase and tax the total amount of your payments, including the interest portion. But there are exceptions.

Some states tax the entire capitalized cost, as if you were purchasing the vehicle. Among them are Arkansas, Illinois, Iowa, Maryland, Montana, North Dakota, Oklahoma, South Dakota, and Texas. The total tax is often due at the commencement of the lease, meaning the lessor must pay it and either collect it from you up front or roll it into your lease. Each state has its own definition of what is included in the agreed upon price of the car, and at least one (Kentucky) defines the gross purchase price for tax purposes as 90 percent of the sticker price.

A few states have hybrid taxation schemes that combine elements of the alternatives covered above. In Maine, for example, the entire tax is due at the time of inception, but the amount is calculated based on the sum of all monthly payments. In Vermont and New Jersey, a tax is imposed up front on the difference between the adjusted capitalized cost and the residual value, so you don't pay tax on the interest or "rent" charges.

Other typical lease items subject to taxation are up-front cap cost reductions you may decide to make, acquisition fees, lease-end disposition fees, termination fees, excess mileage charges, excess wear and tear charges, and collection and repossession fees. If your state has a personal property tax, expect the leasing company to add that in.

Direct-to-customer incentives such as rebates and "loyalty discounts" are usually taxed. And believe it or not, many states treat the equity in your trade-in vehicle as if it were a down-payment check you had written and require that you pay tax on it, too. (If this is beginning to tax your brain, you're not alone.)

Sales tax regulations can change from year to year. To determine how they currently tax leasing where you live, call your state's taxing authority or ask your accountant. If you're an auto club member, check with your local AAA office; someone there should be able to provide that information.

These Lemons Don't Make Lemonade

All states have lemon laws, which protect consumers from getting stuck with chronically ill cars. And most of these laws give the lessee (you) the same rights as the lessor.

But why should you have to go through that hassle, when it's the leasing company's lemon? They buy all those cars, so they've got the leverage with dealers and manufacturers. Ask how they'd handle a lemon situation. If you like their answer, get it in writing. If you don't, lease from someone else.

Miscellaneous Fees

The leasing company gets much of its income from fees, which are typically not negotiable. The most common one: a *lease acquisition fee,* sometimes called a *bank fee,* of $400 to $700. Then, when you turn in the car, there's a *disposition fee* of $250 to $400 if you don't exercise your option to purchase the vehicle. These extra charges may seem like rip-offs, but they really aren't. Here's why.

When a financial institution or finance company makes a typical four-year auto loan, it earns a profit by buying money at one interest rate and loaning it at a higher rate. After checking the customer's credit and approving the loan, there are virtually no additional expenses unless the borrower defaults on the loan and the car has to be repossessed. The financing entity receives 48 monthly payments, then mails the ownership document to the borrower.

A lessor's world is more complicated because the financing entity actually owns the leased car. If the lessee doesn't purchase the car at the end of the lease term, the lessor must inspect the vehicle, determine whether the lessee must pay for excess wear and tear, and make any needed repairs. The leasing company must then transport the vehicle to a wholesale auction location and pay the cost of auctioning it to retail dealers. These are all costly steps. In addition, the leasing company needs to hire extra people to do these things and provide office space for them—incremental overhead expenses that wouldn't be required if it weren't in the leasing business. Yet, they can't necessarily charge a higher interest rate for a lease than for a purchase. So how do they cover these extra expenses? With the lease acquisition fee on the front end and the disposition fee on the back end.

Occasionally an automaker is so desperate to move cars that its captive finance company waives one or both of these fees. But with most leases, you will have to pay them.

FACTORY-SUBSIDIZED LEASES

As we noted earlier, people who lease come back for a new vehicle more often than people who buy. That's the main reason automakers funnel big incentive money into leases—even those that shun customer rebates and factory-to-dealer cash incentives because they think those things cheapen the perceived value of their brands. Using incentive dollars to reduce monthly lease payments allows automakers to cut the price under the table, so to speak, without the stigma of open price-cutting.

Instead of offering you a $1,000 rebate, or giving dealers a $2,000 cash incentive, the manufacturers take the same sales promotion dollars and shift them over to their captive finance companies. The finance companies use that money in two ways to lower your monthly lease payments. They can inflate the residual value to an artificially high level, reducing the depreciation charge. They can also "buy down" the interest rate to a level below the market rate, reducing the finance charge. The net result can be a very attractive deal.

It's not unusual for different vehicles of the same make to have very different residual value percentages and interest rates, depending on how aggressively automakers are pushing certain models in specific time periods. They usually don't need lease subsidies to sell the most popular products, but when the market is soft you might find special lease deals on almost any vehicle. Manufacturers' different lease incentive programs can come and go like the wind, and tracking them all would be impossible. We know of no reliable source of information on current offerings, but many of them are advertised in newspapers. (*Note:* The factory-subsidized lease deals are available only through the manufacturer's financing arm, not through independent banks and leasing companies.)

Do You Get the Incentive If You Lease?

You might logically ask whether the purchase incentives offered to buyers by automakers are also given to customers who lease. They are, but not necessarily in the same way.

A lessee usually won't qualify for a rebate because he's not buying the car, though sometimes manufacturers apply a rebate to either a purchase or a lease. From your perspective, it doesn't matter whether they do or not. If you don't get the rebate on the front end to lower the capitalized cost, you'll see an equivalent value on the back end, in the form of a higher residual value and/or a lower lease interest rate from the automaker's captive finance company. You won't care whether the capitalized cost is $1,000 lower or the residual value is $1,000 higher, because your monthly payment will be the same either way.

Similarly, the benefit of a factory-to-dealer cash incentive shows up either on the front end or the back end, depending on whether the lease is with the captive finance company or another financial entity. If it's a third-party lease, the dealer gets that cash and you can use it to negotiate a lower capitalized cost. But if it's a factory-subsidized lease, the captive finance company usually gets the cash, not the dealer, and you see it in the form of a higher residual and/or a lower interest rate.

Occasionally, when the lease subsidies are particularly heavy, the dealer may even be required to pay part of the cost. For example, when there's a super-low interest rate, such as 0.9 percent or 1.9 percent, the automaker is selling money at a rate well below the rate it must pay for the same money. In that instance, a dealer may have to contribute several hundred dollars to help defray the extra expense, and you may find dealers less flexible on transaction prices.

NEGOTIATING A LEASE WITH CONFIDENCE

Because the key elements of a lease sound like a foreign language to many people, car salesmen can use that language barrier as a smoke screen while they make some of the most profitable deals in the business. As soon as a prospect mentions leasing, the only thing a salesman wants to talk about is the monthly payment. Indeed, the dumbest opening question anyone can ask a car salesman is, "How much per month to lease this car?" That's like walking in with a big sign that reads, "I Just Fell off the Turnip Truck." The payment quoted will be based on the full sticker price or more. As we noted earlier, showing the purchase price under the heading of "capitalized cost" may not alert the uninformed. And because the monthly payment on a terrible leasing deal can be a lot lower than one on a good purchase deal, it's relatively easy for consumers to get fleeced if they haven't done their leasing homework.

THE INFORMATION YOU NEED

The first part of that homework is the language of leasing; the other is the arithmetic. You need to do that arithmetic yourself to be sure the leasing company hasn't added an extra $30 or $40 a month. Fortunately, it's easy to do if you have the information on these four key elements that determine the size of the payment:

1. The **term of the lease,** typically three years to four years, but occasionally two years.

2. The **capitalized cost,** which should be the purchase price you negotiate, plus any additional elements that you agree to include (such as a lease acquisition fee, if you'd rather not pay it up front).

3. The leasing company's **finance charge,** expressed as either an interest rate or a money factor. If they give you the interest rate, divide it by 24 (a constant factor unrelated to the length of the lease) to get the money factor. (For example, 7.5 percent or .075, divided by 24 equals a money factor of .003125.) If they give you the money factor, multiply it by 24 to get the approximate equivalent of the annual percentage rate (APR) for a loan. (A money factor of .003125 times 24 equals .075, or 7.5 percent.) If the rate is above the current APR on conventional auto loans at your local bank, you should ask the dealer to shop for a better rate from another leasing company.

4. The **residual value** of the car, or its estimated value at the end of the lease. This is stated in the lease agreement; it's the price at which you may buy the vehicle at lease-end. It is shown as a dollar value but figured as a percentage of the gross sticker price (MSRP), before any equipment package discounts. Different vehicles depreciate at different rates, depending on the demand for them as used vehicles. Your monthly lease payment could be lower for a more expensive car that holds its value well than for a less expensive car that depreciates more rapidly.

The industry's "bible" for residual values is the Automotive Lease Guide's *Residual Percentage Guide.* Published bimonthly, this guide lists each vehicle's estimated wholesale value, as a percentage of the original sticker price, after two, three, four, and five years. These estimates assume that you won't buy the car when the lease ends, and that the leasing company will sell it to dealers at an auction.

In our experience, the residual values in lease agreements almost always exceed those in the *Residual Percentage Guide* by anywhere from a few percentage points to ten or more points, depending on how aggressively manufacturers are subsidizing leases. The exception: If a vehicle is hot and in short supply, and you have to take a number and get in line to buy one, the manufacturer can easily move every car without subsidizing leases. For all other cars, you should view the values in the *Residual Percentage Guide* as low-end, red-flag numbers. Those numbers are wholesale, not retail prices. They are realistic estimates of the prices leasing companies can expect to get for reconditioned, clean vehicles at auction. If a dealer quotes you a number that low, you should ask him to shop other leasing companies; if he quotes a lower number, they are trying to charge you for "phantom depreciation," and you should walk away and lease from someone else.

Unfortunately, we are aware of no free source one can turn to, on or off the Internet, to get the Automotive Lease Guide's (ALG) current residual values for the cars on our shopping list. You could purchase a one-year subscription to the ALG's bimonthly publication for about $80 by calling (805) 563-0777 or by visiting the ALG's web site at www.alg.com. There are also leasing software programs you can buy that include current residual values, one of which (Expert Lease Pro) is discussed later in this chapter.

It's common for different leasing companies to assign different residual values to the same vehicle. When leasing began to grow dramatically, many banks and finance companies lost a lot of money guessing wrong on residuals. As a result, some lessors estimate more conservatively than others. For example, assume you're considering a three-year lease of a sedan with a sticker price of $22,000. One leasing company estimates a 55 percent residual value of $12,100; another uses 48 percent in its calculation, or $10,560. Anyone leasing from that second company will pay that $1,540 difference—an extra $42.78 per month, plus interest.

Tell your contact that you are aware of these potential differences. You know that the residual percentage may not be negotiable at any specific leasing company, but you expect him to check several sources to determine which is the most favorable. Understand, however, that your objective is to get the best overall deal, and that a higher residual frequently comes with a higher interest rate and won't necessarily net you a lower payment. (As noted earlier, the highest residuals and lowest interest rates often come from the automaker's captive finance company when incentive money is allocated to subsidize the lease deal.)

Here's a helpful tip: Call two or three dealerships selling the car you want and ask to speak to the finance manager. Tell that person you're considering leasing two different cars, one of which his store sells, and you need to know the current residual values and money factors the automaker's captive finance company is putting on 3-year leases allowing 15,000 miles a year (or whatever your specifications are). There's no reason why he wouldn't share this information with you in this "competitive browsing" phase, especially if you tell him you'll shop at his store if you decide to lease the car he sells.

RUNNING THE NUMBERS

Now let's assume you've negotiated a transaction price of $20,000 on a car with a $22,000 sticker price, and that the car's residual value after three years will be $10,000. If you were to *buy* it and finance the whole purchase, part of each payment would pay off the $20,000 principal, and the rest would pay interest on the loan. You'd owe $20,000 at the beginning and nothing at the end.

When you *lease,* you still pay interest on the whole amount because the financing entity (the leasing company) has put up $20,000 to buy the car from the dealer. But unlike a conventional auto loan, the only "principal" you pay off is the $10,000 of depreciation—the difference between the capitalized cost of $20,000 (your negotiated price) and the residual value of $10,000. You don't "pay off" that residual value, but you pay interest on it because you're borrowing it and driving it around for the term of the lease.

Now let's do the arithmetic, assuming a 36-month lease with a 7.5 percent interest rate. We'll do it using the **constant yield method,** which is used by all major leasing companies except Ford Motor Credit. This isn't brain surgery, but it's different, so stay awake.

1. Figure the monthly depreciation charge. Divide the $10,000 depreciation by 36 months to get $277.78.

2. Determine the monthly finance charge. Add the $20,000 capitalized cost to the $10,000 residual value. Multiply that $30,000 by .003125 (the money factor, figured by dividing .075 by 24) to get $93.75. It appears that we're double-counting the residual value, but we're not. The money factor has a built-in assumption that everything gets paid off, like the principal of a conventional car loan, so it cuts everything in half—assuming that on average, the outstanding "principal" is half of the total. That works for the depreciation, since you pay it off over the term of the lease. But you don't pay off any of the residual value. So you must double it before you apply the money factor, which brings it back to its original value.

3. Add the $277.78 depreciation and the $93.75 interest, for a total monthly lease payment of $371.53. Plus tax.

To calculate the effect of making a down payment, or "cap reduction," just reduce the capitalized cost by the amount of the payment and do the arithmetic again.

That's it. Knowing this relatively simple calculation can be very empowering. With it, you can easily "solve" for any of the three factors if you know the other two. Since you negotiate the capitalized cost, and the residual value is stated in the lease agreement, the only missing factor is usually the interest rate. Dealers are not required to disclose this rate, or the money factor, though many will do so when they understand that you can perform this simple calculation.

To solve for an interest rate, start with the monthly lease payment (before sales tax) and subtract the monthly depreciation charge. The difference is the monthly finance charge—$93.75 in the example here. Then divide that finance charge by the sum of the cap cost and the residual value ($30,000 in our example), and you get a money factor of .003125. Multiply that money factor by 24, and *voilà,* there's the interest rate—7.5 percent.

With just a few minutes' practice and an inexpensive calculator, you can figure hypothetical lease payments based on different assumptions of cap costs, residual values, and money factors. Take your calculator with you and run the numbers at the salesman's desk. You will thrill and amaze him. Chances are, he doesn't know how to do it—not because he couldn't perform these simple calculations, but because the dealer wants him to think that only a computer can do anything that complicated. You'll be in complete control, which is the way it should be.

If there's an exception to every rule, Ford Motor Credit Corporation is the exception on leasing arithmetic. Ford uses an antiquated method to determine lease payments, applying one mysterious money factor to the capitalized cost and another to the residual value. Ford's money factors include a built-in administrative fee that makes the effective APR of the lease 1.5 to

2 percent higher than the "internal" interest rate quoted to you by Ford dealers—a discrepancy that you'll discover when you run the numbers.

There's an alternative method that Ford dealers sometimes use to calculate lease payments. They figure the monthly depreciation charge in the standard way, as we have done here. But they perform two nonstandard calculations to figure the finance charge. First, they develop a money factor by dividing Ford's internal interest rate by 12. Then they multiply this money factor by the capitalized cost to get the finance charge. This method also generates a higher effective APR than the more commonly used constant yield method.

Of course, you can easily determine the real rate Ford and its dealers are charging by using the arithmetic outlined here. While it appears that they'd like to hide that rate from you, Ford isn't necessarily padding the interest rate. If a dealer quoted Ford's internal rate at 7.5 percent, but the current bank rate on conventional auto loans were 9 to 9.5 percent, the company's calculation shenanigans wouldn't really be costing you anything. But if the market rate were also 7.5 percent, you'd draw the opposite conclusion.

Back in chapter 12, you learned that car stores earn a commission or fee from lenders when they arrange the purchase financing. That's also true with leasing. Whenever the lease rate is at or near the going market rate for auto loans, the dealer is probably getting a few basis points. (A basis point is one-tenth of a percentage point.) That's neither illegal nor immoral; it's an important income source for auto dealerships. Unfortunately, there's no way to determine the dealer's cut. Your protection against getting ripped off on lease financing will come from (a) knowing the current rate in your market for standard auto loans, and (b) doing the arithmetic yourself to uncover the real interest rate on a proposed lease deal.

Dealers probably get less financing income from leases than from purchases. Based on several years' experience going through lease deals with Fighting Chance customers, we've concluded that the typical lease rate is usually somewhat below the going rate for car loans. That's because the marketing battles are fought in lease ads featuring low monthly payments; to keep those payments low, automakers must hold down interest rates. In this competitive climate, there's less financing profit for leasing companies to share with dealers, and sometimes none at all when the rates are highly subsidized and well below market.

Most people will find the simple arithmetic of the constant yield method more than sufficient to help them negotiate a lease effectively. However, if you have computer skills and would like to own software that performs all the calculations forward and backward, you should check out the "Expert

Lease Pro" program published by Chart Software. It enables you to analyze lease terms, perform lease-versus-buy analysis, compare leases, and print payment tables for use during negotiations. It also includes current residual values. For current information on specs and prices visit the company's web site (www.autoleasingsoftware.com) or call Chart Software at (800) 418-8450, which is also their customer support number.

THE ONE-PAYMENT LEASE

If you don't want the hassle of writing a check every month and can afford to write one very large check, you might consider the alternative of a single-payment lease. This will save you some interest expense, maybe a lot.

When you write that one big check, you'll avoid paying interest on the depreciation, since you'll be paying the entire depreciation charge up front, instead of paying it month by month. You'll still pay interest on the residual value, since you're borrowing it and driving it around for the lease term. But you might negotiate a somewhat lower interest rate because you'll pay all the interest on day one, instead of in monthly installments.

Let's assume you're leasing the same vehicle we used in the earlier example—a 36-month term, a $20,000 capitalized cost, a $10,000 residual value, and a 7.5 percent lease rate. The monthly payment was $371.53, for a 36-month total of $13,375. With a one-payment lease, you'd write a check for $12,250—$10,000 for depreciation plus $2,250 for interest (7.5 percent times $10,000 residual value times 3 years). Your net interest savings: $1,125. You'd save another $150 if they cut the rate to 7 percent.

THE "FAX ATTACK" WORKS FOR LEASING, TOO

First, review the advice in chapter 19 on how to structure the fax if you're leasing. Then send it to fifteen dealers on a Tuesday or Wednesday at the end of the month.

When the respondents contact you, first settle on the price of the car. Remember, you're negotiating the price at which the dealer will sell the car to a leasing company. Most often, that will be the automaker's captive finance company, but it might also be a bank or other financial institution.

Then ask what residual value and money factor will be used in your lease and what the final or "adjusted" capitalized cost will be. If that cap cost is more than the agreed-on price of the car, ask what other items are included. Tell him you need to know about any other applicable charges (acquisition and disposition fees, security deposit, gap insurance, etc.). Finally, ask what the drive-off check will be, both in total and item-by-item.

After you've got all the information you need from each contact, thank each dealer again for responding, say that you're hearing from other dealers, and you expect to get all the responses within the first two days. Tell the dealers you'll call them back either the next afternoon or the following morning to tell them where they stand.

Once you've done the lease arithmetic on the best of the proposals, you don't need to get into the internal numbers on the others. You're simply comparing dollars with dollars. So when you call the dealers who have responded, you'll simply say, "Well, the best lease proposal I've received is $354 per month and a drive-off check of $895. So I guess that's the one I'll take, if no one beats it." Then bite your tongue and wait for a response. If a dealer makes a lower offer, thank him and tell him you'll get back to him once more, after you've talked to the other participants. And now you've got a better proposal to report on your next call.

When you've chosen the dealer you want to lease from, call your contact there and finalize the deal, following the pointers at the end of chapter 19.

Here are a few more suggestions that may help you negotiate the most favorable lease.

Rule 1: Lease Early in the Model Year

Timing can be as important in leasing as in buying, and the right time to lease in some instances is early in the model year. You usually get a better lease deal then, for two key reasons:

1. Most auto manufacturers have at least one price increase during the model year. Some have several. If you lease after an increase, you'll have a higher capitalized cost, which means a higher monthly payment.

2. The later it gets in the model year, the closer you'll come to leasing a car that will be four years old in only 36 months. The numbers go down a little with each bimonthly issue of the Automotive Lease Guide's *Residual Percentage Guide*. Unless the automaker is subsidizing the lease to offset this shrinking value, the leasing company will establish a lower residual value as the model year progresses, which will require a higher monthly payment. This can become a very significant issue if you're considering leasing last year's model after this year's model has arrived. Without big manufacturer subsidies, it will actually cost you more to lease the older model. So if it's July, August, or September, it may pay to wait until October, November, or December and lease next year's model.

The caveat: If the manufacturer is aggressively subsidizing the lease, it doesn't matter where you are in the model year, and this rule doesn't apply.

Rule 2: Don't Gild the Lily

Don't overaccessorize a leased car. There's a maximum retail-price number leasing companies will residualize for each model. This residual value is based on the estimated value of the car to the next owner. If you go hogwild with bells and whistles the next person won't pay for, you can assume you're buying them for him.

If you're a music nut, spring for the six-disc CD changer if you must, but forget the $1,200 aluminum wheels, the $400 decorative "gold package," the $100 pinstriping job, and the $300 walnut-trimmed dashboard. They'll have little or no residual value. And think twice about whether you really need four-wheel drive, a moonroof, or an eight-cylinder engine. This isn't your car, it's a rental car, and it's silly to spend another $50 or more a month for unessential equipment or unnecessary ornamentation. (Would you buy a diamond engagement ring for someone if you knew you wouldn't be together three years later?)

It's also silly to put a fancy security system in a leased car. Think about it: You've got your regular car insurance, plus gap insurance, so if the car is stolen, you'll come out whole financially. Aren't the insurance companies the only ones you're protecting with that $500 security system?

Rule 3: You Can Often Beat the Numbers in Lease Promotion Ads

You will periodically see ads promoting factory-subsidized leases, where the manufacturer has allocated money to inflate the residual value and/or lower the money factor, either of which will reduce the lease payment. In preparing those ads, the automakers must assume a negotiated price of the car that's high enough to avoid angering dealers. Chances are, you can negotiate a lower price by making dealers bid competitively and end up with a lower monthly payment than that featured in the advertising.

Rule 4: Beware of the Lowball Lease Offer

The lowball opener has found its way to the leasing side of the business. Whenever you see a "no money down, only $199 a month" offer, read the fine print. You may find that it's for a stripped-down model no one would want. The purpose, of course, is to get you into the showroom, where the salesman will move you to a more profitable model—one with much higher payments.

Rule 5: Examine Each Thread Individually, but Make Your Decision on the Whole Fabric

You should analyze each element of the lease. Have you negotiated a slim-profit capitalized cost? Is the lessor's residual value attractive compared to the number in the *Residual Percentage Guide,* given the supply and demand situation for the vehicle? Is the interest rate favorable compared to the current market rate for auto loans?

After answering these questions, step back and look at the lease as a whole. If the cap cost is just marginally over the invoice price, the lease rate is an eye-popping 1.9 percent, and the residual is only one or two percentage points above the number in the *Residual Percentage Guide,* it's probably an excellent lease overall. It's unrealistic to expect both a below-cost interest rate and a ten-point inflation of the residual value. Sometimes you have to say, "Two out of three ain't bad."

Rule 6: Read the Fine Print—All of It— Before You Sign Anything

Signing a lease is like signing a mortgage. You've got to make those payments, or else. Understand exactly what you're signing. If the lessor won't give you a copy to study, there's a reason—one good enough for you to find another, more cooperative lessor.

When you've narrowed your vehicle choices and are almost ready to start negotiating, consider ordering the specific information you need from Fighting Chance. As you now know, you need the same information to lease intelligently as to buy intelligently, and then some. One feature you'll appreciate: a customer service number you can call to talk to us and ask questions as you go through the shopping process. We'll look up residual values for customers in the latest issue of the Automotive Lease Guide's *Residual Percentage Guide,* and even go through the payment calculation with you before you sign the lease. See chapter 24 for details.

Rule 7: Don't Take Possession Until the Leasing Company has Approved the Deal

A Fighting Chance customer drove a leased car home, assured by the dealer that the lease would be approved, though the final documents hadn't been signed by the leasing company. Almost two weeks later, the dealer called to say that there were problems with the customer's credit application, and that the interest rate (and the monthly payment) would be significantly higher.

Don't let this happen to you. A deal isn't a deal until it's a done deal.

CLOUDS ON THE HORIZON THREATEN LEASING'S FUTURE AS A FINANCING ALTERNATIVE

In recent years, juries in trials involving accidents with leased cars have gone after the entity with the deepest pockets and assessed multimillion dollar damage awards against the leasing companies. In effect, they have said that the lessor, not the lessee/driver, was responsible for the victim's injuries or death. Which is ridiculous.

This is affecting consumers negatively in a couple of ways.

• Some automakers' captive finance companies and other financial institutions have increased their up-front acquisition fees to $1,000 or more to cover their potential liability in states where these unfair verdicts have become common.

• Others have simply stopped writing leases in those states. Instead, residents there who wish to lease are offered a "balloon payment" purchase contract. The monthly payments are figured the same way, but legally, the customer is buying, not leasing the vehicle, thus limiting the financing company's liability exposure. At the end of the contract term, the customer may buy the vehicle for the balloon-payment price or return it to the financing entity. The bad news: customers opting for this alternative must pay the sales tax on the entire purchase price.

We can only hope that our state and national legislatures will pass laws that limit the ability of trial lawyers to go after leasing companies in this way.

*Ethically, we should quote pay-
ments on a stripped vehicle to
customers. But that cuts out the
finance and insurance manager,
so we are told at the meetings to
quote loaded payments. You can
always come down, but you can't
go up.*
　　　—Salesperson quoted in
Automotive News

22

Are Extended
Warranties
Warranted?

T he sale of an extended warranty contract, which pays for repairs
that occur after the initial factory warranty runs out, is a big back-
end profit item for every car store. These contracts typically cost
$700 to $1,200 and can exceed $2,000, depending on what they cover and
what the traffic (you) will bear.

Extended warranty contracts have become increasingly popular in recent years. According to the National Automobile Dealers Association, consumers bought them on nearly 30 percent of new vehicles sold in 2002 and

more than 40 percent of used vehicles. An estimated 8.7 million such contracts are sold per year, putting the market for them in excess of $10 billion.

You can expect to get a strong recommendation to buy one, frequently from the store's finance and insurance (F&I) manager. Watch out for this guy. You may have negotiated the price of the car without walking into the

Manufacturer	Basic Warranty	Powertrain Warranty	Rust-through Warranty
Acura	4/50,000	4/50,000	5/unlimited
Audi	4/50,000	4/50,000	12/unlimited
BMW	4/50,000	4/50,000	6/unlimited
Buick	3/36,000	3/36,000	6/100,000
Cadillac	4/50,000	4/50,000	6/100,000
Chevrolet	3/36,000	3/36,000	6/100,000
Chrysler	3/36,000	7/70,000	5/100,000
Dodge	3/36,000	7/70,000	5/100,000
Ford	3/36,000	3/36,000	5/unlimited
GMC	3/36,000	3/36,000	6/100,000
Honda	3/36,000	3/36,000	5/unlimited
Hummer	3/36,000	3/36,000	6/100,000
Hyundai	5/60,000	10/100,000	5/100,000
Infiniti	4/60,000	6/70,000	7/unlimited
Isuzu	3/50,000	7/75,000	6/100,000
Jaguar	4/50,000	4/50,000	6/unlimited
Jeep	3/36,000	7/70,000	5/100,000
Kia	5/60,000	10/100,000	5/100,000
Land Rover	4/50,000	4/50,000	6/unlimited
Lexus	4/50,000	6/70,000	6/unlimited
Lincoln	4/50,000	4/50,000	5/unlimited
Mazda	4/50,000	4/50,000	5/unlimited
Mercedes-Benz	4/50,000	4/50,000	4/50,000
Mercury	3/36,000	3/36,000	5/unlimited
Mini	4/50,000	4/50,000	6/unlimited
Mitsubishi	3/36,000	5/60,000	7/100,000
Nissan	3/36,000	5/60,000	5/unlimited
Pontiac	3/36,000	3/36,000	6/100,000
Porsche	4/50,000	4/50,000	10/unlimited
Saab	4/50,000	4/50,000	6/unlimited
Saturn	3/36,000	3/36,000	6/100,000
Subaru	3/36,000	5/60,000	5/unlimited
Suzuki	3/36,000	7/100,000	3/unlimited
Toyota	3/36,000	5/60,000	5/unlimited
Volkswagen	4/50,000	5/60,000	12/unlimited
Volvo	4/50,000	4/50,000	8/unlimited

car store, but you must walk in there to complete the transaction. And you'll typically sign all the paperwork in the office of the F&I manager. Understand that you'll be in the clutches of a commissioned salesman—a low-pressure operator who wants you to trust his advice as you would your father's. He's not your father; he's interested in your wallet, not your welfare.

BE PREPARED FOR THIS ONE

You should determine beforehand whether this purchase makes sense for you. The decision hinges on your answers to these two questions:

1. What's the basic bumper-to-bumper warranty on the car you're buying?

2. How long do you plan to keep the car, and about how many miles will you drive it?

BASIC WARRANTIES ARE NOW CLOSE TO PARITY

The old standard bumper-to-bumper warranty of one year or 12,000 miles (whichever comes first) is a thing of the past, thanks to Toyota, Honda, and Nissan. The Japanese Big Three provide a basic warranty of 3 years or 36,000 miles, and starting with the 1992 models, Detroit's Big Three finally matched their key competitors. (Ford and Chrysler maintained the ancient 12-month/ 12,000-mile warranty on most vehicles through the 1991 model year.)

The basic bumper-to-bumper warranty covers most parts of the car. An additional powertrain warranty covers the things that make the car go (the engine, transmission, and drivetrain), frequently for a longer period than the basic warranty. And a longer corrosion warranty covers actual holes in the body caused by rust. Separate warranties cover the battery, tires, emission control system, and accessory items you may add to the vehicle. There are no warranties covering parts that must be replaced owing to normal wear, such as brake pads, clutch linings, lightbulbs and fuses, wiper blades, filters, and so on.

Of course, to keep that warranty in effect you must maintain your car according to the guidelines in the owner's manual. Be sure to retain copies of all the paperwork detailing the regularly scheduled maintenance performed on your car.

You should be aware that some dealer-added options can void a manufacturer's warranty. The main one to avoid is dealer-installed cruise control. Check with the manufacturer before you authorize the installation of any option that might jeopardize your vehicle's warranty status; if they say there's no problem, ask them to confirm the answer in writing.

The warranties in effect as we're writing this are shown on page 196 stated in terms of years and miles. For example, "3/36,000" means the warranty is good for 3 years or 36,000 miles, whichever comes first. Since warranty policies can change, you should check the current specifics for the makes you're considering.

The most important warranty, by far, is the basic bumper-to-bumper coverage. For most people, it doesn't make sense to accept below-average basic coverage from an automaker, even in return for superior powertrain coverage.

In the past, powertrain warranties covered most of the major problems you might encounter after the original warranty expired because the only really expensive repair bills came from powertrain problems.

Today's automobiles, however, are loaded with complicated new systems that have nothing to do with the things that make the car go. Electronic instrument panels with all kinds of gadgets. Power equipment options. Anti-lock braking systems. Cruise control. Air bags. Sophisticated steering and suspension systems. Diagnosing and fixing problems with these systems is more difficult and expensive than it was with their predecessors. And when they need fixing after the basic warranty period, it's your money that's on the line.

Worth noting: Several import makes have competitive basic warranties and separate powertrain warranties extending beyond the bumper-to-bumper coverage. This makes their warranties somewhat better, overall, than some domestic companies.

THEY'VE GOT SECRETS

If a vehicle problem is serious enough for the federal government to require a recall, all owners are notified by mail. But with less serious but persistent problems, sometimes automakers decide to pay the repair cost on their own, even after the original bumper-to-bumper warranty expires. Trouble is, they don't publicize the availability of these "secret warranties." Some owners learn of them only after repeated complaints for the same problem; most don't know they exist. And only a few states have passed laws requiring their disclosure.

The automakers say that secret warranties don't exist. They call this practice "goodwill service" or "policy adjustments" instead. Dealers learn the specifics of each program from the manufacturer's regular technical service bulletins, which tell them how to fix the problem.

You can learn about the service bulletins for your car from the National Highway Traffic Safety Administration (NHTSA). The best way to do this is to visit NHTSA's web site on the Internet at www.nhtsa.dot.gov/cars/problems. You can get copies of bulletins on file by writing to NHTSA, Technical Reference Library, Room 5108, Washington, D.C. 20590. Ask for "service bulletins" and state the make, model, and year of the car and the year you think the service bulletin was issued. You may also call NHTSA at (800) 424-9393.

With most major manufacturers now at or near parity on basic warranty coverage, your decision on whether to buy an extended warranty contract will depend more on how long you'll keep the vehicle and how far you'll drive it.

THIS CAN BE EXPENSIVE OVERINSURANCE

Remember, these extended warranties don't kick in until the basic coverage kicks out. If you buy a car with an initial factory warranty of 36 months or 36,000 miles, your extension coverage doesn't begin until either mile number 36,001 or the first day of month 37.

Will you keep the car that long and/or drive it that far? If you will, how much longer and farther do you think you'll own and drive it? If you plan to keep the car only about one year or 12,000 to 15,000 miles beyond the initial warranty period, don't buy an extended warranty. Instead, put $500 to $1,000 into a rainy-day account and pray for sunshine. (This alternative may be very attractive if you're buying a vehicle that comes with an extended powertrain warranty.) But if you're planning to drive the car until the wheels fall off, an extended warranty can be a wise investment. Inevitably, something expensive happens between 50,000 and 100,000 miles.

If you're leasing the car, don't even think about buying an extended warranty. One of the major advantages of a lease is that the car is covered by the original bumper-to-bumper warranty for most, if not all, of the lease term. Ideally, you shouldn't lease a car for longer than the warranty period. If you have to stretch the lease one year beyond that period to keep the payments affordable, set up the rainy-day account recommended in the previous paragraph, but don't buy an extended warranty contract.

Note that you don't have to make this purchase decision when you buy the car. In most cases, you may buy this contract months after you buy the car, but it makes sense to do it when you've negotiated the price. And here's the best part: You can buy the factory-backed policy from any dealer who sells the same make.

NEGOTIATING WARRANTIES

"You Better Shop Around"
—Smokey Robinson and the Miracles,
number-two song in January 1961

Salesmen will tell you that an expensive postwarranty repair could cost you over $2,000, making this $1,000+ "insurance policy" a good investment. What they won't tell you is that this $1,000+ extended coverage contract costs them only about 50 cents on the asking-price dollar. This is one of the highest-margin items a car store sells. And most car stores would rather sell it and make a $100 or $200 profit than not sell it and make nothing.

To get the best price, you have to make the negotiation as competitive as that for the car itself. The place to start is with the dealers who want to sell you the car. First, you need to determine which contract you want; they come in many flavors—"premium care" vs. "extra care," deductible vs. no deductible, 6 year/75,000 miles vs. 6 year/100,000 miles, etc.

Whether you use the "fax attack" or some other method to make it a competitive bidding situation, broach this subject with each dealer contact *after* you've discussed the price of the car. Say that you're also considering buying an extended warranty for that vehicle, and ask about the different alternatives available from the manufacturer. Choose the one that's right for you by writing down the key details, and ask for his best price. You will, of course, be getting back to him after hearing from the other responding dealers.

Then, knowing exactly which contract you want, you can ask each successive dealer contact for a price on that specific warranty.

If you decide to consider an extended warranty *after* agreeing to a deal on a car, explore the automaker's alternative contracts with the selling dealer and ask for his best price on the one you want. Tell him you're going to shop other dealers and you'll buy from them if their price is the lowest. Then call the finance and insurance (F&I) managers at several other dealerships for that same make and ask for their best prices. Your target will be somewhere between half and two-thirds of the asking price (the manufacturers' suggested retail price).

Factory-backed extended warranty contracts can cost significantly more than competitive alternatives. Given that fact, why do we recommend them so strongly? Because they will be there for you when you need them, which is more than we can say about the contracts sold on the Internet and by many dealers that are backed by companies you've never heard of. Over the years, several third-party underwriters have gone bankrupt, leaving unwary consumers holding worthless contracts that neither the manufacturers nor their dealers would honor.

Many of these business failures occurred in the late 1970s and early 1980s. Among them: American Warranty Corporation, a division of United Equitable Insurance and National Colonial Insurance Company. The reason: The companies didn't charge enough for their contracts to cover the cost of the repairs for which they had promised to pay. (Duh!)

We'd like to think that the industry would have learned from its past errors and cleaned up its act by now. But it hasn't. The temptation of a quick buck from easy sales of cheaper warranty contracts over the Internet has spawned a horde of new entrants, none of which you've heard of before. They've swarmed over automotive-oriented web sites like hungry dogs on a bone and our in-boxes have been crammed with their junk e-mailings.

And countless numbers of foolish consumers, convinced they are getting a bargain on a sure thing, have flocked to these Pied Pipers of cheap warranties and followed them . . . right over a cliff. Forgetting that we still live in a world where you get what you pay for, these folks got a lot less than they paid for; they got nothing.

In late May 2003, the National Warranty Insurance Company of Lincoln, Nebraska, filed for liquidation. National Warranty was incorporated in the Cayman Islands as a "risk retention group" that administered several brands of service contracts sold by auto dealers and over the Internet. Among the affected warranty brands: SmartChoice, OmniCare, and Encore—all names chosen to inspire consumer confidence.

Although these products are called "extended warranties," they are "service contracts" and therefore not subject to federal regulation. And since National Warranty is a risk retention group and not a bona fide insurance company, it can't be regulated by state insurance departments. This means that consumers duped into buying its contracts can't look to state insurance guaranty funds for relief.

But that's just the good news. The bad news, reported by the *Chicago Tribune* on September 3, 2003, is that National Warranty covered 950,000 existing service contracts when it went belly-up after its underwriting losses in 2003 were approaching $74 million. Consumers paid anywhere from $600 to $2,000 for those contracts. Many thousands had purchased them on the Internet through an Austin, Texas, based company called Warranty Gold—surely another name chosen to inspire consumer confidence.

It gets worse. The *Chicago Tribune* reported that Warranty Gold learned of National Warranty's financial plight on June 6, 2003.

But that September 3 article indicated that Warranty Gold deposited a customer's $200 check paying off the balance due on his contract on July 28, 2003, without mentioning that it had stopped honoring warranties covered by National Warranty. Nice, eh? The article goes on to report that when a Chicago customer called Warranty Gold to complain a second time, a sales representative pitched him to buy a new contract. "He was ready, willing, and able to sell me a new policy. I asked, how can you do this when you can't make good on the ones they sold? Their credibility with me is zero," he said.

There may be some well-run no-name companies selling extended warranty contracts on the Internet and through auto dealers, but there's no reliable way to separate those in good financial health from those on the verge of liquidation. On September 23, 2003, the *Wall Street Journal* reported that A.M. Best Company, which monitors the financial strength of insurers, rated National Warranty highly just months before it stopped paying claims. Best's response: "The rating opinion in our view was correct based on the available information we had at the time."

What's a poor consumer to do? Clearly, buying a factory-backed warranty is the safe choice. But there is at least one other safe choice worth considering.

• GEICO Multirisk Insurance — If you have GEICO auto insurance, go to the company's web site at www.geico.com and check out its excellent mechanical breakdown insurance (MBI) coverage, which provides more protection than the typical extended warranty. It covers all mechanical parts of the car except for maintenance and wear-and-tear items. To add this coverage, you must have a car that's less than 11 months old and an odometer reading of less than 11,000 miles. Added advantage: You don't have to spend extra money up front for an extended warranty. MBI coverage becomes part of your GEICO auto insurance policy. You purchase coverage for only 6 months at a time, just like your auto insurance, and you can renew it each policy period for up to 7 years or 100,000 miles, whichever comes first.

If you're not a GEICO policyholder, you may want to consider becoming one when your next auto insurance bill arrives. The company is also known to have very competitive rates for folks with good driving records.

TWO IMPORTANT LAST-MINUTE SUGGESTIONS

1. Read the fine print before you sign the contract. Understand which parts are not covered, whether there's a deductible charge per repair, whether the contract is transferable to the next owner if you sell the car, and whether you'll get any money back if you cancel.

2. "Use it or lose it." With both the initial bumper-to-bumper factory coverage and the extended protection, why have it if you don't use it?

This question is especially relevant as you approach the end of the coverage periods.

During the last month or the last 1,000 miles of coverage, ask your dealer's service department to go over the car thoroughly to determine whether any major problems are on the horizon. Request that they do something now about these problems, while your car is still under warranty. A good service operation will be glad to do this for a regular customer.

23

The buyer needs a hundred eyes, the seller not one.

—George Herbert

Resisting the Final Temptation

Now comes the fun part: uninhibited emotional involvement without financial risk! Driving that new baby home . . . being seen by envious friends and neighbors . . . inhaling that new car smell . . .

Not so fast! There's one more piece of unfinished business, some work to do now to avoid a potential pile of grief next week: *the inspection.* Smart buyers allow at least one extra day at this juncture to ensure that they'll be happy with the car they drive home.

WHAT YOU DON'T SEE IS WHAT YOU GET

That new car or truck belongs to the dealer until the minute you pay him, sign the delivery receipt, and drive the front wheels off the lot. If it's got any problems, they're going to get fixed much quicker while he still owns it, before you've given him the final check. Once you drive away, he can claim that any defect happened after you took delivery.

Prepare the salesman in advance. Tell him that when the car is ready, you plan to inspect it carefully, and that you'll expect him to correct any problems before you take final delivery. Tell him to be sure to leave the dealer's tags on the car because you want to test-drive it while they still own it. That message should motivate the dealer to pay even closer attention to his checklist for the car before you get there.

MAKE THIS A DAY GAME . . . ON A NICE DAY

You can't inspect a new vehicle properly in the dark or in the rain. Put the trip off until you can do it in broad daylight on a reasonably nice day. Take a friend or relative to help; four eyes and ears are better than two.

Carry a pad and make a list of any problems you discover. Here are the things you should do on your inspection trip:

1. Check the odometer. If it shows more than about 300 miles, the dealer better have a good explanation. (Maybe he made an exchange with a dealer 200 miles away. But maybe he's trying to slip you a demonstrator that someone's been driving for a few weeks.)

2. Make sure all the optional equipment you ordered is on the car. Then have the salesman take you through the operation of all the equipment. The air conditioner, cruise control, lights, sliding sunroof, stereo system (the basics only for now), electric windows, washer-wipers, remote side mirrors, remote fuel cap opener . . . everything. Make sure it all works. (Incidentally, this is part of his job.)

3. Use your accomplice to help check all the lights. The turn signals, backup lights and brake lights, dome light and other interior lighting, even the glove compartment, trunk, and engine light (if there is one). Ask whether the manufacturer has set the interior lights to go on briefly when you leave the car at night, and if so, how long they stay on.

4. Go over the interior fabric areas very carefully. On cloth areas, make sure that the fit is perfect everywhere, and that there are no stains or tears. Ditto for the carpets and the headliner (the cloth or plastic covering between your head and the roof), which should show no sloppy glue stains.

5. Pay close attention to the exterior finish, both body and chrome. It should be perfect, without scratches or dents. (New-car owners should be allowed to put the first dings in their own doors.) If there are small scratches, they can be buffed out without too much difficulty. *But if the scratches are long enough and deep enough to require repainting, you should refuse the car, period!* The original factory finish is very difficult for even the best body shop to match, and partial-panel matching is next to impossible. The body shop would probably end up repainting the whole side or panel to fix a small imperfection, and chances are, you'd be unhappy with the result.

6. Check for previous body damage. It's rare with new cars, but it happens—on test drives or in transporting dealer exchanges. Look for mismatched paint on adjacent body parts or ripples in the surface. (Federal law says the buyer must be given a disclosure statement on previous damage.)

7. Check the fit and finish on all things that open and close. Windows, passenger doors, hood, trunk, glove box—and make sure all the tires match.

8. While the hood is up, ask the salesman to show you where all the fluids go and how to use the dipsticks to check the levels. The engine oil. The brake fluid. The automatic transmission fluid. The power steering fluid. The radiator anti-freeze, and even the windshield washing solution. If any of these is not at the proper level, either the dealer has done a poor job of prepping the car or there's a leak.

9. Most important, take the car for a test drive, ideally while the dealer's tags are still on it, not with temporary or permanent tags assigned to you. That way it's still under his insurance coverage, and he can't claim you've taken delivery. Drive the car reasonably aggressively to test it. If it's an automatic transmission, do the gears seem to shift smoothly and at natural progression points? Does the cruise control work? Accelerate to about 30 mph on a straight, flat, dry road with little or no traffic, and take your hands off the wheel. If the vehicle pulls left or right, it may have alignment problems. Slam on the brakes. Does it stop squarely? And find a road with some bumps to drive over to see if there are any annoying squeaks and rattles.

The dealer won't love you for all this, but you will. Give your list of problems to him to copy (keep the original yourself), and tell him you'll come back after he calls to say he's fixed everything. At that time, examine the car again and, if it's perfect, turn over the final check, sign the delivery receipt, and drive it off into the sunset.

An important detail: *Be sure you've communicated with your insurance agent,* so that you're covered the moment the wheels hit the street in front of the dealership.

One last word to the wise: *If you're financing the car, don't drive it home if the loan documents have not been approved and signed by the lender.* More than one buyer has done that, then learned a week or two later that because of a problem with the credit application, the interest rate (and the monthly payment) would be much higher.

24

Buying a new car without the Fighting Chance information is like going to the beach without sunblock. You're gonna get burned.
—Tom Gargiulo, Westport, Conn.

Tom leased his BMW 5-Series sedan for a capitalized cost just $1,190 over dealer invoice. At the sticker price, the dealer profit would have been $7,000.

You've Got a Powerful Resource @ www. fightingchance. com

We cannot tell a lie; this chapter is a commercial. It's for an information package called Fighting Chance that will increase your negotiating leverage with car dealers—a package that others have rated the best of its kind. You can order it anytime online at our web site www.fightingchance.com, or by calling (800) 288-1134 weekdays between 9:00 A.M. and 4:00 P.M. Pacific time.

As you surely understand by now, if all you have is the correct dealer invoice price, you don't have nearly enough to negotiate from a position of strength. You know that to shop smart for that new car or truck, you must arm yourself with current information about the model or models you're considering. That information falls into two different areas:

1. First, you need all the facts you can gather about the dealer cost of your vehicle. Those elements are (a) the dealer invoice price, (b) the factory holdback, and (c) any traditional factory-to-dealer cash incentives that have been reported. You also want to know about any customer rebates. (As noted in chapter 16, there are' often undisclosed incentives that are based on dealers reaching or exceeding specific objectives set on a store-by-store basis. There's no way to learn how much any given store is earning on your car, but if you make dealers bid competitively for your business, these secret incentives are usually reflected in the price proposals you receive.)

2. Second, you'll bargain from a position of greater strength if you have a feel for how your vehicle is doing in the marketplace. Are sales up or down so far this year? Does the average dealer sell many of that model each month or just a few? Were the most recently reported inventories high or low? Is there a redesigned version of the vehicle coming next year? And what prices are informed shoppers negotiating in relation to the invoice price?

Fighting Chance is a unique consumer service that provides all of this information in one package. One customer described it as "the Swiss army knife for buying or leasing a new car." We created this business because we concluded that the traditional sources of new-car data were not providing consumers with the information they needed to fully empower them in their price negotiations with dealers. We know of no other source that has put together a package this complete and made it so easy to order. (Think of this book as the crossbow you'll use and Fighting Chance as the arrows.)

Fighting Chance has been featured in articles in *Smart Money, Reader's Digest, Forbes, Road & Track, Good Housekeeping, Business Week,* and *Money* magazine, plus newspapers from coast to coast. When the *San José Mercury-News* rated the major national car-buying information services, Fighting Chance was the only one to receive four stars. (The *Consumer Reports* Auto Pricing Service got just two stars.) That *Mercury-News* article infuriated the local car dealers, who canceled their advertising for a full month, costing the paper over a million dollars in lost revenue. It would be fair to say that the dealers don't want you to know about us.

Since its introduction in June 1993, the Fighting Chance information package has helped more than 60,000 consumers avoid getting ripped off when buying or leasing their new vehicles. We are continually improving the product, based on what we learn in our daily contacts with them. And much of the business comes from repeat customers and the friends they refer to us.

The following are the four key elements of the package.

1. COMPLETE DEALER INVOICE DATA

For each car or truck, you'll get a printout showing all the configurations the manufacturer offers, with both the sticker price (the manufacturers' suggested retail price) and the dealer invoice price. That way, you'll be able to make price-value comparisons between different trim levels. (Remember, a higher trim level often represents a better value because it includes standard equipment in the base price that would be extra-cost items in a lower trim level.)

These printouts show the standard equipment included with each trim level. They also include both retail and dealer invoice pricing for all the factory-installed equipment packages and other options.

We get regular updates from our pricing supplier every week or two and often have pricing data on new models before most other sources. Frequent updates are important because automakers sometimes raise prices several times throughout the model year. You can check www.fightingchance.com anytime for a current list of available pricing.

The basic package price of $35 to $40 includes dealer invoice price data for one vehicle. Pricing information for additional vehicles on the same order costs $9 to $10 each. (We list a range because this book will be in print for several years and on library shelves for decades, and pricing can change. Please check our web site for current pricing.)

2. THE *CARDEALS* REPORT ON CURRENT INCENTIVE PROGRAMS

The second element in the Fighting Chance information package is the latest issue of *CarDeals,* a report covering the current manufacturers' incentive programs—both the consumer rebate offers and any traditional factory-to-dealer cash incentive programs that have been announced. This biweekly report is compiled by the Center for the Study of Services, a nonprofit consumer service organization in Washington, D.C.

As you might guess, we subscribe to just about every publication that covers the retail automobile market, and this is the most comprehensive report available on incentives. *Automotive News,* the industry's weekly newspaper, publishes an incentives section, but *CarDeals* often has twice as many listings. It's four to five pages long, with separate sections for subcompact, compact, midsize, large, and sporty cars, as well as minivans, pickups, and sport utility vehicles. (You can view a sample of a previous *CarDeals* report on our web site.)

Having a report covering the current incentive offers for all vehicles has another advantage: It can open other attractive options. Reviewing the *CarDeals* report, you might discover there's a significant offer on another vehicle you hadn't considered buying—perhaps even a model more expensive than you thought you could afford.

You should reread the caveats on incentives in chapter 16 and remember that you won't find them on all vehicles. Many popular models seldom get incentive dollars because they sell well without them. And some automakers avoid customer rebates and traditional dealer cash because they work against the image they're trying to project and erode the value of the brand's franchise. If *CarDeals* shows no incentives for your vehicle, please don't shoot the messenger; we don't create the news, we just report it. Vehicles without reported incentives usually are not difficult to deal on if you make dealers compete. If there are secret, undisclosed dealer incentives, they are typically reflected in the price proposals you'll receive.

3. OUR BIG PICTURE ANALYSIS— A POWERFUL NEGOTIATING TOOL

As we noted in chapter 15, there is real power in knowing how the makes and models you are interested in are doing in the marketplace. That's why each Fighting Chance package includes "The Big Picture," our model-by-model analysis of the current sales and inventory status for each nameplate on your list. Updated bimonthly, this report enables you to gauge the relative sales strength of different vehicles and determine which are likely to be more flexible on price. You'll also learn whether the average dealer sells 30 of your model every month or just 1 or 2. We'll tell you if there are major changes in the design of your vehicle scheduled for the next model year. And if there have been changes in a manufacturer's holdback policy, we include the latest information in this summary.

Perhaps most important, you'll benefit from the continuous feedback we get from the actual shopping experiences of other Fighting Chance customers
We receive daily reports from them on the actual transaction prices they pay (in relation to the dealer invoice price), and we include this information in our Big Picture summaries for each nameplate. Understand that this is anecdotal data, not real research. Since we are not your parents, you don't have to send your report card home if you aren't proud of it. But lots of folks do, and if people in several markets across the country report buying a given car for $200 to $300 over invoice, that's strong evidence that you can negotiate a similar deal where you live.

This up-to-date perspective can provide extra leverage in your price negotiation, especially if sales of your vehicle are flat or down. You'll be able to say in your "fax attack," "I also know that sales of this car were down 10 percent nationally in the first nine months of the year, and the average dealer is selling just three a month. And I have a good feel for the transaction prices paid by knowledgeable customers."

Another bonus you'll typically find in our package: The nameplate rankings from the most recent industry studies on initial quality and long-term reliability, which are usually published in both the automotive and national press in late spring and summer.

Why is Fighting Chance the only information service for new-car shoppers that provides these kinds of insights? We've asked ourselves this question for years. The automobile industry is the most overreported business in the world, and we try to read everything. Anyone who took the time to analyze the available information could do what we do. The only extra edge we have comes from our "insider contacts" with thousands of Fighting Chance customers every year. They make us smarter every day, so we can make you smarter.

The fact that *you* know this information—and 99.9 percent of the other shoppers don't—stamps you as a knowledgeable prospect and changes the way dealers respond to you. It also changes the way you feel about what you're doing, bolstering your confidence in your ability to negotiate a good deal. As much as anything else, that feeling is what we're selling.

4. A UNIQUE FEATURE: A REAL PERSON TO TALK TO

Thanks to the miracles of technology, we now live in an automated, computerized, voice-mailed, digitized, and impersonal world—a world where you get to talk to machines, not people. That's not our world. The Fighting

Chance package comes with an endangered species: someone to talk to as you go through the process of purchasing or leasing a new car.

Are you puzzled about how to interpret a pricing printout or by something a car salesman said that doesn't ring true? Call our customer service number, and we'll be happy to answer any questions you have. We work with this information every day, but you use it only every few years, so there's no such thing as a silly question.

If you're negotiating a lease, think of us as your informal "coach." We invite Fighting Chance customers to call us to go through the numbers before they sign the lease. We'll look up residual values in the latest issue of the Automotive Lease Guide's *Residual Percentage Guide,* to make sure no one's trying to low-ball you by charging for phantom depreciation. It'll be a toll call, but it'll save you the cost of purchasing the guide. We'll take out a calculator, go through the monthly payment calculation with you, and tell you whether we'd sign that lease. But we're in loss prevention, not triage, so be sure to call us *before* you sign the agreement. Once you've signed, it's a done deal.

Remember that we're in the Pacific time zone, which may be a few hours behind you. *And please note that we provide this service only for customers who have ordered the Fighting Chance package described in this chapter.*

Important notes: This is a service for *new vehicles only.* We have no information on used vehicles. Also, we have no Canadian pricing data. (For Canadian pricing, visit www.carcostcanada.com.) Finally, we have no information on travel trailers, truck campers, motor homes, van conversions, boats, airplanes, or motorcycles.

TO LEARN MORE, CHECK OUT OUR WEB SITE

If you'd like to learn more about Fighting Chance, you can find us on the Internet at www.fightingchance.com, where there's a more detailed description of the package, including a look at a typical vehicle pricing printout, a Big Picture analysis, and a *CarDeals* incentive report. You'll also find a current listing of available vehicle pricing, which is updated regularly as we get new data. And if the price of our package has changed, the web site will always have the current information.

In addition, you can play the "Car Name Game." We invite web site visitors to treat car names as acronyms and submit their ideas on what a make's name really stands for. (For example, did you know that Jeep means "Journey Eventually Ends Perpendicularly?")

HOW DO YOU ORDER?

You can order the Fighting Chance information package anytime you wish on our web site, www.fightingchance.com, where you can also print out an order form that you can fax or mail to us. If you prefer, you may order by calling (800) 288-1134 weekdays between 9:00 A.M. and 4:00 P.M. Pacific time.

You may charge the purchase to Visa, MasterCard, American Express, or Discover. If you'd rather order by mail and send a check, our mailing address is Fighting Chance, 5318 East 2nd Street, No. 242, Long Beach, California 90803.

The package price includes delivery by either first-class mail or e-mail. E-mailed packages are transmitted as portable document files (PDF) that you would open and print using Adobe's Acrobat Reader software. (You can download the latest version of Acrobat Reader for free from www.adobe.com.) We can also send the package via U.S. Priority Mail, fax, or Federal Express. Additional costs for these alternatives are listed on our web site. We usually fill orders within two or three business days.

HOW DO OUR CUSTOMERS RATE US?

When we created Fighting Chance, our objective was to provide a service that was demonstrably better than the existing alternatives.

The most well-known and probably the largest new-car pricing service is the one offered by *Consumer Reports*. Many Fighting Chance customers report that we frequently have new pricing data well before *Consumer Reports*. Customers who have used both services also tell us that our information is more complete.

Although we believe Fighting Chance is more timely, more comprehensive, more personal, and a better choice overall, we have great respect for some of the other work of *Consumer Reports*. Indeed, the annual April auto issue is probably the best single source of information on vehicle safety, reliability, comfort, convenience, and economy.

The best source of any company's business is customer referrals, and a very high percentage of Fighting Chance's business comes from old customers telling new customers. As one Fighting Chance customer put it, "Your service is deeper, more insightful, more interactive and personal, and ultimately more helpful than anything else out there—including the free stuff on the Internet. I've told everyone I know they shouldn't think about buying a new car without it."

We get fan mail like this every day, and you will find a generous sampling of recent customer testimonials on our web site.

The best testimonial we've ever received actually came from a car dealer, who said to a customer who had used the fax attack, "This is the only way to buy a car. But if everyone did it this way, we'd be out of business."

25

Frugality is the other thing money can't buy.

—W. James Bragg

The
Used-Car
Alternative

Let's start with the caveats.

We are not experts on used cars; our business is helping people buy or lease new cars. But we're not sure a true used-car expert exists. By definition, every used car is different from every other used car. That makes expertise very difficult to attain. When knowledge is harder to come by, nobody knows that much.

The books we've read on the subject seem to do a poor job of focusing the buyer on the best used-car options. Maybe that's because they're trying to talk to everyone, right down to the person with only $2,000 to spend who will end up with a 10-year-old car with over 120,000 miles on the odometer.

This chapter is not for everyone. It's for people who are seriously considering a new vehicle but have a strong left-brain orientation and wonder whether a previously owned vehicle would be a smarter buy. (If your left brain could talk, it would say, "Nobody needs a brand-new car to get from A to B.") These folks understand that every new car becomes a used car very quickly, and that in a sense we're all really driving used cars—it's just a matter of timing. They also know that when it comes to cars and humans, there's more than a dime's worth of difference between "used" and "used up."

THE ECONOMICS ARE COMPELLING

There's a strong dollars-and-sense argument for used over new, especially if you're a relatively young person convinced that you'll live forever but concerned that Social Security won't.

If you're in your twenties or early thirties, the slam-dunk way for you to put an extra $300,000 into your retirement kitty is simply to decide never to buy a new car. Instead, every four years, buy a two-year-old car. Let that first driver take the big depreciation hit. (The average car's wholesale value drops to 45–55 percent of its original sticker price in two years.) On a car with a sticker price of twenty to thirty grand, you'll save a thousand or two a year. For the rest of your life.

You won't be buying someone else's problem either. Today every automaker is building longer-lasting, more reliable cars. And the average two-year-old car even comes with some of its original three-year/36,000-mile bumper-to-bumper warranty. (We've focused on two-year-old cars for that reason. If you're shopping for a used luxury car with a four-year/50,000-mile warranty, you can consider buying a three-year-old. See the table in chapter 22 for warranty specifics by make.)

But saving $1,500 a year won't inflate your retirement kitty unless you invest that money religiously. Pick an aggressive no-load mutual fund. Start when you're 25, and if you average only a 7 percent return after taxes, you'll have an additional $320,000 when you're 65. Average 10 percent, and you'll have an extra $730,000. Doing that will require more financial discipline than most people have, but we told you this chapter isn't for everyone.

ADOPTING THE RIGHT TWO-YEAR-OLD

Whether you want to bolster your retirement savings or just cut your transportation budget, the strategy of buying a two-year-old car every four years makes a lot of sense. People are spending money more carefully these days, and with the average new-car transaction price over $26,000 and climbing, the stigma of driving a used car isn't what it used to be. Since body styles change only every four to eight years, most of your neighbors won't know whether you're driving new or used anyway.

How Do You Choose the Most Desirable Two-Year-Old Car?

By doing a little homework to narrow your choices. Go to the library and check the *Consumer Reports* annual auto issue, published each April. The substantial used-car section contains the key information you need to narrow your choices: (a) lists of the most reliable and least reliable used cars; (b) model-by-model reliability summaries, based on an annual survey of over 500,000 readers; and (c) frequency-of-repair records for several recent model years, with trouble spots detailed. While you're in the library, you may also want to check out the current annual editions of the *Consumer Reports Used Car Buying Guide* and *The Used Car Book* by Jack Gillis.

After you've selected a few likely candidates, ask the reference librarian for the library's copy of the *Kelley Blue Book's Guide to Used Car Values* or the *NADA* (National Automobile Dealers Association) *Official Used Car Guide.* As we've said before, these books purport to show trade-in/wholesale and market/retail used-car values, but don't take them too literally. They usually don't reflect the specific situation in your market, but they'll give you a feel for the percentage differences between what dealers pay for used cars and their retail asking prices. They'll also let you assess the differences between one car and another and one model year and another. Of course, you can also do this research on the Internet. Start by visiting the *Consumer Reports* web site at www.consumerreports.org, where you can purchase access to all the data for a modest fee. You can find ballpark used-car values at the web sites of Kelley Blue Book (www.kbb.com), Edmunds (www.edmunds.com), and the National Automobile Dealer Association (www.nadaguides.com). Another web site, www.autotrader.com, is also an excellent site on the Internet to browse through a large inventory of used cars and check asking prices. You will find cars offered there by new-car and used-car dealers, as well as by individuals.

Are All Two-Year-Old Cars of the Same Make and Model Equally Desirable?

We don't think so. Assume two apparently identical cars are side by side on a dealer's lot, each with 25,000 miles on the odometer. One has just returned from a two-year lease to a private individual or family; the other has been in a car rental company's daily rental fleet. Which would you choose?

We'd choose the off-lease car over the rental fleet car in the blink of an eye, and we'd pay a premium for it. It's likely to be the highest-quality used vehicle you'll find. The difference isn't in the way the two cars have been maintained, for both have surely had all the required maintenance work done. The difference is in the number of different drivers they've had and the way they've been driven. The leased car probably had one or two regular drivers who treated it lovingly because they knew at lease-end they'd have to pay to fix anything beyond normal wear and tear on the vehicle. By contrast, the daily rental car had 300 to 500 different drivers, none of whom spent even one minute worrying about wear and tear. Some accelerated quickly and screeched to a halt at every light or stop sign, maximizing the strain on the powertrain and brake systems. Others drove it on rough roads and over potholes, bottoming out the suspension system. For many car renters, anything goes as long as there's no visible damage when they return the car.

The major car rental companies sell their own used cars at facilities similar to new-car dealerships, where the prices are non-negotiable. The smaller rental outfits send theirs cars to wholesale auctions, where they are sold to franchised new-car dealers and independent used-car dealers. In our view, these are cars to avoid.

Here's an experience that brings the point home. Returning our daily rental to the local office of a major national car rental company, we asked the manager of the office if he'd rather buy that Ford Taurus with 25,000 miles on it or an identical one with the same mileage that we had leased for two years. His immediate answer: "I'd rather have yours with 45,000 miles on it than ours with 25,000." Now, there's a testimonial worth remembering!

Where Do You Find Your Target Vehicle?

The two-year-old used car you want is most likely to be on the lot of a franchised new-car dealer who sells the same make. Remember, most new-car dealers sell as many used cars as new cars. But since they don't get all the late-model trade-ins they need, they must look elsewhere to stock their used-car operations. The two-year-old cars you'll find on a new-car dealer's lot come from several sources:

- Some are the better ones he's taken as trade-ins on new vehicles or purchased from private individuals who know they'll get the highest wholesale price from a dealer who sells the same make.

- Others are cars the dealer has purchased from leasing companies when customers returned them at the end of the lease term. A dealer will buy them if the price is close to the wholesale value, but he'll pass on cars from highly-subsidized leases with sky-high, non-negotiable buyout prices. Three to four million vehicles come off leases every year, split about equally between two- and three-year-olds. If a leased car is not purchased by the lessee or the leasing dealer, the leasing company will have it trucked to a wholesale auction. (As many as 80 percent of off-lease units on two-year leases end up in the hands of the leasing company.)

- Most of the other cars on a new-car dealer's used-car lot come from those wholesale auctions, where 2.5 to 3.5 million cars of all ages and backgrounds are sold to dealers each year at prices 20 percent or more off retail prices. Some auctions offer only one automaker's cars, sent there by the company's captive finance arm, and only that manufacturer's dealers are invited to attend. Other auctions are open to all dealers and offer cars from many different sources.

Most late-model cars from wholesale auctions fall into four categories:

1. Some are excellent cars coming off leases to private individuals, mostly those that dealers decided not to buy at lease-end because the residual values were too high. These cars sell for significantly less at auction.

2. Others come to the auctions from daily rental company fleets. These are typically less than two years old and have high mileage for their age. They are frequently called "program cars" because they're programmed to leave the rental fleet at a certain age and mileage.

3. Some are finance company repossessions from buyers who failed to make the required payments.

4. And some are refugees from corporate auto fleets. These can be high-mileage, high-wear-and-tear vehicles that have been poorly maintained. They can also be attractive lower-mileage cars driven by auto company executives.

The car you want, of course, is one that's been driven by an individual or family as a personal car. These are more likely to be off-lease cars, since relatively few car buyers trade cars after only two years.

What About Those Chains of Used-Car Superstores?

You're less likely to find the car of your dreams there. What you will find are a lot of cars from daily rental fleets and auctions at "no-dicker" prices. These stores don't get to buy the best cars leased through an automaker's captive finance company; the manufacturer's franchised new-car dealers get first crack at those. Superstores like CarMax do, however, get cars from leases financed by third-party lenders, as well as from individuals.

These no-dicker used-car superstores are good places to shop prices, but we think your local new-car dealer will have better late-model used cars. You may pay less there, too, because the prices will be negotiable. (See the research findings on comparative transaction prices in chapter 14.)

Overall, these stores may be better places to sell a used car than to buy one, but if there's one near you, it's worth checking its inventory and asking prices. (We have heard from several Fighting Chance customers who have been offered more for their used car by CarMax than by any new-car dealer. The CarMax web site is www.carmax.com.)

BACKGROUND CHECKING
How Can You Tell Where a Late-Model Used Car Has Been?

For openers, the dealer who bought it has the previous title document, so he knows where it came from. Ask for the car's history, in writing; if he won't give it to you, that's a signal that he has something to hide and you should buy from someone else. And don't sign a "power of attorney" form when you buy a used car. That enables a dealer to process the title transfer papers without showing you the certificate of title.

Some states require that a dealer disclose whether a used car is a former rental or salvage vehicle or a "lemon law buyback." But those laws aren't universal. Fortunately, there's a universal source you can use to check any vehicle's background.

The Carfax® Vehicle History Report

To reduce your risk when buying a used vehicle, order a report on the car from Carfax, a database firm with over 550 million vehicle records. You give them the 17-character vehicle identification number (VIN) found on title documents and on the driver's side of the dashboard, near the edge of the windshield. With that number, Carfax can generate a detailed history report on virtually any used car or light truck built since 1981.

This report helps you answer these questions.

- Has the vehicle ever been declared a total loss by an insurance company, been sold at a salvage auction, or been damaged extensively in a flood?

- Has the odometer been rolled back?

- Has the manufacturer ever bought it back under the lemon laws?

- Was it used as a rental vehicle?

Carfax says it finds a red flag for one of nine cars.

The Carfax database may not have the history of every vehicle. The information on any given car depends on how long it has been on the road, how many times it's been titled, and where it's been driven. Carfax obtains its information from state motor vehicle departments (except Rhode Island and Vermont), auto auctions, used-car wholesalers, and emission inspection stations. It does not collect the names of vehicle owners, repair service records, stolen vehicle data, or the dollar value of vehicles.

We ordered a report for a 1995 Toyota Camry that was purchased as a used car from Avis several years ago in California. The four records it contained showed that:

- The car was registered in California as a rental vehicle by a major rental car company on October 1, 1994. (Avis was not identified by name.)

- The original title or registration was issued on October 13, 1994.

- A new title was issued on August 18, 1995, which is when the new owner borrowed money to buy the car from the rental company and a California financial institution put a lien on the vehicle. The odometer reading then was 20,674.

- A California inspection station performed an emissions inspection on September 14, 1996, when the odometer reading was 29,809.

- There were no problems found for the vehicle.

You may order a Carfax report on the Internet (at www.carfax.com). The price is $19.99 for a single history report, but you can order an unlimited number of reports over a 30-day period for just $24.95. You enter the vehicle identification number and your credit card number on a form and receive the report by e-mail in less than 30 minutes. (*Note:* Many dealers use Carfax regularly and may order a report for you if you ask.)

GIVE THAT CAR A COMPLETE PHYSICAL

Have a mechanic look before you leap. When you find a car you're serious about buying, any offer you make should be contingent on the vehicle passing a thorough inspection by an independent mechanic, ideally one who knows the model well. The service department of another dealership that sells the same make would be a good choice. Tell them exactly what you're doing, and make it clear that you don't own the car and won't buy it if it has mechanical problems. That will eliminate any incentive for them to recommend unnecessary repairs.

Many dealers will do a thorough used-car inspection for $50 to $150. This should include a compression test on all cylinders, a body integrity check for accident damage, a brake inspection, and checks of the front wheel bearings and suspension system, the transmission, and the exhaust, cooling, and electrical systems. Ask them to road-test the car for you. And get a cost estimate for any repairs they recommend.

This may seem to be overkill for a nearly new car with plenty of its original bumper-to-bumper warranty remaining, but it's not. If it's a car headed for mechanical trouble, you don't want it. If the selling dealer won't let the car off his lot for an inspection, and if you can't find one of those traveling inspection outfits that will do it there, find another dealer.

SHOULD YOU BUY A "DEMO"?

Several times a month, customers call us and say they've got an opportunity to buy a dealer's "demo" vehicle; they wonder whether that's a good idea and ask how they should negotiate a realistic price. This is a gray area with no established guidelines, but here's an approach to dealing with the question.

Strictly speaking, a demo is not a used car. It's a "used new vehicle" that's owned by the dealership and has never been sold. It might be the current year's model or last year's. It typically has from 1,000 to 10,000 miles on the odometer—most often 4,000 to 6,000.

You need to know who put those miles on the car. These are seldom true "demos," in the sense that they've been used mainly for test drives with prospective customers. Usually the vehicle has been driven for a few months by someone in the business or the dealer's family—perhaps a spouse, the sales manager, or the salesperson-of-the-month. Those are not tough miles; they're the same kind any individual would put on the vehicle. But if a car has been rented or loaned to service customers, and if 6,000 miles means 300 different people have driven it 20 miles each, those are not wonderful miles. (It's rare for a brand-new car to be used for this purpose, but it happens.)

Assuming you're comfortable with the car's history, there are three key issues to consider when you're trying to put a price on one of these cars.

1. Loss of Warranty Protection—Assume you find a demo with 6,000 miles on the odometer, and the car's original bumper-to-bumper warranty was 3 years or 36,000 miles. The mileage count started with the first demo mile driven, so one-sixth of the car's original warranty is gone. If you drive only 12,000 miles a year, you'll be out of warranty after two and a half years, and any big repairs in the following six months will come from your checkbook instead of the automaker's.

The time clock may also have been ticking on that warranty. Ask the dealer whether he established an "in-service" date on the car when he started using it as a demo. He may have, since he can't make warranty repairs on a car that's not yet in service. You need to know that in-service date, because that's the day the three-year warranty started. Ask him to print out a warranty history on the car. If warranty work has been done, an in-service date has been established.

A dealer might say he'll extend that original warranty by 6,000 miles or 6 months, but don't fall for that. That warranty is between you and the manufacturer, period. No dealer has the authority to extend any manufacturer's warranty.

2. Loss of Trade-in Value—Someday, years from now, you'll sell that car or trade it in on another new one. It will have an extra 6,000 miles on it that you didn't put there, and it'll be worth less because of those miles. That loss must be factored into the price you pay.

3. The Cost of the Same Car with No Miles on It—This must be your reference point. There are two relevant questions: (a) What would you have to pay for an "unused" version of the same new car? (b) How much would you have to save to make the used version a smart buy?

So What's the Right Price for a Demo?

The dealership has driven significant value off the vehicle; it must compensate the buyer for those miles. Our rough rule of thumb is 25 to 30 cents per mile—$1,500 to $1,800 on a car driven 6,000 miles. Why? Because 10 or 15 cents isn't enough, and they'd never agree to anything like 50 cents. (If it had 20,000 miles, you wouldn't get a $10,000 price reduction.) Assuming you could buy an "unused" version of the same model for $500 over invoice, you'd want to pay $1,500 to $1,800 less—or $1,000 to $1,300 *below* invoice—for one with 6,000 miles.

And if that 6,000-mile demo is last year's model? Figure that five years down the road, you'll get about $1,000 more for this year's model than for last year's with the same mileage. That's *another* $1,000 you'd have to save just to break even. So your total purchase price would have to be $2,500 to $2,800 below what you'd pay for this year's "unused" model to make it a smart buy.

One more concession you should ask for: an extended warranty at dealer cost. Emphasize that you are very concerned about buying a car with a chunk of its original warranty gone, and the only way you'll do that is if they'll sell you the extended warranty at cost. They just might.

THE PICK OF THE USED-CAR LITTER:
MANUFACTURER-CERTIFIED CARS

There's another alternative you should consider strongly: a "certified" used car. These are typically cars coming off lease that are inspected and reconditioned according to the automaker's specifications and come with a manufacturer's warranty. They cost an extra $500 to $1,500 compared to "uncertified" cars, but that modest upcharge buys a lot of long-term peace of mind. (With these cars, you don't need a Carfax vehicle history report or a separate mechanic's inspection.)

Automakers initiated these certification programs to deal with the glut of late-model used cars spawned by the leasing craze. It all started with the high-end luxury cars, but today everyone from Toyota and Ford to Lexus and Mercedes has a certification plan that runs quality exams on used cars. Depending on the manufacturer, these cars must undergo a 75- to 150-point inspection. Dealers fix whatever needs to be fixed, and the cars are sold with relatively comprehensive manufacturers' warranties.

Most used cars are sold "as is" and carry the dealer's 30-day or 1,000-mile warranty. But the manufacturer-backed warranties on certified cars typically run at least one year or 12,000 miles and come with roadside as-sistance. (Lexus backs some certified cars with 2-year/20,000-mile cover-age.) And this extra protection is often added to the end of any new-car warranty still in effect.

Most franchised new-car dealers sell certified used cars today. Manu-facturer certification programs are a potent weapon for traditional dealers in the battle for used-car market share—a weapon the superstores can't match. Only franchised new-car dealers can get these cars.

USED CARS ARE FOR LEASING, TOO

If you're a candidate to lease, you should consider leasing a used car. This alternative makes the most sense for someone who'd rather be driving a luxury or semiluxury car, but can't afford a new one.

You reference point should always be the cost of leasing the current model of the same car. After determining that number, check the cost of leasing a two- or three-year-old version. In most cases, you won't save much by leasing a car that listed for under $20,000 when new. With all the subsidized new-car leases for vehicles in that price range, a used-car lease might save you only $20 a month. But leasing a three-year-old, factory-certified BMW 5-Series sedan might save you $200 a month compared to a new one.

TALKING TURKEY

Okay, you've done your homework and chosen the car you want. You've checked the logical sources of estimated trade-in/wholesale and mar-ket/retail used-car values, recognizing that those sources aren't per-fect. You've also checked local asking prices for the car you want on dealers' lots, in the classified ad section, and online at sites such as www.autotrader.com.

There's no "dealer invoice price" for used cars. But we know that deal-ers make about as much total profit selling used cars as new ones, and they probably build at least a 20 percent gross margin into their asking prices.

Once you've located the car you want, tell the salesperson you have a feel for both the wholesale prices and the asking prices in your market. You expect him to make a profit, but you're not going to finance his next trip to the Super Bowl by yourself. Then offer 15 percent below the asking price and bite your tongue; the next person who talks will lose. When he counters with a higher number, bump your offer to 90 percent of the asking price. If he turns that down, say you've got an appointment at a competitor who has the same car and leave. But leave your phone number; he'll probably call.

26

Education is what you have left over after you have forgotten everything you have learned.

—Anonymous

The
Executive
Summary

Our objective is to make this guidebook the most comprehensive and useful information package available to people shopping for new vehicles. While it would be impossible to compress it into a pocket-size checklist, we have tried to highlight below the major points covered for use as a memory trigger as you go through the shopping and negotiating process.

• For openers, have a current overview of the automobile business. Which automakers have been winning and losing in the brutally competitive retail auto market (chapter 3)? What's the sales and inventory picture for the vehicles you're shopping? The poorer the sales and the higher the inventories, the better the deal is likely to be (chapter 15).

• As you consider your vehicle choices, give serious weight to the quality and safety differences between one car and another. Higher-quality vehicles break down less often, last longer, and are worth more when you sell or trade them (chapter 4). And some vehicles are inherently safer than others in a serious accident, so check the crash test data on all your finalists (chapter 5).

• Adjust your attitude. You are shopping for a commodity, and you'll always get a better price on a commodity by making suppliers bid competitively for your business. Only a solid, gold-plated fool would walk into a car store to negotiate the price of a car. And you are nobody's fool (chapter 6).

• Watch all three ways the car store can make money on you: (1) the price you pay for the new car, (2) the financing and other back-end add-ons they try to sell, most of which are of little value, and (3) the real price they pay for your trade-in vehicle (chapter 7).

• Develop a smart buyer's plan. Learn what your current car is really worth at wholesale and retail. Decide whether you'll trade it or sell it yourself. Shop for money before you shop for cars. Visit car stores to narrow your choices. Gather information on invoice costs and current consumer rebates and traditional dealer cash incentive offers. Make timing work for you. Put all the pieces together in an aggressive plan to make several car stores bid competitively, playing them off against each other to maximize your leverage. And resolve to let them do the stewing (chapter 8).

• If you're going to trade, keep the discussion of the price you pay for the new car separate from the discussion of the price they pay for your current car (chapter 9).

• Learn the true wholesale value of your current car before you talk with any car stores about a trade-in (chapter 10). And sell it yourself if you expect to get top dollar for it (chapter 11).

• Deal with the key financing issues before you deal with the dealer. Shop smart for money to provide a basis for determining if the dealer's financing proposal is attractive (chapter 12).

- Make your tire-kicking and test-driving visits "away games" if you can. And try to retain two or three equally attractive vehicle alternatives, perhaps by exploring "family relations" (chapter 13).

- Learn everything you can about what those vehicles really cost the dealer. Bone up on dealer invoice prices, traditional factory-to-dealer incentives, and dealer holdback and make a work sheet showing the key elements. Understand that it's not possible to learn a dealer's true "dead cost" for any vehicle, but if you make dealers bid competitively, those secret cash incentives will usually be reflected in their price proposals (chapter 16).

- Make timing work for you. Gather data early in the month, but negotiate price only at the end of the month (chapter 17).

- Understand that it may not be possible to get a car without some unwanted factory-installed options, but just say no to the high-profit add-on options dealers will try to sell you (chapter 18). Determine beforehand if you're a candidate for an extended warranty contract, but beware of those sold by companies you've never heard of; they may not be there when you need them (chapter 22).

- Seriously consider using the "fax attack" to make several dealers bid competitively (chapter 19). This approach consistently turns up the best price available. If you don't want to do it yourself, either by fax or phone, consider hiring CarBargains to do the work for you (chapter 20).

- If you're considering leasing, ask yourself the right questions to determine whether it makes sense for you, learn the language and the arithmetic, negotiate via the fax attack to get the best deal, and read the fine print before you sign anything (chapter 21).

- Be sure to give that car or truck an inspection that would make a marine colonel proud before you give the salesman the final check and sign the delivery receipt (chapter 23)

- Prepare yourself to bargain effectively for the vehicle you want by having (a) up-to-date dealer invoice pricing for the vehicle, (b) a current overview of its sales performance in the marketplace, including a feel for the actual transaction prices being paid in relation to invoice price by other educated shoppers, and (c) a report of current incentive activity, including any traditional factory-to-dealer cash offers in effect. You may obtain this information directly from us by ordering the Fighting Chance information package on our web site (www.fightingchance.com) or by calling us at

(800) 288-1134, or you may obtain it elsewhere. But be sure to have it. (See ordering details in chapter 24.)

- If you're considering buying or leasing a late-model used vehicle as an alternative to a new one, be just as disciplined in your approach. Do your homework to learn which previously owned cars to covet and which to avoid. And take a long look at those "factory-certified" used vehicles (chapter 25).

Appendices

Contacting the Auto Manufacturers

I f you can't get all your important questions answered by people at a dealership, try contacting the manufacturer. Here's a list of their customer assistance 800 numbers and web site addresses. Identify yourself as a consumer who is considering the purchase of one of their vehicles and say you have a question the dealer can't answer. The automakers have become much more consumer-oriented, and the operators should be able to find someone who can help you. You will find product information and links to dealers on the manufacturers' web sites.

Acura Division
American Honda Motor Company,
Inc.
(800) 382-2238
www.acura.com

Audi of America, Inc.
(800) 822-2834
(800) 367-2834
www.audiusa.com

BMW of North America, Inc.
(800) 831-1117
www.bmwusa.com

Buick Motor Division
General Motors
(800) 521-7300
www.buick.com

Cadillac Motor Car Division
General Motors
(800) 458-8006
(800) 333-4223
www.cadillac.com

Chevrolet Motor Division
General Motors
(800) 222-1020
www.chevrolet.com

Chrysler Corporation
(Chrysler, Dodge, and Jeep)
(800) 992-1997
(800) 227-0757 (for news of current
    consumer incentives)
Chrysler: www.chrysler.com
Dodge: www.dodge.com
Jeep: www.jeep.com

Ford Division
Ford Motor Company
(800) 392-3673
www.fordvehicles.com

GMC Truck Division
General Motors
(800) 462-8782
www.gmc.com

Honda Division
American Honda Motor Company,
Inc.
(800) 999-1009
www.honda.com

Hummer Division
General Motors
(866) 486-6376
www.hummer.com

Hyundai Motor America
(800) 633-5151
(800) 826-2277
www.hyundaiusa.com

Infiniti Division
Nissan Motor Corporation in
U.S.A.
(800) 826-6500
(800) 662-6200
www.infiniti.com

American Isuzu Motors, Inc.
(800) 255-6727
www.isuzu.com

Jaguar Cars
(800) 452-4827
www.jaguarusa.com

Kia Motors America, Inc.
(800) 333-4542
www.kia.com

Land Rover North America, Inc.
(800) 637-6837
(800) 346-3493
www.landrover.com

Lexus Division
Toyota Motor Sales U.S.A., Inc.
(800) 255-3987
www.lexus.com

Lincoln-Mercury Division
Ford Motor Company
(800) 392-3673
Lincoln: www.lincolnvehicles.com
Mercury:
    www.mercuryvehicles.com

Mazda Motors of America, Inc.
(800) 222-5500
www.mazdausa.com

Mercedes-Benz of North America, Inc.
(800) 367-6372
www.mbusa.com

MINI USA
BMW Group of America
(800) 831-1117
www.miniusa.com
www.bmwusa.com

Mitsubishi Motor Sales of America, Inc.
(800) 222-0037
(888) 648-7820
www.mitsucars.com

Nissan Division
Nissan Motor Corporation in U.S.A.
(800) 647-7261
www.nissanusa.com

Pontiac Division
General Motors
(800) 762-2737
www.pontiac.com

Porsche Cars North America, Inc.
(800) 767-7243
www.porsche.com

Saab Cars U.S.A., Inc.
(800) 955-9007
www.saabusa.com

Saturn Corporation
General Motors
(800) 553-6000
www.saturn.com

Subaru of America, Inc.
(800) 782-2783
www.subaru.com

American Suzuki Motor Corporation
(800) 934-0934
www.suzuki.com

Toyota Division
Toyota Motor Sales U.S.A., Inc.
(800) 331-4331
www.toyota.com

Volkswagen of America, Inc.
(800) 822-8987
www.vw.com

Volvo Cars of North America, Inc.
(800) 458-1552
www.volvocars.com

B

The
All-American
Speedster

THE ALL-AMERICAN SPEEDSTER

Factory Code No.	Model/Trim Level	Dealer Invoice	Retail (MSRP)
S88	AAA 4-door wagon	$15,700	$18,400
S87	AA 4-door wagon	13,000	15,200
S86	A 4-door wagon	12,800	15,000
S85	AAA 4-door sedan	14,300	16,800
S84	AA 4-door sedan	12,200	14,300
S83	A 4-door sedan	11,900	13,900

STANDARD EQUIPMENT BY TRIM LEVEL

A trim level:

Driver-side airbag
Power front disc brakes/rear drum brakes
Dual power mirrors
Digital clock
3.0-liter V-6 EFI engine
Full wheel covers
Fuel cap tether
Lights for ashtray, door courtesy, trunk,
    glove box, under hood, headlight switch,
    cargo area, dome

AM/FM radio w/4 speakers
Split bench seats w/dual recliners;
    65/35 split fold-down rear (wagon)
Power steering
Map pockets
P205/70R14 SBR all-season tires
    (blackwall)
Tinted glass
Cloth upholstery
Luggage rack for wagon

AA trim level (in addition to or in place of A trim level):

Deluxe cloth upholstery
Diagnostic warning lights
Remote release, decklid/liftgate

Paint stripe
Cast aluminum wheels

AAA trim level (in addition to or in place of AA trim level):

Air conditioning
Convenience kit
Illuminated entry system
Reclining front bucket seats w/6-way power
    driver seat and lumbar supports
P205/65R15 SBR blackwall tires

Full console w/armrest and storage
3.8-liter V-6 EFI engine
Automatic on/off/delay headlights
Speed-sensitive power steering
Tachometer
Luxury cloth upholstery

PREFERRED EQUIPMENT PACKAGES

Factory Code No.	Model/Trim Level	Dealer Invoice	Retail (MSRP)
444B	AA	$1,500	$1,800

Includes 725 manual air conditioning; 757 rear window defroster; 211 f&r floor mats;
129 power door locks; 888 AM/FM stereo radio w/cassette; 254 cruise control; 343
power windows; 298 power driver seat; 765 P205/65R15 tires. Prices reflect discounts
of $600 dealer invoice and $730 suggested retail.

(continued)

THE ALL-AMERICAN SPEEDSTER *(continued)*

Factory Code No.	Item	Model/ Trim Level	Dealer Invoice	Retail (MSRP)
291	Passenger airbag	All	$400	$500
725	Manual air conditioning	A, AA	700	850
735	Automatic air conditioning	AAA	150	190
525	Anti-lock brakes	All	500	600
754	Cargo cover	Wagons	60	75
254	Cruise control	All	190	225
757	Rear window defroster	All	140	170
129	Power door locks	A, AA	210	250
222	California emissions	All	75	110
947	3.8-liter V-6 EFI engine	AA, AAA	470	560
143	Engine block heater	All	20	30
211	Front and rear floor mats	All	40	50
888	AM/FM stereo/cassette	All	140	175
861	High-level audio system	All	250	300
	(includes controls for bass, treble, balance, fade; seek-scan turning; AM stereo; Dolby noise reduction; 80 watts power)			
862	Compact disc player	All	400	500
	(includes cassette; requires 861 high-level audio system)			
311	Power moonroof	AAA	700	800
	(requires 725 manual air conditioning when 735 automatic air conditioning is not ordered)			
298	6-way power driver seat	AA	250	300
299	Dual 6-way power seats	AAA	250	300
314	Rear-facing third seat	Wagons	130	160
301	Leather bucket seats	AA	500	600
	with console	AAA	400	500
524	Leather steering wheel	AAA	65	90
	(requires 254 cruise control)			
343	Power windows	A, AA	300	360
106	Rear window washer/wiper	Wagons	100	150
	(requires 757 rear window defroster)			
765	P205/65R15 blackwall tires	AA	130	150
608	Conventional spare tire	All	60	75
	(replaces rear-facing third seat on wagons)			
Destination charges		All	500	500

Note: This chart contains fictitious information about a vehicle and a manufacturer that do not exist. It was created solely as an aid in helping the reader learn to build a new-vehicle worksheet (see chapter 16).

Index

satisfaction with dealer service, 41
warranties, 196
Cap reduction, 178
Car and Driver, 90
CarBargains, 162–164
Car-buying services, 166
  Internet, 161–162
CarDeals, 124, 162
Car family tree, 92–95
Carfax, 221–223
CarMax, 221
Cars
  attitudes to adopt to shop and negoti-
    ate. *See* Attitudes to adopt to
    shop and negotiate
  brokers, 164–166
  buying. *See* Buying
  dealer cost. *See* Dealer cost
  extended warranties. *See* Extended
    warranties
  financing. *See* Financing
  leasing. *See* Leasing
  manufacturers, contacting, 235–237
  "no-dicker" dealers. *See* "No-dicker"
    dealers
  options. *See* Options
  preownership inspection, 204–207
  present car, selling. *See* Selling your
    old car yourself; Trade ins, get-
    ting enough for
  quality of. *See* Quality, car
  retail selling system, knowing in
    order to save money, 53–54
  safety of. *See* Safety
  shopping for without buying. *See*
    Shopping without buying
  U.S. market for. *See* Market for cars,
    changing face of
  used. *See* Used cars
Cash rebates, 117
Chevrolet
  initial quality ranking, 37
  long-term reliability, 38

manufacturer contact information,
    236
  market share, 18
  number of dealers, 106
  satisfaction with dealer service, 41
  warranties, 196
Chrysler
  initial quality ranking, 37
  long-term reliability, 38
  manufacturer contact information,
    236
  market share, 20
  number of dealers, 106
  satisfaction with dealer service, 41
  warranties, 196
Chrysler Group
  "family relations" vehicles, 94
  foreign assembly plants, 33
  market share, 13, 15, 20
  mergers, 14
Closed-end leases, 176
College graduate (recent) offers, 118
Commercial user discounts, 118
Consumer Reports, 41, 90, 214, 218
*Consumer Reports Used Car Buying
    Guide,* 218
Crashworthiness, 44–47
Credit life insurance add-on rip-off, 87
Customer loyalty discounts, 118

Daewoo
  long-term reliability, 38
  satisfaction with dealer service, 41
Daimler-Benz, 14
Dealer cost, 108–126
  dealer advertising association
    charge, 125–126
  dealer holdback, 113–116
  dealer invoice price, 110–111
  document processing fees, 126
  incentives, 116–123
    getting information on, 123–124
    manufacturer-to-customer offers,
      117–119

About the Author

W. James Bragg could name every car on the road when he was three years old, long before he could read. As a teenager, his fancy was fueled by a fire-engine-red Ford convertible, and he's been an avid student of the automotive world ever since.

Today, he is a consumer advocate helping people become more knowledgeable new-vehicle shoppers. Much of his counsel is based on the actual shopping experiences reported by over 60,000 customers of Fighting Chance, the unique information service he founded in 1991. Fighting Chance has been featured in articles in many national magazines (including *Smart Money, Reader's Digest, Forbes, Road & Track, Money, Business Week,* and *Good Houskeeping*), as well as in newspapers from coast to coast.

A graduate of both Yale and Harvard Universities, he has written on the subject for *Money* magazine and has been a periodic commentator on *Marketplace,* Public Radio International's daily business program.